POST ROAD

Post Road publishes twice yearly and accepts unsolicited poetry, fiction, and nonfiction submissions. Complete submission guidelines are available at www.postroadmag.com.

Subscriptions: Individuals, $18/year; Institutions, $34/year; outside the U.S. please add $6/year for postage.

Post Road is a nonprofit 501©(3) corporation published in partnership with Literary Ventures Fund and the Lesley University MFA program. All donations are tax-deductible.

This issue of Post Road is made possible in part by generous support from The Cotton Charitable Trust.

Distributed by:

Ingram Periodicals Inc., LaVergne, TN

Printed by:

BookMasters, Mansfield, OH

Post Road was founded in New York City in 1999 by Jaime Clarke and David Ryan with the following core editors: Rebecca Boyd, Susan Breen, Hillary Chute, Mark Conway, Pete Hausler, Kristina Lucenko, Anne McCarty, and Michael Rosovsky

post road

Table of Contents

Art

Etcetera

Recommendations

Contributor Notes

Eve Abrams is a freelance writer, radio producer, and educator living in New Orleans, Louisiana. Her most recent work can be read in *Fourth Genre* and heard on *This American Life*.

Kathleen Aguero is the author of three books of poetry: *Daughter Of, The Real Weather*, and *Thirsty Day* and editor of three volumes of multicultural literature published by the University of Georgia Press. She is a Professor of English at Pine Manor College in Chestnut Hill, MA, teaching in their low-residency MFA and undergraduate programs.

Jami Attenberg is the author of the short story collection, *Instant Love*. A novel, *The Kept Man*, will be published in 2008.

Stephen Ausherman is the author of *Fountains of Youth*, a novel, and *Restless Tribes*, an award-winning collection of travel stories. He was the 2005 Writer-in-Residence for Devils Tower National Monument in Wyoming and Buffalo National River in Arkansas. Visit his site at restlesstribes.com.

Rusty Barnes grew up in rural northern Appalachia. He received his B.A. from Mansfield University of Pennsylvania and his M.F.A. from Emerson College. His fiction, poetry and nonfiction have appeared in journals like *Memorious*, *Red Rock Review*, *Small Spiral Notebook*, and *SmokeLong Quarterly*.

Nathaniel Bellows is the author of *On This Day*, a novel, and *Why Speak?*, a collection of poems.

Elisabeth Brink worked in publishing, high-tech marketing, and counseling before earning her PhD in American Literature in 1993. Since then she has taught writing and literature at Harvard, Tufts, and Boston College. Her essays and stories have appeared in *The Gettysburg Review*, *Alaska Quarterly Review*, *Manoa*, *Orchid*, and other publications. Her recently published comic novel, *Save Your Own*, is a Booksense Notable Book.

Jericho Brown holds a Ph.D. from the University of Houston Ph.D. Program in Creative Writing and Literature and an MFA from the University of New Orleans. He has received fellowship, grants, and scholarships from Cave Canem, the Breadloaf Writer's Conference and the Polish Poetry Seminar in Krakow. His poems have appeared or are forthcoming in *jubilat*, *Prairie Schooner*, *New England Review*, *AGNI*, *The Journal*, and *Callaloo*. He teaches creative writing as an assistant professor of English at the University of San Diego.

Nickole Brown is the author of the forthcoming *Sister*, her first poetry book. She lives in Louisville, Kentucky.

Kevin Canty lives in Missoula, Montana, where he teaches in the MFA program at the University of Montana. He has written two short story collections and three novels, the most recent of which is the novel *Winslow in Love*.

Shannon Connelly is a graduate student at Columbia University. She is currently at work on a project exploring the links between Neue Sachlichkeit portraiture and the comic grotesque.

Michael Czyzniejewski grew up in Chicago. His fiction has appeared or is forthcoming in *American Short Fiction*, *The GSU Review*, *Other Voices*, and *Redivider*, and has been reprinted in Pushcart Prize XXXI. He currently teaches at Bowling Green State University.

John D'Agata teaches creative writing at the University of Iowa.

Quinn Dalton is the author of a novel, *High Strung*, and a story collection, *Bulletproof Girl*. Her third book, *Stories from the Afterlife*, was published last October.

Meghan Dunn was raised in upstate NY but has been a converted Bostonian for the past several years. She received her MFA in creative writing from Emerson College.

Debra Gitterman received an MFA from Warren Wilson in 2006. She lives in New York City.

Maria Halovanic holds an MFA from the University of Maryland, College Park. She is currently working on her doctorate at Boston University where she is studying the intersection of cognition and poetic language.

Michael Hearst has written a novel, lots and lots of short stories, and about two-hundred pages of a narrative memoir, but most of his writing has never been published. He is, however, a founding member of the band *One Ring Zero*, which has released seven CDs. Most recently, he released a solo album called "Songs for Ice Cream Trucks."

Trans-Pacific writer **Alex Kuo**'s collection of short stories *Lipstick and Other Stories* received the American Book Award in 2003. His most recent book is the novel *Panda Diaries*.

Evan Lavender-Smith attended the University of California, Berkeley, and New Mexico State University. His writings appear in recent or forthcoming issues of *Colorado Review*, *Denver Quarterly*, *Glimmer Train*, *Land-Grant College Review*, *The Modern Review* and *Opium*.

Ronnie E. Maher is a photographer, living in Norwalk, CT. She predominantly photographs portraits and weddings. She also teaches photography to high-risk youth in both Norwalk and Nicaragua, and much of her personal and professional work centers around local non-profits. More photographs can be viewed at www.ronniemaher.com.

Jill McCorkle is the author of five novels: *The Cheer Leader*, *July 7th*, *Tending to Virginia*, *Ferris Beach* and *Carolina Moon* and three story collections, most recently *Creatures of Habit*. Her work has appeared in *The Atlantic*, *Ploughshares*, *Best American Short Stories* and *New Stories from the South*, among other publications. The recipient of the New England Book Award, the John Dos Passos Prize and the North Carolina Award for Literature, she has taught creative writing at UNC-Chapel Hill, Tufts, Harvard, Brandeis and Bennington College. She is currently on faculty at NC State University.

Mameve Medwed (named for two grandmothers, Mamie and Eva) is the author of the novels, *Mail, Host Family, The End of an Error, How Elizabeth Barrett Browning Saved My Life*, and the forthcoming *Men and Their Mothers*. Her stories, essays, and reviews have appeared in *Yankee, Boston Globe, Missouri Review, Newsday,* and *The Washington Post.* Born in Bangor, Maine, she lives in Cambridge, MA.

Lydia Millet is the author of five novels, including *My Happy Life,* which won the 2003 PEN-USA Award for Fiction, and most recently *Oh Pure* and *Radiant Heart,* about the physicists who worked on the first atomic bomb. Her next novel, *How the Dead Dream,* will be published in late 2007.

Mary Morris is the author of three collections of short stories, including the prize-winning *Vanishing Animals & Other Stories.* Her stories have been widely anthologized in such places as *The Paris Review, TriQuarterly,* and *Vogue.* She is also the author of six novels and four travel memoirs, including, most recently, *The River Queen.* The recipient of the Rome Prize in Literature, Morris lives in Brooklyn, NY and teaches writing at Sarah Lawrence College.

Mark Mothersbaugh, a founding member of Devo, is a successful artist and musician whose scores for film and television include *Bottle Rocket, Rushmore, The Royal Tenenbaums, The Life Aquatic with Steve Zissou, 200 Cigarettes, Drop Dead Gorgeous, Rugrats, Clifford the Big Red Dog, Felix the Cat,* and *Pee-Wee's Playhouse,* among others. He also produces music for commercials and video games through his production company, Mutato Muzika.

Logan Perkes is an Austin-based writer and instructor. *Making the Bed,* a collection of essays and poems, is her first book-length project. Over the summer she was an intern for the National Theatre Workshop for the Handicapped in Maine. She earned her MFA degree from Fresno State University.

Mike Scalise is a freelance writer and editor living in Washington, DC. His essays and short stories have appeared in publications such as *Inkburns* and *Two Note Solo.* He is currently working towards his MFA in creative nonfiction from George Mason University.

Robert Anthony Siegel is the author of two novels, *All Will Be Revealed* and *All the Money in the World.* He was born in New York City and educated at Harvard, the University of Tokyo, and the Iowa Writers' Workshop. He teaches creative writing at the University of North Carolina Wilmington, where he lives with his wife, the writer Karen E. Bender, and their two children, Jonah and Maia.

Debra Spark's most recent book is *Curious Attractions: Essays on Writing.*

Craig Morgan Teicher's first collection, *Brenda Is in the Room and Other Poems* won the Colorado Prize and was published in fall 2007. His poetry has appeared in *The Paris Review, Seneca Review,* and *The Yale Review,* among other magazines. He lives in New York.

Sam Weller is the author of *The Bradbury Chronicles: The Life of Ray Bradbury,* winner of the Society of Midland Authors Award for "Best Nonfiction" in 2005. The book was also short-listed for the Bram Stoker Award. Weller is a professor in the creative writing program at Columbia College Chicago.

Jeffrey Yang published a translation of classical Chinese poems titled *Rhythm 226,* as well as a translation of *Su Shi*'s East Slope. His book of poems, *An Aquarium,* is forthcoming.

Track 4: Reflections
as performed by Diana Ross

Jericho Brown

I wanted to reflect the sun.

I wore what glitters, smiled,
Left my eyes open, and,

On the ceiling of my mouth,

Balanced a note as long as God allowed,
My head tilted backwards, my arms stretched

Out and up, I kept praying,

If the red sun rising makes a sound,
Let my voice be that sound.

I could hear the sun sing in 1968.

I learned the word *assassin*
And watched cities burn.

Got another #1 and somebody

Set Detroit on fire. That was power—
White folks looking at me

Directly and going blind

So they wouldn't have to see
What in the world was burning black.

Track 1: Lush Life

Jericho Brown

The woman with the microphone sings to hurt you,
To see you shake your head. The mic may as well
Be a leather belt. You drive to the center of town
To be whipped by a woman's voice. You can't tell
The difference between a leather belt and a lover's
Tongue. A lover's tongue might call you *bitch*,
A term of endearment where you come from, a kind
Of compliment preceded by the word *sing*
In certain nightclubs. A lush little tongue
You have: you can yell, *Sing bitch*, and, *I love you*,
With a shot of Patrón at the end of each phrase
From the same barstool every Saturday night, but you can't
Remember your father's leather belt without shaking
Your head. That's what satisfies her, the woman
With the microphone. She does not mean to entertain
You, and neither do I. Speak to me in a lover's tongue—
Call me your bitch, and I'll sing the whole night long.

THE BOOKSHOP, by Penelope Fitzgerald

Nathaniel Bellows

The *Bookshop*, by Penelope Fitzgerald, is 116 pages long. This doesn't seem to make sense because, despite the small story—Florence Green, a newly widowed middle-aged woman, decides to take her minimal inheritance and start a bookshop in a small coastal town in England— the book is flush with deeply felt, perfectly drawn characters; a living, breathing landscape; and a sensibility that is so generous with emotion, wisdom, and fine, tart humor, you'd think the book would need to be at least three times the length in order to accommodate it all.

How is this possible? I ask myself every time I finish it. How does someone master such economy of description while creating such a vivid, rich world? How does someone, in such a short space, connect us to these characters—and sustain this connection well beyond the final, heartbreaking pages?

I have read *The Bookshop* four times, and I still don't know the exact answers to any of these questions. But a good deal of Fitzgerald's alchemy, I think, can be attributed to her voice—an instrument of such pitch-perfect subtlety, it has the ability to communicate many levels of narrative at once, while maintaining a quiet, elegant, unquestionable authority.

In the opening of the book Florence, wandering the wild moors outside of the town, comes across Mr. Raven, the marshman. He asks for her help—his horse's teeth are blunted; it can't properly chew the grass, and therefore it can't get the nutrients. Mr. Raven asks Florence to hold the horse steady so he can file down the horse's teeth, and she obliges.

> He slipped his finger under the loose skin, hideously wrinkled, above the horse's jawbone and the mouth gradually opened in an extravagant yawn. Towering yellow teeth stood exposed. Florence seized with both hands the large slippery dark tongue, smooth above, rough beneath, and, like an old-time whaler, hung gamely on to it to lift it clear of the teeth. The horse now stood sweating quietly, waiting for the end. Only its ears twitched to signal protest at what life had allowed to happen to it.

The genius of this passage, and many, many others like it throughout all of Fitzgerald's books, is how this curious encounter, rendered perfectly plausible by its visceral realness, possesses an interpretation of the events that extends beyond the description of these three poor souls, standing out on the windy, wet moors. Fitzgerald is able to offer commentary of a deeply human kind—superimposed seamlessly onto the horse—on how instantly susceptible we can be to an unpredictable world.

It seems this layering of purpose within the language—a kind of narrative told in three dimensions—is what allows Fitzgerald's books to remain so slender while possessing such weight. However, what keeps her tone and voice from feeling overengineered, or too prim or mannered, is her ability to be direct, just when it matters.

Called to the house of Mr. Brundish, the town's most noble and most reclusive resident, Florence sits across from him at tea at his dining-room table.

> She knew perfectly well, sitting in the dull afternoon light, with the ludicrous array of slop basins and tureens in front of her, that loneliness was speaking to loneliness, and that he was appealing to her directly.

It is these people—these embodiments of "loneliness"—that are Fitzgerald's muses. I have read all nine of Penelope Fitzgerald's novels at least twice, and they all contain these kinds of characters; often wayward, often lost—well meaning, but blighted, struggling to stay afloat in an inhospitable world. Florence Green, like the other characters in Fitzgerald's trove, isn't pitied and isn't needlessly abused; Fitzgerald gives her the same simple, aching kind of tribute she bestows upon all those whose stories are left untold, and therefore unknown.

In *The Afterlife*, a collection of her essays and criticism, published after her death in 2000, Fitzgerald, in her own words, states her goal as a writer:

> I can only say that however close I've come, by this time, to nothingness, I have remained true to my deepest convictions—I mean to the courage of those who are born to be defeated, the weaknesses of the strong, and the tragedy of misunderstandings and missed opportunities, which I have done my best to treat as comedy, for otherwise how can me manage to bear it? ✧

Possum

Mary Morris

I didn't see it, but Marisa did. At least that's what she tells me one morning as I'm dragging out the trash. "You can't believe what was in your
garbage last night" are her exact words. It's the kind of thing Marisa
would see. She sits on her stoop late at night—in her bathrobe, no less—
smoking or talking to her boyfriend, more like yelling at him, or them, on
her cell phone, though I've asked her, and so has James, to keep it down.

Marisa tells me how she was just sitting there with her cigarette and
glass of scotch when it walked by, heading west. "I couldn't believe it," she
says when I see her as I'm leaving for the school where I teach special ed.

Then Marisa goes up and down the block, in her high heels and pen-
cil skirt, telling everyone. She stops neighbors right and left as they're
walking their dogs or moving their cars. "I thought it was a rat and then a
big fat cat." She's getting all the mileage she can. She did the same thing
when her marriage broke up. She walked around saying, "I figured it out
myself. From the E-ZPass bill."

Since Marisa told me about the opossum, there've been other sight-
ings as well. Sam Martins, who lives on the other side of the street, report-
ed seeing something strange when he got home from his graveyard shift
at the hospital. And up the block some teenagers, smoking a hookah on a
front stoop, thought they were seeing things. Over dinner one night
Jimmy Jr. says he saw it.

"Oh, yeah, what was it doing?" his father says.

"It asked for a cigarette," Jimmy tells us, "but I didn't have one, so it
kept going."

I start laughing, but James snaps, "I don't see the humor in this.
There's nothing funny about cigarettes."

"So, did you see it?" I ask my son.

"Maybe," he quips back.

"I doubt it," James says. "He's just trying to be a big man." James says
"big" in a long, drawn-out way, and there's a palpable pause at the table as
dinner comes to a halt. The frozen family, Jimmy called us once, as we
wait to see where James is going with this, but then he shakes his head and
gives a little laugh. We're used to his little flare-ups. They come and go like
brushfire, a little flicker that can flash, then fade just as quickly. We all stop
to see where it's going to lead, but it leads to nothing and we just go on
with our meal.

"Don't even think about cigarettes, kid," James says, poking at his
creamed corn. I've always called him James. Never Jim or Jimmy. Once or
twice, joking, Geronimo, but mostly it's James. To everyone. He won't tol-

erate it when a pal, someone who thinks he knows him says, "Hey, Jimmy Boy, how's it going?"

"It's James," he always says. "Diminutives are for pets and children, and women," he might add.

"Oh, James," I say, "leave the boy alone. So, did you see it?" I give Jimmy Jr. a nudge, and grinning, he shakes his head.

Still, something is roaming our block, taking the lids off garbage cans, vaulting off of people's decks. Peering into windows as supper is being served. Dogs are growling. Cats refuse to go outside. The block blog is all abuzz.

Marisa made the first posting. She's a woman with time on her hands. Marisa was married to Fred until she realized he was driving across the Triborough Bridge four times a week, when he worked downtown. No one could have imagined Fred doing that. You never can really know people, can you? Even if they live right next door. Marisa got the house in Brooklyn, and Fred took the place upstate, but they used to spend every weekend there. "I know an opossum when I see one," Marisa wrote.

We use the block blog for all kinds of things. When a neighbor is ill or somebody needs a good middle school. Births, deaths, congratulations, all get posted there. Volunteers for the holiday party, cleaning out the tree pits. Can anyone babysit tonight? Can we stop the new drive-through bank? When Tuna the cat went missing, that went up on the blog. And later when the cat was found, the owner wrote, "Our thanks to all who helped bring our beloved Tuna home."

Last summer our block president inadvertently posted his family vacation to Orlando. We gazed at pictures of his kids with Mickey Mouse, or his wife in a bikini, sipping a drink with a lime green paper umbrella in it, by the pool. A picture of our president himself, a slight paunch falling over his trunks, waving on water skis. "Good thing it wasn't his visit to the strip joint," James said.

"A bushy-tailed, not a ring-tailed," Marisa wrote. "And it looks a little mangy." "Like it had been in a barroom brawl?" someone shot back. I suppose that's the disadvantage with blogging. But wild animals have been coming into the city. Hawks now soar overhead and make our lapdogs nervous. A coyote, dubbed Hal, found his way into Central Park. And once the Millers, just across from us, found a boa constrictor in their backyard, but that turned out to be an escaped pet.

I've seen evidence of raccoons. Our garbage can lids have chew marks around them, but the opossum took us off guard. It's hard to imagine North America's only marsupial cavorting in a Brooklyn neighborhood. I didn't believe Marisa at first. She's not exactly the kind of woman you would believe. She's flashy. An attention seeker. A drama queen. An "Oh, you won't believe what happened to me" kind of person. Once, years ago, a man named Frederick Dillard was murdered in Prospect Park—a gay murder, it seemed. Well, that was coincidentally Marisa's husband's name, and Marisa told everyone, "I just want you to know that's not my Fred." She rang people's doorbells so she could tell them.

We used to be friends with Marisa and Fred. We had them over to dinner a few times, and we'd go over there. When the kids were small, we'd throw hot dogs on the grill. Fred was a quiet guy. It was easy to forget he was there. The invisible husband, we joked. Jimmy's good with the quips. But James and Marisa could go at it for hours, bantering, slapping each other on the back. Bathroom humor, especially if they'd had a couple drinks. They had a hoot, while Fred sank deeper into himself, until one day he was gone and, last we heard, living in their place upstate with a younger woman he'd been seeing for years.

I don't know why I haven't seen the opossum. I'm nocturnal in my own way too. Well, not exactly nocturnal. It's more like I don't really sleep. I drift somewhere between being awake and asleep, so that the line between the two is pretty thin. I have been like this for years. Or I'll start off asleep, then I'm up. When I'm up, I wander through the house. Check on the kids. Then go back to bed. "You're like a sleepwalker," Jimmy Jr. once said.

I can go back to sleep unless I start to listen to James snore. Once he starts snoring, that's it. I'm awake. It's not a loud, insistent snore. It's just a heavy breathing in and out, like the way I imagine a bear would breathe if I were curled up next to one in its cave. If I lie beside him and listen, I never get back to sleep.

Sometimes when I wake up, James isn't there. Either he hasn't come home or he's downstairs, passed out on the couch. Then he's usually not snoring, and on those nights I feel a sense of relief, and I can just go back upstairs without worrying and try to sleep. And sometimes I actually do. But other times I listen to the quiet of the house—the wind through the trees, our son, rolling in his bed . The creaking of the house at night. The strange sounds it makes.

So I thought if there was an opossum on our block in the wee hours of the night, I'd have seen or heard it too. But then the fish disappeared. I didn't notice at first because in the cooler weather they tend to swim deeper in the pond. But one morning in March when it was starting to get warm, I walked out with a cup of coffee and found the remnants—a tail fin and a head.

I stared at the fish for a long time. I had raised them with my own hands. I hadn't believed Marisa until now. I shouted up from the garden. "James," I called, "James. Caesar and Augustus are dead."

James came onto the deck with his plate of toast. He stared down at me. "I'm sorry, Cathy." He made his way down the stairs leading from the deck and stood over me. He was all ready for work, decked out in his navy blazer and a creamy red tie. I'm assuming it was a day in court. "Well, I don't want to be an 'I told you so.'"

"So don't be," I said, tears welling up in my eyes. "What do you think did this?"

James knelt down, putting his hand on my back. "I don't know, Cathy. Anything could . . . ," James said.

"But it's never happened before."

James kissed the top of my head. "I gotta get to work."

The pond was here when we bought the place, but it hadn't been used in years. It was just a hole in the ground, really, but I wanted to fix it up. I got down on my knees and cleared out the muck. I had the water pipe reconnected. I bought the fish and named them after famous Romans. I raised them in a small tank in the living room. James said, "What're you going to do with them?"

"I'm going to put them in the pond," I told him.

"Oh, boy." He made a face and walked away. He's never been big on plants and household pets. He's never taken that great an interest in the fish or in the pond. He never likes to sit beside it and do the crossword puzzle or read a book the way I do. I can sit on the bench and stare into that pond for hours. James is an assistant DA and he's very busy, really. He is always writing appeals, filing briefs. He works all the time, so we rarely see him, which at times, I think, is for the best.

James isn't a bad man, not really. Only if he drinks, and he's been trying to stop. He's been going to meetings, and for long periods of time he quits. But then he starts up again. The other night James came home late and found Jimmy Jr. on the front stoop with a couple of his pals. There may have been a beer can or two and a cigarette being smoked. And maybe there was some stuff going on with a girl.

But it was all innocent, in good fun. The boys didn't see him coming, or they'd have put the smoke out. They were just being boys, having a good time. It was a warmer night than usual, so it was easy for them to be outside and lose track of the time. Probably Jimmy Jr. forgot that his father wasn't home. I was already in bed. But James came huffing up to the house and started shouting, "What the hell do you kids think you're doing? I could have you arrested."

I heard the shouting and went to the window. The kids scattered like roaches, but Jimmy Jr. had nowhere to go, and his father told him he was grounded and there'd be no smoking or drinking or hanging out on the front stoop until all hours.

I heard Jimmy say to his dad, "Yeah, and where've you been?"

"Earning a living to support you," his father said.

"Yeah, well, I can smell it on your breath." I was proud of Jimmy for standing up to his dad, but even from the window I could see that James got that furious look you hardly ever see, and I thought he was going to hit him.

Instead he just called him names. "You're a lazy bum," he said, "and you're never going to amount to a goddamn thing." A few more things were said between them that I couldn't make out.

I stood at the window, waiting to see how it was going to end, and then Jimmy came inside and clomped up the stairs. I wanted to go to him, but his door slammed and I thought it was best if I left him alone. Then James headed into the living room to watch TV, and I crawled back into bed.

I hardly slept after that, and I'm certain my eyes were a little red the next morning when I ran into Marisa. She probably heard the fight. I'm sure the whole block did. Marisa's our closest neighbor, and she's up at all hours doing God knows what. But I didn't mention a thing. She was dressed to the nines. Those tight black capris she wears and a short blue jacket, just to go to the Department of Housing, where she works. "Did you see it? It was here, last night. It was in the garbage."

"You saw it again?"

She smiled at me proudly and held up two fingers, as if this was a victory. "I've seen it twice."

More people were seeing the opossum as well. Bucky Robertson saw it when he was leaving early for swim practice, and Claudia Watson came home late and found it sitting on her front stoop. And the Australian couple said they got it on film, but that turned out to be a raccoon. You'd think Australians would recognize a common marsupial. Now it's all over the block blog. Messages have begun to flow. "Have you seen it?" "Have you?"

It's become a joke, really. With lots of bantering around. Sam Martins posted that he'd seen a koala. Stephanie Rubenstine asked if anyone had noticed a kangaroo hopping through the yards. Someone came up with "Required Reading": An Opossum Grows in Brooklyn, by Betty Smith; One Flew over the Opossum's Nest, by Ken Kesey; A Room with an Opossum, by E. M. Forster; and To Kill a Possum, by Harper Lee.

It's all in good fun, I suppose. Who ever heard of a marsupial wandering around Brooklyn? I've always liked marsupials. Koalas, kangaroos, and whatnot. I like the idea of the babies sleeping right inside their mother's pouch, safe and protected there. Jimmy always thought they were cute, with their little heads poking out of their mommy's belly. "If I had a pouch," I'd tease him, "I'd keep you there." I thought how nice it could be—to protect your children that way in your pouch.

But what about the animal smell? And don't they shit in there? I started to think what it would be like. To live so close to your mother's skin. To smell her. To shit right in that pouch.

That night over dinner I tell James, "You know, Marisa says she saw the opossum again."

"Oh, yeah?" James smiles. "That's the booze talking?"

That Saturday at our annual stoop sale James runs into Marisa and starts teasing her. "I want evidence," he says in his big lawyer's voice. "I want proof."

And Marisa, who'll talk your head off if you let her, just starts to go on. "You want proof? I'll give you proof."

"What about our fish?" I pipe in. "Isn't that proof?"

"A cat could've done that, sweetheart," James says.

James is very popular on the block. Everyone loves him. He's a big, funny man, a sprawling six feet, with a beer gut, and quick to bring out the Irish whiskey whenever there's caroling or some cold wintry event. The life of the party, really.

That's what I fell in love with, I suppose. James and I went to school together. Middle school! You might say we grew up together. I've never been with anyone else, but he, well, I'm not sure where he's been or what he's done.

It's just a few days after Marisa has had her second sighting. I want to sleep, but I can't. Every sound I hear outside, I think it's the opossum. Acorns being hurled, garbage lids tossed aside. I picture little paws dipping into the pond, one by one, devouring my fish. Beady red eyes glaring at me. That rancid animal smell.

I can't sleep, so I go online. I've never really seen opossums, so I look it up. This red-eyed creature stares back at me. It looks naked, but with mottled, sick flesh, an ugly, pointy nose. "Opossums have prehensile tails, used for grasping." Prehensile. That's a word you don't hear very often anymore. There is something about this creature's bareness that disgusts me. No wonder it is nocturnal. Who'd want to be seen in public if you looked like that?

Once, before Jimmy Jr. was born, I had this dream. I dreamed I was sitting under a tree and I gave birth to this naked creature that turned itself inside out, into this bloody, fleshy thing. It pulsated and grew larger as I lifted a stick to try and beat it back. It wanted to devour me. It would eat me from head to foot if it could.

I turn off the computer and go upstairs. I'm sitting at the window, staring down, when I hear the door open. James is coming in. He's stumbling, banging into walls. In the dark I can almost see his bloodshot eyes. In a moment he'll be beside me. I'll smell it on his breath.

I slip back in bed as he staggers into the room. "Cathy," he says, pulling me near. I hate the sour smell he brings with him. Like cheese that's been left in the fridge too long. With his calloused hands lifting my nightgown, pawing my breasts.

"James, not now," I tell him. "Not when you're drunk . . . stop it." I try to push him away, but he's not really listening. He's a big man, as I've said, and he pulls my nightgown over my head, but it gets stuck. For a moment I can't breathe and I think he'll suffocate me in my own nightgown. But he rips it off. With his rough hands he's prying open my legs. I tell him to leave me alone, but he's too drunk and hot-and-bothered to hear.

Finally I go along because it's the easiest thing to do, and it's over pretty soon, as I assumed it would be. Afterward he goes right to sleep, and I crawl out of bed. I slip into my nightie and press my face to the glass. Acorn after acorn comes hurtling down. I want to see what's making that sound.

In the morning I go outside with my coffee and see another fish. Brutus is dead.

A reporter got wind of our opossum. A guy who reports on urban wildlife came snooping around. Someone posted his name on our blog. "If anyone has a sighting," a neighbor wrote, "contact this guy." I drop a note to the reporter. I tell him about our fish. I feel this might be useful information to him. "I haven't actually seen the opossum," I tell him, "but I think I've heard it up in the tree. They climb, don't they? But it has eaten my koi." The reporter writes me back a few minutes later. "If you see it, take a picture. Then call me right away."

Well, I don't have a picture of it because of course I haven't even seen it, but I decide to post it on the block blog. "Does anyone have a picture of our little critter?" I write as the subject line. I get a number of answers. Some helpful. A few not so night. One guy suggests that the block invest in a FLIR night-vision electron magnifier and infrared camera. A FLIR, he tells us, costs $7,500, can detect heat behind solid walls, and can see in total darkness.

To see in total darkness. It's an idea that actually appeals to me. I suppose that is what nocturnal creatures do. It's something in their eyes. I do a little reading up on "America's only marsupial." One site I find says that "opossums are poorly understood creatures. They are vulnerable and utterly harmless. They never attack and pose no health risks. Yet people confuse them with vermin such as rats and raccoons."

I'm reading up on opossums on the Internet and grading some papers when James comes in. He's still got his briefcase in his hand. "Have you talked to your son about what he's been up to?"

I shake my head. "He's your son too, I believe."

"Is he . . . well, he's heading for trouble. I've seen him hanging out late at night."

I push myself away from the computer, trying to stay calm. "Maybe you could spend a little time with him. Be more of a father . . ."

James sucks in his cheeks the way he does when he's about to blow his stack. "Be more of a father? What the hell is that supposed to mean?"

James heads into the kitchen to pop a beer, and I follow him. "I don't know . . . hit some balls with him. Take him to a game."

"Cathy, he's sixteen."

"Well, he still needs his father. . . ."

But James puts the beer back in the fridge and is already out the door. I see him heading up the street, and I have no idea what he's doing. I start to make dinner. Pasta with sausage. A salad, bread. When he's not back for dinner and Jimmy doesn't come down, I eat alone. I made the pasta with a good meat sauce, and I savor each bite as I listen to the news.

That night I go down to the pond. I've got a Polaroid with a flash attachment. It's not the same as that FLIR, but I figure for the purpose of finding this opossum it will do. There's a bench in the garden, and I sit off to the side. Maybe I'll catch it in the act.

It's a cooler night, with a chill in the air. The wind blows through the branches. All the acorns are down. Soon the leaves will fall. It's late as I sit at the edge of the water. Deep down I see the movement of one or two remaining fish. I see my own reflection. I am looking a little haggard and tired, but not that much worse for wear.

I am surprised at how much I can see in total darkness. And how oddly soothing it is. To see the fish, my face. The ripples on the pond. I look up and see the branches and leaves of the oak tree. I see the telephone and cable wires. It is not that difficult, really. The darkness is amazingly clear. Then I hear laughter. Voices are coming from Marisa's house. She laughs in that high-pitched, trashy way. I look up at her living room and I can see that she's laughing with someone on her couch.

From my vantage point deep in the garden I see them, their glasses clinking. I recognize the raised arm, the shape of the head. The wide, assured shoulders. James hasn't laughed like that in years. Not with me, anyway. I am surprised to hear him now—a deep, hearty laugh as they get drunk. I watch them for a while, just drinking and laughing, until the lights in her living room go dim.

I don't know how long I sit there, with my Polaroid and flash in my bathrobe, waiting for the opossum to come. But I know it won't. Certainly not if I'm waiting for it like this. If it comes at all, it will be when I least expect it. When I don't even want to see it anymore. It's probably hanging above me right now from its prehensile tail.

I'm shivering, sitting by that pond. At last I head into the house and go upstairs. It isn't much later when I hear James come in. He's making a racket, banging into chairs. He opens cabinets, then slams them shut. He clomps up the stairs, and I hear him in the bathroom, where he pees like a horse. Then he makes his way into our room, stumbling against a chair.

But I know what to do. He slips into bed, but I don't budge. I lie very still, and he doesn't even know I'm awake. ✧

Phillip Lopate
Adam Braver

*Phillip Lopate was born in Brooklyn, New York, in 1943 and received a BA
from Columbia University in 1964 and a doctorate from Union Graduate
School in 1979. He has written three personal essay collections,*
Bachelorhood *(Little, Brown, 1981),* Against Joie de Vivre *(Poseidon,
1989), and* Portrait of My Body *(Anchor, 1996); two novels,* Confessions of
Summer *(Doubleday, 1979) and* The Rug Merchant *(Viking, 1987); two
poetry collections,* The Eyes Don't Always Want to Stay Open *(Sun Press,
1972) and* The Daily Round *(Sun Press, 1976); a memoir of his teaching
experiences,* Being with Children *(Doubleday, 1975); a collection of his
movie criticism,* Totally, Tenderly, Tragically *(Anchor, 1998); an urbanist
meditation,* Waterfront: A Journey Around Manhattan *(Crown, 2004); and
a biographical monograph,* Rudy Burckhardt: Photographer and
Filmmaker *(Harry N. Abrams, 2004). In addition, there is a Phillip Lopate
reader,* Getting Personal: Selected Writings *(Basic Books, 2003).*

1. The Holy Genres

ADAM : When I was reading over the Ten Commandments the other day,
I noticed a new one—an Eleventh Commandment that apparently established genres. Now, so many millennia later, do you think that genres are
falling down—especially between fiction and nonfiction?

PHILLIP: I don't think they're falling down. There's admiration and envy
across the lines; some writers care more about the distinctions, and others care more about blurring the distinctions. The power of experience,
of the real, of what actually happened, continues to affect writers and continues to be very attractive. I'm attracted to nonfiction, probably because
I do sense a kind of shape underneath experience. And I try to bring up
that shape by working with the materials. So something happens, and
then I think, What was that all about? Then I try to work with it till it
yields some formal meaning. And often in my own mind there's something uncanny about the way something actually happened. I don't want
to invent anything, because it's so beautiful or so odd, the mesh of circumstances in real life.

ADAM: How do you know if what happened needs to be written as fiction
or nonfiction? Is there an obvious line?

PHILLIP: I've written fiction in which I've invented whole characters
and whole situations. My novel *The Rug Merchant* was about a
Zoroastrian rug merchant living in New York City. I'm clearly not

Zoroastrian, nor am I a rug merchant. I recently completed a novella about somebody Hispanic and Catholic and wealthy. That's the biggest distortion of my own life. So I knew that I was writing fiction. I also knew that I was calling upon certain psychological elements in myself that was much the way I might in a personal essay. So to me, possibly because I do write fiction, the line is much clearer. That is, I go to fiction as a kind of holiday from nonfiction and a chance to project my character into other lives so that it becomes a kind of route not taken.

ADAM: That's some holiday, Phillip.

PHILLIP: It's a holiday that proves to be more taxing and excruciating than writing nonfiction. That is, I think of myself as a natural nonfiction writer and a labored fiction writer.

ADAM: And why is that?

PHILLIP: It comes much more naturally to me to write nonfiction because I've learned to command my voice on the page. What interests me in fiction is partly the more distorted voice, and the unreliable narrator, to some degree. But I think even in my nonfiction, in my first person, I play with elements of unreliability. That is, what I say actually happened and is factual, but I tease the reader into wondering how much of a monster I am.

ADAM: The beast in Lopate.

PHILLIP: Actually, I consider myself in the lineage of mischievous writers. That is, when I was younger, going to college, some of the authors that meant the most to me were Italo Svevo, and Machado de Assis, and Ford Madox Ford's *The Good Soldier*, [André] Gide's *The Immoralist*. I was attracted to a kind of ironic style. And I think that ironic style is very useful in the writing of personal essays. What gets me going very often in writing is to find some mischievous relationship to material or to technique.

ADAM: In finding those relationships, do you have self-imposed rules about "what actually happened"? For example, are you willing to distort a fact for the flow of the essay?

PHILLIP: Yes, up to a point. For instance, the distortions may come in the forms of condensation. I may compress and combine materials for economy's sake. Instead of going through five meetings, I may go through two meetings. You know what I mean?

ADAM: All too well. And would you do that with people? Combine several into one person?

PHILLIP: I don't actually do combined characters, which some of my friends, like Vivian Gornick, do. I don't. I don't disapprove of it, but I don't do it. It's not a moral sense. It's a sense of delight in things as they are.

ADAM: Fictionalized scenes?

PHILLIP: I like to think that reality has enough amplitude and plenitude to draw on already.

2. Thinking on the Page

ADAM: There is a lot of talk in the nonfiction world about scenes versus exposition in the essay. I assume that is where the borrowing from fiction starts to come in?

PHILLIP: Yes. I am much more drawn to the expository voice, the summarizing voice, the aphoristic voice, when writing nonfiction than I am to the scene-making voice. I will make scenes, but I definitely disagree with this idea that nonfiction should be as much like novels as possible. I don't think you need dialogue and scenes all the time. The key to being a good nonfiction writer is actually developing a flowing, mellifluous, articulate voice on the page. By that I mean a telling voice.

ADAM: It seems as though students are more attracted to scenes.

PHILLIP: Yes, definitely. To some degree they've been told to do this, and to write everything in kind of visual detail and description, and to show, don't tell. I think that comes about because the mores and examples of fiction workshops have penetrated into nonfiction. There isn't as articulate a nonfiction pedagogy as a fiction pedagogy. So out of laziness or a zeitgeist teachers tell students to follow the rules of fiction. This is this resistance to thinking on the page. And if everything is done in scenes and dialogue, it seems to go down more easily. I, on the other hand, really am attracted to thinking on the page. What draws me to nonfiction writers is a lively mind as much as anything. I certainly don't pick up an essayist or memoirist in order to read a series of scenes. I want to hear an intelligent voice, you know, grappling with each sentence.

ADAM: It almost seems contradictory on some level, since a good part of the contemporary fiction pedagogy demands that the writer be absent from the story completely. And it seems as though with an essay the writer is the story.

PHILLIP: Yes. I think that's true, and I think that one of the attractions of nonfiction is this very old-fashioned idea that there is a writer, that there is a self, that there is still such a thing as the individual self, which is an old concept of humanism that's been under attack by a lot of critical theory and structuralism and things like that.

3. Experience

PHILLIP: I think very often young writers want to give the reader the sense that they're experiencing something for the first time in the somewhat baffled, dreamlike, sleepwalker way that the author may be experiencing the event. My own perspective is that it's not so much what happened; it's what you make of what happened. That's where memory comes in; and that's where assessing memory and judging it and turning it upside down and realizing that you're no longer the same person that you once were come into play.

ADAM: The narrative events are really a means of assessing what it means to you as the writer.

PHILLIP: Yes. Yes. Yes. What you make of it. Like in George Orwell's "Such, Such Were the Joys." He doesn't want to just conclude that it's terrible to cane children. He wants to say that some of the misunderstanding and some of the grief of childhood may be inevitable—may be structural, even—as opposed to it just being the kind of abuse situation.

ADAM: There certainly is more of a seduction to writing the dramatic moment or situation, in contrast to discovering the beauty within an ordinary moment or day.

PHILLIP: There's a lot of pressure to reinterpret your past as based on some victimized situation or some abuse or some trauma or some overcoming of a disability or overcoming of an addiction. And I think that the assessing of the every-day is still fascinating. It takes a lot of guts, you know. You have to have confidence that your mind is interesting enough that you can meditate on the events of everyday life in a way that keeps the reader's interest. Readers will be interested in those things. But certainly a lack of confidence might push somebody in a melodramatic direction.

ADAM: Is that coming from the feeling that that's what it takes to get published?

PHILLIP: That's part of it. But in the case of students, adolescence is a very dramatizing, self-dramatizing, time. It's a time when even the sanest kids are given to moodiness, suicidal impulses, drama-queen tantrums, and so on.

ADAM: So I've heard.

PHILLIP: You have to have lived awhile for the perspectives to even out, for you to realize what really is major and what's minor. That equilibrium is almost a function of middle age. Some people get it when they're much younger than middle age. But in general, if you look at it developmentally, young people need to project a dramatic sense of themselves to believe they have a self and to get it across to others. To give you a little example, when I was younger, I used to try to be the life of the party all the time and to be very lively in social gatherings. And now I'm more likely to hold back at first and just to watch, because I don't have to project myself as a clown all the time.

ADAM: Can you expect younger writers to have that level of introspection to step back and assess why they need to be the life of the party?

PHILLIP: I do think introspection is a tendency that can be taught. For instance, I want young people to start to get into the habit of thinking beyond how somebody hurt their feelings, but how they might have hurt someone else's feelings, or that the person who hurt their feelings may have been goaded into action by something you, yourself, did.

ADAM: Sure.

PHILLIP: That ability to look at a question from all angles, not just from the defensive angle, from the self-righteous angle, is an important part of the introspection needed to be a good nonfiction writer. Self-reflection is very important, not just in being a writer, but in being a human being.

ADAM: I was thinking about this with people I've taught who are essentially writing memoirs—even if they call them fiction. The younger ones often write about themselves in that moment. But the same type of people who are more middle-aged are suddenly writing about the town they grew up in, and the history of the town, and how the town they grew up in shaped them—understanding their environment in order to understand themselves. As we get older, it seems we become more interested in the relation of ourselves to the rest of the world, with the priority of getting a handle on the rest of the world first. Then seeing how we fit ourselves into that space.

PHILLIP: Yes. The balance between the self and the world changes. For instance, I think one of the important developmental experiences that can occur with a nonfiction writer is to go from writing only personal memoir to writing material that requires research and going out into the world and talking to other people.

4. Researching

ADAM: Do you think people are concerned that research will compromise their memoir?

PHILLIP: I don't think they think it compromises, as much as they're afraid they don't know how to do it well. It is difficult. You have to assimilate large amounts of disparate materials in a dry style, and you have to reposition them in your own writing style. You have to integrate materials and voices from elsewhere into your voice. For instance, when I was researching The Waterfront, at first I had a lot of quotes because I felt, modestly, "I don't know this stuff. I'd better quote somebody who does know." I was literally told, "You have too many quotes." I had to reconfigure it, recast it in a Lopatean prose style. I had to find a way to make it more ironical, mischievous, or provoking, you know, in an enjoyable way. I was reading reports by engineers, by scientists, and I couldn't allow it to be too dry. There are some writers, of course, like John McPhee, whose greatest talent is in taking the materials of research and recasting them in a very understandable and illuminating way. But he doesn't work with the self as much.

ADAM: So when you're researching, do you find yourself also at times looking for that nugget that does seem like a Phillip Lopate view of the world?

PHILLIP: Yes. Something I can seize on that has some contradictory quality. Something that will go against expectations.

ADAM: Do you find it hard to convince people it is actually there for them as well?

PHILLIP: It is there. To give you a specific example, I know a lot of students who are politically engaged, more on the left than on the right. Sometimes they want to write personal memoirs or accounts of the involvement in some struggle, some movement, anti-war or anti-poverty or anti-mobilization and so on.

ADAM: Right.

PHILLIP: I have to try to convince them to find their own ambivalence and their own internal contradictions, in spite of the fact they'll tell who the good guys are and who the bad guys are. It would be much more interesting if they could show their own divisions between the utopian and the pragmatic.

ADAM: And only using the event as a backdrop.

PHILLIP: Instead of preaching to the converted, mouthing the same things that you believe in, show where your faith faulted.

ADAM: Finding the vulnerability.

PHILLIP: And finding the doubt. Finding the doubt is very important.

ADAM: Do you find resistance to that? Is that liberating to people when they see that?

PHILLIP: In my experience, sometimes students start to do it and get very excited, and then they relapse. And maybe they do it again. The politically committed side of them is used to mouthing pieties for the sake of morality; nothing else. It's a kind of group speech. What I try to encourage them to do is to find their own individual speech within the group speech.

ADAM: Makes sense.

PHILLIP: And also to look at historical context. That's where research comes in also. Again, research—everybody starts out with morality and politics. But you've got to be open to research information that will contradict your morality and your politics, and you should be intrigued by that, not disturbed by it.

ADAM: The goal is to get people out of the black-and-whiteness of how they see an issue.

PHILLIP: Exactly. It's like an environmentalist fighting the unions. The unions see it as jobs. The environmentalists see it as the environment. You have to be able to look at both sides of the question.

ADAM: Along these lines, how much do you expect an audience to know coming into the story or essay, versus how much do you feel you're also educating them? Say you're writing on the environment. Is it also your job to educate on the issue?

PHILLIP: Sure. Interesting question. When I wrote *Waterfront*, there was a vast literature of New York's history. Many people don't know any of it, and [those] in the field know it so well it's the same thing over and over again. What I did, in order to cover some ground quickly, I wrote a chapter called "A Quick Start-Up of Manahatta," like a video game where everything is speeded up. I purposely did that. I plotted history in a light tone so I could get the information in and not take up hundreds of pages. The Dutch. The pre-Revolutionary period. The Grid Plan and so on. I had to get it in the book and not insult the intelligence of people who knew the stuff already.

ADAM: And clue people in who were new to it.

PHILLIP: I like to write in such a way that I'm not lecturing people. I try to write for people as intelligent and possibly more intelligent than I am. I try to write up rather than down.

5. The Double Portrait

PHILLIP: Something that always interests me in a self-portrait or any portrait is its relation to the figure in the background and what items or objects are in the background. For instance, when I write a self-portrait, I need other people to bring out my personality. I can't possibly just write about myself in a void. Sometimes I use a sense of place. Sometimes I use other people. But you need that kind of figure-background relationship. I'm very fond of something I think of as a double portrait, which is where a writer writes about another person the way James Baldwin wrote about Richard Wright, or Gore Vidal wrote about his relationship to Tennessee Williams. I've written about Donald Barthelme and how one's own character comes into play by encountering someone very different.

ADAM: It's so often about the relationship to the setting.

PHILLIP: No painter paints a figure against a void. There usually is something in the back. Even Francis Bacon, you know. There's a chair. There's a sky or something. How we place ourselves, and against what, is very important. I go so far as to say that a self-portrait is not the main thrust but is necessary to bring back the other piece of it. I couldn't write about Donald Barthelme without writing about myself. I think of it as a portrait of Barthelme and me, a double portrait. It's almost as if you're taking a photograph and there was a mirror in the photograph, so we saw the person being photographed and the photographer.

ADAM: Again, when you're teaching people or working with people, part of it is reminding them to fill in the back of the portrait.

PHILLIP: Exactly. So true.

6. Autobiography, Memoir(s), and the Biopic

ADAM: We were talking earlier about the idea of truth, and how far one is willing to go. And how different people will go to different lengths in terms of what they will allow into their nonfiction. I read a piece the other day about all the biopic films that are coming out. The article was attempting to separate out which ones are most faithful to the actual story of the person, as opposed to those that are merely cinematic stories that happen to involve the real people. Considering the latter, why do you think we're willing to accept distortions of truth and fact in film, but not on the page?

PHILLIP: I think we understand that in making a movie, it takes an awful lot of money and you have to appeal to a large mass of people, so there's going to be a lot of shaping in order to keep the story line going. Also, I think films are much more plot oriented than character oriented —any screenwriter will tell you that—whereas in a book the sense of atmosphere and character can matter more than plotline, so we do expect more veracity. There's no need to distort in the book. There's plenty of need to distort in film.

ADAM: Coming back to Vivian Gornick and her composite characters— that could really bother a reader, but it's less likely to bother a filmgoer.

PHILLIP: Right. Exactly. It happens all the time. They create a character who is like a friend, something like that. Exactly. These are considered, I suppose, par for the course, valid distortions. You don't go to a film for the truth of biography. We go to get a good story. Sometimes the biopic is an opportunity to take materials in real life and make them into good stories. The problem with biopics so often is that they're episodic. There's a sense of, in spite of the pressure to keep the plot going, that you have to pass through too many time zones, in effect. Chronology, one thing after another, and the one-thing-after-another undercuts the cleanliness of the plotline. Plus, some biographies are something in between biographies and myths.

ADAM: In terms of autobiography or memoirs—especially when talking about great figures—it most often is the early part that is the most compelling, before the second half turns into "and then we flew to London. . . ."

PHILLIP: ". . . And had lunch with the Duke of Windsor." Charlie Chaplin's autobiography is fascinating. He's poor. He's trying to cobble together a self. He's trying to figure out what his talent is. He's up against one challenge after another. It's riveting. Then he becomes a huge success, and then it becomes an itinerary of the famous people he had lunch with.

ADAM: I guess it's not so much a sense of form, but a willingness to maintain a level of introspection and what this means to you.

PHILLIP: You have to keep finding tension. The first half of any life is the tension of Am I going to make something of myself? Assuming you do make something of yourself, you have to find a way to recast the second part as another tension.

ADAM: That makes sense, as opposed to I made it.

PHILLIP: So you made it. So then it's Can I maintain my success? Or Can I be a loving person? What about my private relations? Are they going to be satisfying? What about all these things? You have to find some other kind of tension. Relationship to God. Relationship to one's community. Political upheaval.

ADAM: I suppose that's the attraction to the memoir.

PHILLIP: It's true that we've shifted from autobiography to memoir. There used to be a category called memoirs, with an s, more like autobiography. They're not writing about how time changes everything. They're writing about a slice of life. So a writer like Mary Karr, in *The Liars' Club* she wrote about one slice, and in the next book she wrote another slice. And so did Frank McCourt. I do think that the whole shape of a life, whether it's [Henri] Rousseau, [Benvenuto] Cellini, or Saint Augustine, continues to be a fascinating challenge, and I would hate to see it go. I still think there's something profound and important in looking at our whole life; to look at the shape, rhythms, and the ups and downs of our whole life. It's difficult to do. And of course younger writers, who haven't lived a whole life, are necessarily going to fasten on a smaller time period. It's a limited number of writers who can do it, because you're really looking for people middle-aged or older to reflect on their whole life.

ADAM: You have to have the end.

PHILLIP: We didn't get to the end yet. Just near the end. ✧

The Illusion of Symmetry

Logan Perkes

I shrug into my sweater, regretting a recent haircut that bares the back of my neck to the cold.

"I don't know what to do about him," a friend says. "We're together almost every day, but—he's seeing other people. I know he is. I guess, well, we aren't official or anything, so it's not like I can say something to him about it."

I've heard this before. I almost tap my fingers on the lunch table, but I stop myself.

"I wish . . . ," she starts.

"What?" I say, trying to be supportive.

"I wish I could become somebody else for a day just so I could look at myself. I mean, I really want to see myself objectively," she says. "Don't you wish you could see yourself from the outside? As a stranger does?"

"I don't know. I've never really thought about it," I say. It takes a few days for my lie to surface and bob in the slush puddles of memory. I'm waiting at a stoplight, staring at a scoliotic woman walk down the street limping, her left hand gripping a wooden cane, when I realize my thoughts inevitably circle the question of how others see me.

While I was lying unconscious, a surgical nurse shaved the right side of my head. My mother asked to keep the hair; she'd been told that if I died, the mortician could glue the strands back on my bare scalp for the funeral. Doctors at Valley Children's Hospital in Fresno, California, handed the nearly weightless golden brown mass over to my mother in a clear plastic bag. My hair spent the subsequent years sitting in the downstairs closet among boxes of toothpaste, deodorant, and old shoes—a tucked-away reminder that a blood vessel ruptured in my head when I was ten years old. Later I would open the closet door to grab an umbrella, only to look up and be surprised when I saw that plastic bag full of hair.

After doctors opened my skull, repairing what they could, and I was well enough to be placed in the pediatric ward, a family friend gave me a haircut, roughly chopping the long hair streaming from the left side of my scalp, trying to make the shaved right side less painfully obvious. The chunks fell limply next to the hospital bed and were swept away, discarded for their redundancy. I'd live, although the left side of my body was wholly paralyzed. My neck flopped back and to the side like a newborn's: brain-damage-induced babyhood. It was a reincarnation of sorts, rebirth of the soul into a new body. My girlhood erased—or so it seemed. I had to look at the pictures of myself before June 1990 to believe I'd once swung from bars, braided hair, and held both my parents' hands at the same time.

*

As an unhappy freshman at UCLA, I decided to see a psychologist. It was not the first time. But this psychologist was smarter than the rest, and I, unfortunately, was more self-reflective. After years of watching Oprah and after-school specials, I'd come to the conclusion that the reason I didn't have friends I connected with, and the reason I didn't date, was the blood vessel that had burst inside my head and the brain surgery necessary to remove it. I told this man so. "Hmm," he said in a deep, thoughtful voice, not buying it for a second. "You are you, right? No matter how you got to be that way?"

"Yes, I guess so," I said, not pleased with his answer. "But I've never had a boyfriend. My friends in the dorm think I'm weird. I am weird. I wouldn't be like this if it wasn't for the brain aneurysm."

"Logan, can I tell you for a minute what I see when I look at you?"

"Okay."

"I see a young lady who is intelligent, interesting, maybe a little shy, and attractive. Basically, I don't see anything wrong with you. I don't see anything standing between you and the things you want."

There is no way to escape the paradox of my body. I am paralyzed. I am inert. I am epileptic. I move uncontrollably.

My left calf is atrophied, my right is muscled. My left arm is shrunken below the elbow, my right is meaty. My left toes tighten and curl whenever they wish, my right toes obey.

My left hand does not open at my volition. I have every reason to doubt the existence of my left side—no pulse is present.

My right side moves. My right hand grasps, clutches, holds. My right arm swings, punches, reaches. My right side lives.

Every day I see the effects of the brain aneurysm—every day I do not see the effects of the brain aneurysm.

I am sick and I am healed.

During my senior year of high school I studied my condition online and discovered some words to make sense of the experience. After years of doctors' appointments and afternoons spent with physical therapists, I finally learned about the intricacies of my condition alone in a room with a computer. The adults around me had not described a brain aneurysm as a dilation, bulging, or ballooning of the wall of a vein or artery. They never told me that a small, unchanging aneurysm wouldn't produce symptoms until immediately before the rupture. They never told me that after the rupture the patient (me) would exhibit such symptoms as vomiting, severe headache, and loss of consciousness. They never explained that the area where my dilation-bulging-ballooning was located controls problem solving, judgment, impulse control, and social and sexual behavior.

Doctors simply said I was a lucky girl. As a child, I tried to believe them.

At twenty-four I moved to Fresno to teach and attend graduate school not far from the place where I had been hospitalized. Although Children's Hospital had relocated to nearby Madera four years earlier, my move transported me back inside the pediatric ward. I saw myself once again limping down long white corridors with jagged, boyish hair. Driving the same freeways and same side streets reminded me of my lost equilibrium and forced me to question the new sense of self I'd developed away from the place I'd been born.

Within a few days of moving into my rented house, while my clothes were waiting to be put away and my furniture was waiting to be shifted, I unexpectedly met a guy. I recognized him as a friend of a friend, and we briefly spoke after a documentary film screening. Not even three hours after our meeting our mutual friend Sandra called. "I gave your e-mail to Sammy. He asked for it. I hope you don't mind," she said. "He likes you."

"Oh, no. You think he wants to go out?" I began to ring the black phone cord around my index finger, dexterously with my right hand.

"Maybe he just wants to be friends," she said unconvincingly.

"That'd be great," I said. It wasn't that I didn't like Sam. I barely knew him. I just didn't like the expectation that goes into dating and knowing that someone likes you. My fear of formal dating was not new: Valentine's Day annoyed me with its run-of-the-mill, generic presents, like red roses and chocolate. In high school, prom night, with its corsages and chain-restaurant dinners, was a torture I gleefully avoided. Growing up in California's Bible Belt, my friends were obsessed with meeting the men they would one day marry. One friend started taking prenatal vitamins at fifteen to prepare her body for motherhood.

Another friend, Janna, was one of those girls obsessed with the idea of being half of a pair. She managed to date frequently, and each time she thought her current boyfriend was the one. My sophomore year Janna offered to set me up with one of her boyfriend's friends. I was suspicious about what type of boy this would be, yet intrigued by the prospect of going out on a date—something I had still not done at fifteen. Days after her initial offer she told me the setup wasn't going to work out. "Why not?" I asked.

"He asked me if there was, you know, anything wrong with you."

"Oh," I said in a wisp of sound, turning my head, like I always did, so she wouldn't see my lips flexing and tightening—fighting to remain straight and emotionless.

Sitting in my kitchen in Fresno, talking with Sandra, I knew I had to purge this experience from my memory, purposely erase the boy who haunted me like an apparition. The boy whose name I never knew, whose face I never saw.

A couple of years after my dilation-bulging-ballooning I went to my mother's hairstylist. Virginia was a Mexican woman with a black mushroom-cloud hairdo and stiletto heels. She was so short she stood on a painted wooden box to cut my hair. She smelled stale and artificial, like the synthetic hair spray she always showered my head with when she finished her work. "Time for a wash," she said as I leaned back in the reclining vinyl chair and felt the cold sink hard against my neck. She wet my hair with steaming water and rubbed my scalp with surprising violence. But whenever she neared the horseshoe-shaped dent on the right side, her angry fingers retreated—she was almost gentle. "Did I hurt you there, honey?" Virginia asked.

She told me that I tilted my head far to the right, and it made my hair look crooked. When I sat in the chair, she motioned for me to look in the mirror. I tried to see what she saw, but my reflection shone bright before me, and it hurt my eyes to look. Virginia decided to cut my hair an inch longer on my left side to make my flaw less obvious, so when I tipped my head it would even out. "At least it will look straighter," she said

The first date was a job interview. This is what makes it tricky—you have to pretend to be really interested even when you're not sure just so you're not ruled out as a viable candidate. In this situation I felt like the boss.

We sat across from each other in a brown booth in the center of a busy chain restaurant. My palms were a little sweaty and I was already gulping down my water, despite the large chunks of ice inside the glass and the near-freezing temperature inside the restaurant.

Throughout dinner he and I went through the usual interrogation disguised as casual conversation. He had five siblings. I had three. He came from a traditional Mexican family. I came from a traditional WASP one. I decided to enliven our discussion and jump right into the drug history questions. Our mutual friend Sandra and her boyfriend were dedicated potheads, so I asked him if he liked to smoke.

"No," he said. "I've never tried it." This was the wrong answer. Let me explain—it's not like I wanted to date a habitual pot smoker, but I feel that in order to be a cool twentysomething, you need to have at least tried it.

"So how about you?" he asked.

"I take prescription drugs."

"For what?"

At this point I weighed my options. Thinking of the date as a job interview, I remembered that in college various vocational counselors had told me I should not disclose my disabilities to future employers. ("Don't give them the chance to discriminate against you.") This was a problem. I didn't have a firm policy in place on how or when I told new friends about my body, much less a policy on when I told dates. In that moment with Sam I could've made an inappropriate first-date joke and said I'd gotten herpes from one of the outdoorsy guys on the television commercial, but I decided not to.

"I have nocturnal seizures," I said. I used the term "nocturnal seizures" to soften the blow. It doesn't sound like an unattractive condition, like say fibromyalgia. If I'd been speaking with a friend or a doctor, I would have plainly said "epilepsy," the more clinical term. But I didn't tell Sam this because the word epilepsy evokes images of people who fall over, shake convulsively, and bite their tongue. Even though I wasn't sure how I felt about Sam, I still wanted him to find me attractive, and this newly discovered vulnerability terrified me more than anything.

"So why do you think you don't have a boyfriend?" my psychologist asked me.

"Guys just don't like me."

"Why do you think that? Do you ever try and talk to any of them?"

"No."

"Why not?" he asked. "What are you afraid of?"

"Rejection."

"But what will they be rejecting? Say you talk to a guy for a minute in your dorm, and you like him but he doesn't like you. What will he be rejecting? Will he really have known you?"

"Yes." I paused. "Well, maybe no. He won't really know me."

"Yes!" he said, happy I got the right answer. "Look, I know rejection stings; I won't pretend otherwise, but remember, it happens to everybody and in some way it's not personal. Most rejection is based upon a very limited amount of information."

"Maybe I'm just not ready to date," I said hopefully.

"If you wait until you're ready, it's never going to happen, Logan. We have to push ourselves to do things we are afraid of. It's part of maturing, of being an adult."

I'd been stalling Sam for a couple weeks with excuses. I had a cold. I had so many student essays to grade. I had to read long treatises on composition theory. I wanted to date him, and I didn't want to date him.

Nearly two weeks after our dinner out he called the house. It was Sunday. I had a cold and was wearing an oversize tee and tiny shorts, and I didn't feel like having visitors. "I have a present for you," he said. "I won't stay long. I promise."

When I opened the door, I saw him sheepishly hiding his hands behind his back. Inside my house he held out a thick piece of white art paper. "I drew a picture of you," he said proudly.

I looked down warily. His drawing was black and white. This is how he'd drawn me—in the strapless dress I wore on our first date. My lips were wider, my collarbone more protruding, my cleavage more pronounced. My left hand was loose and open, my fingers looked like they moved. This is how he'd captured me—my head tilted down toward the ground, my body erect, but my eyes were looking away, into the nothingness of the paper's edge.

"This is great," I said, surprised I meant it. Traveling, I'd seen painters and cartoonists selling their skills to draw portraits, and I'd shied away. I'd begun to feel confident in my appearance, but it still seemed like a bad idea to pay someone to draw a caricature of you.

Sam smiled with pride. "I spent all day on it. It's done by hand, not the computer."

Later I showed the drawing to my roommates and various friends. "He really got your hair," they said. "It's flippy."

One good friend said, "You always look down. Why do you do that?"

Looking back on high school, I think my life is best depicted by red exploding circles looming in the periphery of sight. Here's what I remember from freshman year: reading romance novels in the back of math class. (I must have read five a week.) My head was down and my hair shadowed the lower half of my face while I hid the novel behind the large algebra textbook. In biology I gave a presentation in front of the class on nature versus nurture; both hands shook so badly I dropped the note card I'd stuffed in my usually tightfisted left hand. Friday nights I watched *The X-Files* with my best friend. Afterward she and I stood outside my house until her mother picked her up, promptly at ten. Saturdays were spent with Mom—we went to Linda's Used Book Store to resupply. The store was filled with pages and pages of dust, and I sneezed as I walked down the dark rows of paperbacks, passing fifty-year-old women who could have been teachers or homemakers or court reporters. I identified with them; we all sought escape from the humdrum routine of our lives. Inside the store, we didn't have to walk too far to find the good stuff—Linda kept all the romances up front and hid the literature, cookbooks, and children's books in the back room of the store like pornography.

Amid all this one high school conversation stands out, although I was not in it. The school joke, Tammy, was. One grade ahead of me, she habitually wore blue athletic shorts with one of those bright floral shirts popular among retirees. She was not cool. If you spoke to her, you were suspect—unless you were making fun. This day two guys in their Wrangler jeans and muddy boots were talking to her.

"Do you have a boyfriend, Tammy?" one asked.

"No," she said in her high voice. "My parents won't let me have a boyfriend."

"Have you ever kissed a guy?" the other said.

Before I reveal her answer, let me stop here and set the scene. I sat in the back of the class, near the row of computers. My high school was built in the 1980s, and each building was a square block of gray concrete that looked more like a detention center than a place of learning. This room had only one window—a darkened rectangle of glass right next to the door. During this conversation my back faced Tammy and the boys speaking to her. I didn't need to pretend to be occupied; somehow I'd managed to escape notice, being neither popular nor ostracized.

I frequently listened in on others' conversations, always trying to figure out how my high school world worked. I'd become smart about people. I could figure out quickly who was going to give me trouble and who wouldn't. Tammy didn't have the same skill. In that moment I willed her to walk away. I willed her not to tell them if she'd ever kissed a boy. But she sat in the plastic chair, smiling, oblivious to my telepathic urgings.

"Why do you want to know?" she said.

"We think you're cute, Tammy. We were just talking about you. Wondering what your boobs look like."

"Yeah, Tammy. We wanted to know if your nipples were large or small. What size are your nipples? Come on, tell us. We won't tell nobody."

Tammy laughed and laughed. Her laugh was all wrong—loud and high-pitched, like a wail, as if she knew her pain would linger. Her laugh did linger in my head as an audible symbol of how I felt about my own body—that it was wrong and subject to male ridicule at any time.

Middle school. I'd begun figuring out what being a girl was. In the movies and on television I learned that a lady must never eat more than a man and must always look her best. In seventh grade my mother sent me to "puberty camp" every Thursday at the Baptist church. It went like this: in between making crafts and reading from the Bible, we would listen to tapes about sex and our bodies recorded by Dr. James Dobson. The girls and I would avoid looking at one another during the sessions. Our cheeks burned hot like summer sunburns as we listened to Dr. Dobson's deep voice from the speakers of a boom box in the center of our girl circle. This is how I interpret what he said: our bodies were a source of overpowering pleasure that God didn't want us to experience until we got married, until our husbands unearthed our vaginas like buried long-lost treasure. This was our power, he said, in not excavating our gold coins and ruby rings. I wasn't sure what parts of the body he was talking about, exactly—so I just avoided touching myself anywhere that could be labeled private.

*

During a break in my Composition Studies class I told my friend about Sam.

"Can you believe he did that?" I asked her. "Spent so much time drawing a picture of me after one date?"

"Yeah, that's a lot," she said.

"I know. I'm kind of freaking out."

"He must really like you."

"Yeah," I said, restlessly brushing the hair from my face. All I could think about was that he didn't really know me, so how could he like me? I worried his feelings might change once he knew about my dilation-bulging-ballooning.

Later that night I told him everything. Okay, I actually e-mailed him everything. Okay, okay. Actually, I e-mailed him a link to an article I had written for an alt-news Web site a few years before. This article described what had happened in graphic detail. I waited for his reply, anxious. Sam wrote, "Great article," and asked when we could see each other again.

You'd probably never guess I had a dilation-bulging-ballooning at the age of ten. Your eyes wouldn't see the secrets my body hides. At twenty-five my gait has much improved, I've had many nice haircuts that easily camouflage my horseshoe-shaped indentation, and I've learned methods to perpetuate the illusion of symmetry. My head is generally vertical, and my smile is almost straight. When I take pictures, I like to be on the right side. This way my left hand will be hidden behind the other person's body in the photograph. Also, I do not swing my right arm when I walk, as most are apt to do; I don't want to draw attention to my unmoving left arm. Although I no longer fixate on my corporeal self, years of past obsession linger, and I often find myself, unthinkingly, going out of my way to hide my visible flaws.

I stood in my yellow kitchen, frying corn tortillas for dinner with Sam. It was late fall, but the sun still shone through the lace curtains, and the warm air drifted inside the house through the open windows. Sam was on my right, helping to cut the avocados and telling me about work. I finished frying the shells and started making us drinks, and he began playing with the poetry magnets on my fridge.

A minute later he tapped me on the shoulder and pointed to the fridge when I faced him. I saw the daily indicator I'd gotten at my old job. This was a large magnet full of round happy faces—except all the faces weren't happy. This chart had emotions like Tired, Lonely, Bummed, Happy. Sam had moved the square over to the Captivated happy face, which had little hearts above the circle. I laughed, pleased, and a feeling of security bloomed in my stomach like desire. This is when I really thought he and I could work. It scares me to admit this: I thought if my body didn't bother him, maybe it wouldn't bother me. Maybe I'd be free from the nagging insecurity that felt as impossible to shake as my blue eyes. This sense of hope stayed with me the whole night as we sat on the living-room floor eating, as we held each other's hands and watched a movie, and, later, when we played together, like children, but not.

That was the last time I saw Sam.

At first I wasn't worried. I thought we were both two cool, independent people who didn't plan their schedules to spend every free hour together, and I was proud to be independent and have a life of my own. But then he stopped calling and writing regularly. I was upset by his sporadic communication because I could tell he was trying to keep the relationship going, barely. Soon I ended it, realizing he wasn't going to. It was hard for me because somehow I'd begun to associate dating him with my own maturity and self-acceptance, but I was wrong. He wasn't going to give me anything. I had to see myself, alone, and have that be enough.

At UCLA the psychologist gave me homework. He told me that I couldn't just sit around and expect things to change. He asked if I'd agree to go outside my comfort zone. I was wary, but curiosity won out and I said okay.

Task one: meet five new people (male or female) and get their phone numbers.

I bargained him down.

Task one, revised: meet three new people and get their phone numbers or e-mail addresses.

Outcome: I started talking to more people in my classes and asking them questions. What was a fun science course for me to take? What did they think of L.A.? Did they—by any chance—enjoy talking about feminism and the roots of patriarchy in American society? I scored a couple friends this way and got the names of some good professors.

Epiphany: meeting friends requires effort, but it's not impossibly difficult.

Task two: talk to at least three boys.

I bargained him down.

Task two, revised: talk to at least two boys.

Outcome: Guy #1 was at a party. My friend and I were standing out on the balcony of a large apartment that used to be a house. I heard, "Hey, Logan. How are you?" I looked through the haze of cigarette smoke toward the sound coming from a boy's beautiful mouth. My friend, next to me, looked at me with enormous eyes that screamed, This guy is gorgeous. After my initial loss of words he said, "You don't remember me, do you? We met on the bus."

The bus? I was confused. Oh, the bus. He was talking about the

Office for Students with Disabilities bus, of course. I had begun riding the bus shortly after starting at UCLA because I developed a large blister on the inner arch of my left foot from an orthotic that made it painful to walk. The students on the bus were a mix of students in wheelchairs, frat-boy types with crutches who'd injured themselves skateboarding downhill, and student athletes recovering from pulled tendons.

"Right. The bus," I eventually said, still amazed I couldn't remember that face.

Guy # 2 also spoke to me first. He had luxuriously rich skin and shiny white teeth. In International Development Studies class I happened to sit near him, and he said, "Hey, don't I know you from the bus?" I smiled at him and said, yes, probably. We talked in class for the rest of the semester.

Epiphany: I realized what my shrink wanted me to realize. Others did not see me as I saw myself. This statement may seem simple, but I rode the bus for months after my foot healed because it had dark windows and I liked to sit in the front and stare out at the other students walking by. I saw myself like I saw my left side: visible but lifeless.

I found out later that Sam had met another woman a few days after our last dinner. At a loss for how to deal with my emotions, I drank a lot of wine. (I cried, too.) In the campus pub I had a cold beer with a male classmate and earnestly asked him why men were incapable of being straightforward.

Sometimes I swam in Pacific Oceans of self-pity—I didn't even want to date Sam at first, and then I was the one who got dumped. Sometimes I felt elated by my narrow escape—he wore a toe ring, for God's sake. The one feeling that remained consistent was shame. I had put aside doubts about my own feelings to develop what I hoped would be an adult relationship with a guy. I'd fallen for him because of the safety I thought he offered.

I wanted to spread my pain around and mush it into the chairs, the tables, the ground—anywhere away from me. I distracted myself writing a manifesto about my teaching pedagogy for my Composition Studies class. When that didn't work, I talked with my students about power relations in society via traditional and contemporary dating practices. ("Dating sucks and has always sucked" was the focus of my lesson.)

Still, I didn't think the one thing you might have expected me to think, considering my obsessive history—I didn't believe Sam didn't want me because of my body. Even better, why he didn't want me didn't seem to matter at all. I'd pushed myself to open up to the possibility of a healthy relationship for the first time in my life, I had risked rejection, whether I had planned on it or not. Now I understood what real rejection felt like, and it hurt, but I didn't seriously question my own worthiness.

It made it easier because I didn't miss anything specifically or essentially Sam. My memories of the way he'd touch my stomach, the googly look he got in his eyes before we kissed, sparked annoyance. Weeks after the breakup I could barely make out his face in my memory—his features had vaporized like mist on his black-frame glasses. The only other tangible memories of him were the crispness of his styled hair and his flip-flops. I began to wonder if I would recognize him if we passed on the street.

The first boy I let touch my scalp was infatuated with my roommate at UCLA. My attraction for him grew exponentially with my dislike for her. Late one night he injured himself in a silly stunt and fell to the ground, blood gushing out of his head. He was rushed to the hospital. Doctors put sixteen stitches in his scalp, and he had a small scar. I used my dilation-bulging-ballooning to flirt with him. It went like this.

"You're not the only one with a scar," I told him with what I imagined was a voice full of sexy bravado. "Do you want to feel mine? It's huge." When he said yes, I took his hand and guided it to the right side of my head.

"I think I found it," he said.

"It's big, right?" I said. "Like a horseshoe."

He rubbed his fingers up and down and around my indentation. He pushed clumps of hair out of the way to get even closer to my scalp. I leaned into his hand, removing my own from the top of his, surrendering my head to him.

I've heard if you split a head in two—crack it open like a coconut—the two sides are not identical, the two halves do not make a whole.

And this is true for all faces and all bodies.

It is true for my left eyebrow, which droops lower than my right.

It is true for your left foot, which is a half size smaller than your right, or for your right breast, which is half a cup larger than your left one.

It is true for my left leg, which swings out and around, a white crescent moon, while my right foot walks straight as a metal post.

This is the sound of my walk on smooth cement: thwack-whoosh, thwack-whoosh, thwack-whoosh.

It's a kind of music. Can you hear it?

The family friend who gave me the haircut at Children's Hospital still cuts my hair when I visit my parents. I've neglected my hair, it has grown heavy and long, so I call to see if she can squeeze me in.

"How is your boyfriend?" Marta asks me as soon as I plop down in her padded chair. I know she's talking about Sam, but I don't bother explaining that he and I were never officially boyfriend and girlfriend.

Older people, especially my mom, fail to understand the intricacies of twentysomething dating.

"I'm single again."

"What happened?"

"He didn't want me," I say, amazed by the truth and how much it hurts to tell it. "I don't know why."

"You'll find someone else," Marta says consolingly.

"I'm in no rush. This last one wore me out."

She lifts my hair, almost playing with it. "You have so much hair." She lets the chunks fall just below my shoulders as she looks at my face in the mirror. "It's too long. You look better with shorter hair."

"Yes, I know." I offer up a weak smile.

She sprays my too-long hair with water before she gets her scissors out, ready to cut. "Keep your head straight," she tells me. I try to right myself, but I'm still not there. She grabs each side of my face with her two hands and shows me where center is. ✧

A MIRACLE OF CATFISH, by Larry Brown

Jill McCorkle

A *Miracle of Catfish*, Larry Brown's final novel, is one not to be missed. I read it in as close to one sitting as was possible, loving that I was feeling so committed and steeped in these characters lives, immersed in all the possibilities that lay up ahead and around the bend of those Mississippi back roads Brown has given such vivid life and respect to all these years. Then as I got closer to the end, I kept feeling the shock of knowledge that I was moving toward an ending he had not had time to write before his untimely death at age fifty-three. It's a novel without the author's official ending, and yet this does not in any way diminish the satisfaction this story delivers. Editor Shannon Ravenel chose to publish Brown's notes and thoughts about what might or should happen at the end, and though it is a gift to glimpse the suggestions, the power of what has already been woven together has a natural momentum that would have been enough to set the reader's imagination off in any number of possible and satisfying conclusions.

There's much to admire and marvel at in the work of Larry Brown, and for years I have sent writing students to his books for lessons. The sheer beauty of the language alone is enough—a seemingly simple, sharp-eyed clarity that unearths chasms of dysfunction and despair. Then there is his strong appreciation for a place—the natural world as well as those creatures inhabiting it. But the lesson I most often send people to find is one of compassion. Brown can take the vilest person and find some trace of redemption, something that makes it impossible to easily judge and dismiss a life.

In *A Miracle of Catfish* a character known only as Jimmy's Daddy is a poor excuse for a father, letting his son down time and time again with failed promises. Jimmy, a child with bad teeth whose big dreams are getting his go-kart going again and getting to a Kenny Chesney concert, is the ultimate optimist, coming back again and again with a new surge of hope that this time it might be better. His trust and desire are heartbreaking to watch, as is the slow, painful recognition of the reality of his world. The kindness Jimmy does find is from a man named Cortez, who is in the process of building the catfish pond that serves as centerpiece to the novel. And Cortez's kindness to the boy is a gesture that works to weigh against his own dark past and secrets. They all have secrets and worries and desires, and it's the weaving and crisscrossing of these lives that showcases Brown's brilliance both as a novelist and as a chronicler of human emotion.

In an interview Larry Brown once said: "My fiction is about people surviving, about people proceeding out from calamity. I write about loss. These people are aware of their need for redemption. We all spend our time dealing with some kind of hurt and looking for love. We are all striving for the same thing, for some kind of love. But love is a big word. It covers a lot of territory. I try to tell it in a fresh, new way, to be innovative." The author's words say it best, and here again his means are fresh and innovative, allowing us into the world of a giant catfish or a buzzard as easily as into that of a man who has committed murder, or one whose own father's abuse prevents him from being the father he knows he should be, or a woman feeling the burden of raising her children in a hopeless household while longing for something better, or a boy just on the cusp of the reality of his world as he clings to his own innocence with hopes and desires of miracles—a giant catfish or a daddy who won't sell his go-kart out from under him.

In this novel Brown covers a lot of territory with his trademark style—the precise, vivid language and endearing wit; the dark, ugly turns to violence and cruelty; the struggle for compassion and salvation. His innate wisdom about human nature gives the paths his characters' lives take the sure-footedness and clarity he gives to his own geography. And in that way there is something almost reassuring in ending where we do, as if we've been driven way out those Mississippi back roads, past pastures and cotton fields, and left there to survey the routes we might take, to imagine all the lives with stories worth telling down each and every one. Brown's literary world will be traveled for a long time to come, a literary map that reflects all of humanity, and so it is perhaps fitting that the ending is left open, leaving us all, even in the face of a sad reality, lingering and hoping like Jimmy for a little bit more, a miracle of sorts. ✧

The Groaning Cows

Craig Morgan Teicher

One night, as if responding to some invisible signal, all the cows began groaning in unison. They groaned and groaned all the next day and did not stop at nightfall. This went on for days and days. No one could sleep. The children were growing more and more afraid. Nearly driven mad, everyone in town gathered in the meeting hall.

Were the cows sick? Was it a warning? Of what? What should they do? No one could agree. Someone suggested that perhaps there was something wrong with the grass, and the cows were groaning because their stomachs ached. But this did not seem likely, as the other animals ate the same grass and none of them were groaning. Someone else wondered whether the cows had finally tired of their servitude. Perhaps they were groaning to beg for their freedom. But no one else was willing to believe that cows had such ideas. No one could think of a good explanation, and no one could think what to do, so they agreed to meet again in one week's time.

Still the cows continued to groan, night and day, while the farmers milked them, while they were being led out to pasture, when it was dark outside and they should have slept. Their voices never tired of groaning.

After a week had passed, the town gathered again, and the mayor, who, after all, was soon up for reelection, said that something must be done. He determined that all the cows in town must be slaughtered. Then he would go to the next town and buy more cows with the money set aside for the harvest festival, which they would have to do without this year. Since no one could think of a better idea, the people of the town agreed.

That night all the men met in the square. They brought with them every tool of violence they had—scythes and clubs, knives and large iron rods—so no one would be without a weapon. Then, holding torches, the mob made its way to the first farm. They would all kill the cows together.

As they reached the place where the groaning cows were standing, the cows seemed to take no notice of their approach, despite the glint of the torches on the blades the men carried. In truth, the men were nervous, still unsure whether they were truly taking the best course, but the mayor was among them, and he urged them on. They raised their weapons and prepared to strike.

Just then a girl ran into their path and stood between the men and the cows. She was the weaver's daughter, a quiet girl who kept rabbits and loved to make up songs.

"Stop!" she cried. "You must not kill these cows, or else terrible luck will befall us all!" Then she put her hand on the soft muzzle of the nearest cow. To her surprise, and to the surprise of everyone there, as she touched it, the cow stopped groaning. Soon all of the cows were quiet, and precious silence filled the night. Everyone went home and slept for what seemed like the first time in their lives.

The next night, just as the sun finally set, all the pigs began groaning, as if responding to some invisible signal. They groaned and groaned and would not stop.

The poor weaver's daughter. She knew then, when she heard the groaning, that her life would never be her own. It would belong to the pigs and the cows, to the goats and the ducks, to the hens and the rabbits. Most of all, it would belong to the men, who she knew would never let her be.

The Story of the Stone

Craig Morgan Teicher

When the first frost settles over everything, you find you have become a stone. When it grows colder all around you, and things begin to huddle together for warmth, you are only as cold as you were when you first became a stone.

When everything is buried in snow—the trees up to their waists, all the brown leaves on the ground, the burrows and the creatures who live in them—you are only as buried as you were when you first became a stone.

When the world begins to grow warm again, and the ice thaws, soaking the earth with water, you thaw only as much as you thawed when you first became a stone.

When it is finally warm everywhere, and life is buzzing like the bees who anoint every new flower pushing up to claim its life, you claim only as much life as you claimed when you first became a stone.

When great heat beats down like a thousand fists upon the world, and everything is sluggish, sulking like sweat across the grass, you sulk only as much as you sulked when you first became a stone.

And when everything begins to die—when the leaves and the grass and the streams wither and turn brown—you die only as much as you died when you first became a stone.

This is the way it is, the way it was, the way it will always be, until you are no longer a stone. Then it may be some other way.

THE KIN-DER-KIDS, LITTLE ORPHAN ANNIE, and Masters of American Comics

By Shannon Connelly

In fall 2005 curators at the Hammer Museum and the Museum of Contemporary Art in Los Angeles teamed up to organize Masters of American Comics, a dazzling survey of twentieth-century comics innovation, from the early Sunday pages of Winsor McCay to the contemporary graphic novels of Chris Ware. I caught Masters at the tail end of its East Coast run, in January 2007, where it was split chronologically between the Newark Museum in New Jersey and the Jewish Museum on Manhattan's Upper East Side. I'd grown up coveting my uncle's impressive collection of mint-condition, plastic-wrapped Marvel titles. But Masters of American Comics was no staid procession of superheroes. Instead, it was a compact comics education, exploring the colorful, the grotesque, the lyrical, and the strange through the eyes of fifteen pioneering artists.

In Newark, Masters set the scene with the genteel stylists Winsor McCay and Lyonel Feininger, both famous for their innovative Sunday newspaper pages, and tracked the development of weekly and daily strips from George Herriman's *Krazy Kat* to Charles Schulz's *Peanuts*, with stops along the way for Frank King's languid, lovely *Gasoline Alley*, Chester Gould's darkly violent Dick Tracy, and Milton Caniff's exquisite noir set piece *Terry and the Pirates*. Across the Hudson River, at the Jewish Museum, the focus turned to comic books and their offspring, starting with Will Eisner (*The Spirit*) and Jack Kirby (creator of well-known characters like Captain America, the Fantastic Four, the Incredible Hulk, and others, and the only "superhero artist" in the Masters exhibition). The show wound down by winding up, tracing the explosion of underground comix from Harvey Kurtzman and *MAD* magazine to currently active innovators like Robert Crumb, Gary Panter, and Chris Ware.

Conspicuously absent at the Jewish Museum was Art Spiegelman (of *Breakdowns* and *Maus*, as well as 2004's provocative *In the Shadow of No Towers*). One of the fifteen selected masters and an early exhibition instigator—Spiegelman first proposed the show ten-odd years ago—he pulled his work at the last minute to protest the geographically inconvenient Newark/New York installation and the censorship of certain works that had been on display in Los Angeles and the exhibition's second stop, Milwaukee.[1] The Jewish Museum scrambled to fill the void, tacking on a tepid installation of superhero drawings at gallery's end.

---

[1] *Spiegelman wrote an open letter to the press about his decision to withdraw that was posted on the online venue the Comics Reporter. See http://www.comicsreporter.com/index.php/resources/news_story/6231/.*

Despite these curatorial snafus, Masters of American Comics presented a wide-ranging introduction to American comics and familiarized a museum crowd with a medium usually preserved in dog-eared paperbacks or crumbly newsprint. Yet as the curators readily acknowledged in the accompanying exhibition catalog, narrowing the selection from the wide range of possible "masters" was a challenging process, merely the first step in what they hoped would "open the doors for future museum presentations that reflect the diversity of the medium as it further evolves in the twenty-first century."[2] Surely this gambit is too good to pass up. After taking in the Newark/New York exhibition (and after taking part in Spiegelman's Columbia University seminar "Comics—Marching into the Canon"), I have a few preliminary ideas.

I.

Let's start with some basics. How does one define a "master" of American comics? A master of comics voraciously gobbles up information—from the purely aesthetic to the intensely personal, from the high and lofty to the utterly base. A master then unites these narrative and visual elements to create a personalized diagrammatic vernacular. But this artist is not some empty vessel, oozing inspiration like a slug on pavement. He or she works in response to historical predecessors and in relation to a contemporary audience.

Regardless of genre, however, a master both reinterprets the visual medium and carves out new terrain for those who follow. McCay, the earliest master in Masters of American Comics, infused his dreamworlds with art nouveau flourishes and figures that might have been snipped from a book of Victorian paper dolls. The result was a fantastic style of young adventure stories that would be reworked by comics artists throughout the twentieth century. In the 1950s Kurtzman borrowed the spare, expressive line quality of German woodcuts for war stories like "Corpse on the Imjin!" and "Air Burst!" These tales were the testing ground for the broader cultural critique and crowded visuals of MAD magazine, which would in turn inspire a generation of comic satirists. And Crumb excavated even older forms (from Brueghel to Goltzius to Goya) for his drawings of fat-haunched, strong-ankled women covered in yeti hair or shrink-wrapped in Catholic-schoolgirl uniforms. Although these stories were the specific blueprint of Crumb's imagination and desires, they nevertheless emboldened a wide audience of underground artists in the 1960s and '70s.

McCay, Kurtzman, and Crumb are, of course, just three examples of the assimilative and biographically compelling comics auteur, which

---

[2] *Philbin and Strick, "Directors' Foreword," 10.*

Masters of American Comics compiled in its series of mini retrospectives to form its twentieth-century canon. Catalog essays and wall texts encouraged viewers to consider the influence of high culture on comics, including Japanese ukiyo-e prints (Feininger), Mark Twain stories (E. C. Segar), old-master drawings (Crumb), and '6os minimalism (Schulz). While helpful to the non-expert, these allusions also defined the canonical in the mustiest sense of the term: patriarchal, predominantly Caucasian, and legitimized by salty old favorites from art history and classic literature.

The Masters exhibition was successful, however, at establishing a cogent visual narrative and suggesting links between masters at various points on the historical time line. In Newark, in particular, one could see certain installations bleed from one gallery into the next, suggesting formal or narrative affinities between artists—simplicity of line and idiosyncratic characters passed down from Herriman to Segar, for example, or noirish suspense and crime drama from Gould to Caniff. With a good memory, one could even pick up the thread at the Jewish Museum to draw connections across the century, between Schulz and Ware, Eisner and Kurtzman, and so on down the line. Yet this chronology, by its very nature, was riddled with holes. The New York Times chief art critic, Michael Kimmelman, puzzled at several artists who had been "grievously excluded" from the exhibition, asking: "Where's Charles Burns? Daniel Clowes? Lynda Barry? Milt Gross? Jules Feiffer? Alex Raymond?"[3] Indeed, the Masters show left plenty of room for expansion—if only from one's curatorial armchair.

A thematic installation might have allowed for more masters (and avoided the limiting, artist-in-a-vacuum scenario), but it would also have led to overcrowding and oversimplification. The focused, mini-retrospective approach was necessary to introduce American audiences to these comics masters within a museum setting. Yet with space for only fifteen artists, adding or subtracting just one master changes the entire scope of the exhibition—the loss of Spiegelman on the East Coast, for example, left a gaping hole in the narrative of the postmodern, self-referential comic strip and the early graphic novel. Changing the cast of characters modifies the story one sets out to tell. With this in mind, I'm going to suggest the removal of one artist and the addition of another for the fifteen-master lineup of Masters of American Comics.

II.

Each selected master contributed something vital to the development of American comics, to be sure. Yet I would argue that the German-American Feininger (1871–1956), creator of the newspaper comic strips

---

3 *Kimmelman, "Funny Papers!".*

The Kin-der-Kids and *Wee Willie Winkie's World*, was the anomaly in the arc of the Masters exhibition. Feininger was in many ways a quintessential modernist, with a complicated and often contradictory pedigree: a native of New York who spent much of his adult life in Germany, a caricaturist and illustrator who would become one of the original teachers at the Bauhaus, and, later, a celebrated cubist painter. He was also an inventive cartoonist whose brief comics output could not do full justice to his talent and imagination. Certainly, his grasp of color theory and printing technology was masterful, as is evident in his early Sunday pages, soaked in olive green, pale mauve, and lavender. Feininger also devised creative solutions to depicting depth and movement in Kin-der-Kids stories like "Narrow Escape from Aunty JimJam" and "Piemouth Is Rescued by Kind-Hearted Pat" (see fig. 1). The latter introduced Feininger's clever use of colored brackets between the panels, a device he would further develop in the lyrical *Wee Willie Winkie's World*.

What's more, Feininger led the pack of German cartoonists brought on by *Chicago Tribune* editor James Keeley to class up the newspaper's Sunday comics supplement in the early 1900s. Feininger—along with Lothar Meggendorfer, Karl Pommerhanz, and Victor Schramm—was therefore positioned as an old-world master set to hoist the American public up by its bootstraps. The Tribune acknowledged that "the artistic sense of the [American] people has not been developed as highly as in some other countries" and that this was "partly due to the lack of high grade examples for study."[4] To this end, Feininger was called upon to design comics with a sophisticated combination of comic humor and fine-art sensibilities. His efforts echoed the modernist vogue for japonisme, characterized by flat areas of intense color, off-center composition, and low diagonal axes slicing through the picture plane.

Two *Kin-der-Kids* Sunday pages epitomize this orientalist style: in "Piemouth Comes to the Rescue of the Kin-der-Kids" (see fig. 2) a series of steeply peaked waves recall the foamy whitecaps in prints by Ando Hiroshige and Katsushika Hokusai. The roiling, pistachio green sea is set against a sky that shifts from blush to carmine to indigo, all the while punctuated by fat yellow lightning bolts. The page is a graphic tour de force, with Feininger as master colorist and compulsive detailer. (Note the grease bubbles in the water in the final panel, after Piemouth has leaked some of his previous night's dinner.)

A page like "The Kin-der-Kid's Relief-Expedition Slams into a Steeple, with Results" also packs a similar visual punch, with its careful panel arrangements and muted color palette like a tin of pastel butter mints. Yet from a strict curatorial standpoint, Feininger's graphic mastery

---

[4] Chicago Tribune, *"New Comic Supplement."*

is redundant in the Masters exhibition, where McCay's *Little Nemo in Slumberland* and *Dreams of the Rarebit Fiend* serve together as a fine introduction to both the Sunday color supplement and the early twentieth-century popularity of fantastic adventure comics.

Furthermore, Feininger had a short life span as an "American" comics artist—just fifty-one pages of comic strips for the *Chicago Tribune*—and one could also argue that he merely refined a story line that had been well established by 1906. (Here I refer to Wilhelm Busch's German *Max und Moritz*, later reinterpreted by Rudolph Dirks in America as *The Katzenjammer Kids*.[5]) True, Feininger drew it better, but does this qualify him for inclusion in a masters exhibition of limited curatorial scope?

Indeed, the Masters curators might have shown a more diverse sampling of early twentieth-century artists by including a contemporary newspaper cartoonist like Tad Dorgan or Bud Fisher, whose work captured the vitality of urban life in boxing matches, horse races, and domestic squabbles. Or the exhibition might instead have included a master like Harold Gray (1894–1968), whose *Little Orphan Annie* reflected the earnest striving and workaday melodrama of America between the wars.

III.

Like Feininger, Gray got his start at the *Chicago Tribune*, where he was a lettering assistant to Sidney Smith (*The Gumps*). Unlike Feininger, Gray was a committed social realist, with red-state values and a deep sense of moral obligation. He was a cartoonist from the wrong side of the political tracks, but his contributions to the medium would have an enormous effect on later artists, whether they embraced or rejected his ostensibly conservative ideology.

In 1924 Gray pitched a comic strip called *Little Orphan Otto* to the *Chicago Tribune*, then run by the influential publisher Joseph Patterson. Captain Patterson encouraged Gray to change his character from Little Orphan Otto (reportedly telling Gray that "he looks like a pansy"[6]) to Little Orphan Annie; she debuted in the special pink edition of Patterson's *New York Daily News* on August 5, 1924. The early strip was

---

[5] *In a letter to his childhood friend Frank Kortheuer in 1890 Feininger wrote that Busch's comics were "not very finely drawn" but "full of life and humor." American caricatures, however, were "the best in the world." It is clear from his collected correspondence that Feininger intended to become a serious comic artist; an 1894 letter to Alfred Vance Churchill gives us a glimpse of the artist's scheme for* The Kin-der-Kids: *"I mean to assure the position of the* Nonsense-Story, *which title does not preclude the possibility of its containing pure humor, feeling, etc, by any means! . . . I have an idea for an entire book, a series of quaint chronicles, to be written and illustrated by myself." Scheyer,* Lyonel Feininger, *63*

[6] *Marschall,* Comic-Strip Artists, *166.*

spare of ornament and anchored by Annie's unusual physical character-istics: her trademark dress, unblinking eyes, and wild, meringue-like dol-lop of hair. Although it shared in the formal tradition of spare, spidery black-and-white dailies like Fisher's *Mutt and Jeff*, Herriman's *Stumble Inn*, and George McManus's *Bringing Up Father*, *Little Orphan Annie* did not focus on the travails of henpecked husbands or the pranks of mis-chievous children. The strip instead created a tiny universe of purpose-ful, plodding melodrama, driven forward by Gray's mastery of comics structure—a 2-D world populated by darkened doorframes, shadowy staircases, and cold stone walls. When they appeared (as they did in almost every panel), Gray's bloated speech bubbles lent additional form to this composed world of objects.

Gray liked the idea of having Annie as an orphan, he said, because "she'd have no extraneous relatives, no tangling alliances, and the free-dom to go where she pleased."[7] Annie was a spunky do-it-yourselfer, Daddy Warbucks her loving but often absent millionaire father figure. Supported by occasional visits from laconic "Oriental" types like Punjab and the Asp, or like the ageless, nationless Mr. Am, Annie traversed the globe on her adventures, rotating through a cast of stand-in parents who often appeared as less mature and less pragmatic than the eleven-year-old redhead. Annie insisted on paying rent and holding down a job—usu-ally based on her "circus 'sperience"—and even on setting up the hapless, lovelorn adults in her orbit. (The washed-up actress Janey Spangles and loser producer, George Gamble, are just one example.) In this way Annie echoed Gray's personal convictions of Emersonian self-reliance, indus-try, and gumption, and mistrust of fancy, spoiled types from Hollywood to big business.[8] Gray said of Annie: "She is tougher than hell with a heart of gold and a fast left, who can take care of herself because she has to. She's controversial, there's no question about that. But I keep her on the side of motherhood, honesty, and decency."[9]

These basic values would steer Gray through more than forty years of *Little Orphan Annie*, from the Depression to World War II; from the baby boom to the hippie era. As the strip matured, it became more mythic,[10] and Annie and Daddy took on qualities of iconic omniscience. Like Superman or Captain America, Annie never grew old; she remained in spunky tween-age limbo until Gray's death in 1968. And in *Little Orphan Annie*, like in the superhero comics, what has happened before

---

[7] *Gray*, Arf! *iii.*

[8] *Indeed, although many critics attacked Gray for his "pro-capitalist" views, he often skewered greedy businessmen with as much relish as union organizers or lazy gadabouts.*

[9] *Gray*, Arf! *iii.*

[10] *Marschall*, Comic-Strip Artists, *179.*

and what happens after appear hazy and indistinct.[11] Causal chains are not open in Annie's universe; to borrow Umberto Eco's language, this "temporal scrambling" allows Annie to act without consuming herself—in other words, it allows her to live forever. Gray perpetuated this myth through a geographically vague but rhythmically repetitious story line that was grounded in historical events. He reportedly traveled 40,000 miles a year around the country to "keep his ear to the ground," yet he ventured abroad only once.[12] Perhaps this obsessive focus is what lent *Little Orphan Annie* its essentially "American" character—work hard, mind your own business, and don't become hardened or cynical when things don't go your way.

As the years passed, Gray's main character did not age, but *Little Orphan Annie* underwent a steady formal refinement. The dailies of the 1920s and '30s were open and airy, almost as if the figures had been strung together with bits of black thread. In this way they resembled popular newspaper comics like *The Gumps*, *Thimble Theatre*, and *The Bungle Family*. (Annie had one important difference, however, in that it was anchored by a female leading character.) By the 1940s Gray had adopted a harder line, in the style of Gould's popular *Dick Tracy*. The comics historian Donald Phelps has written that the vivid blackness in Dick Tracy is not just negative space but "the supplanting of light by a vigorous, surface-rending presence."[13] Indeed, Gould's inky diagramming conveys dread in those black-and-white dailies—a bold swatch of sidewalk, the pants of the double-crossing Summer Sisters, a villain's suit jacket, and so on. Gray, too, used darkness to uncanny effect, particularly as *Little Orphan Annie* evolved during the war years, when he cut the daily strip from four panels to three.

Whatever its relative size or style, however, Gray's *Annie* was quintessential "termite art," as defined by the film critic Manny Farber in his famous 1962 essay "White Elephant Art vs. Termite Art." In it Farber describes the persistent, burrowing tendencies of art without artifice (he celebrates B-movie directors like John Ford, for example, along with the "slothful-buzzing acting" of Myron McCormack and Jason Robards) as the antidote to bloated and listless "white elephant art." Farber writes: "Good work usually arises where the creators . . . seem to have no ambitions towards gilt culture but are involved in a kind of squandering-beaverish endeavor that isn't anywhere or anything. A peculiar fact about termite-tapeworm-fungus-moss art is that it goes forward eating its own

---

[11] *Umberto Eco has written about this phenomenon in his 1972 essay "The Myth of Superman," recently republished in Arguing Comics.*

[12] *Gray,* Arf! *iv.*

[13] *Phelps,* Reading the Funnies, *1.*

boundaries, and, likely as not, leaves nothing in its path other than the signs of eager, industrious, unkempt activity."[14]

And so it is in *Little Orphan Annie*, where Gray does not hesitate to slow the pace to termite speed, gnawing patiently through situations that other comics dramatists might mark with a brief gesture or one-panel conversation. Gray is also a persistent, no-frills narrator with an industrious sense of forward movement. Beginning on March 9, 1936, Gray introduced the story of Jack Boot, yet another enigmatic father figure in Annie's progression of stand-in parents (see figs. 3–8). Here we see Gray's spartan use of gesture and diagramming to guide the reader through the panels, focusing on Annie's oversize coat and hat as she and Sandy descend the staircase to Jack Boot's repair shop. Inside, Jack's massive back and delicately crosshatched vest stand out against a smattering of objects—a chair, a workbench, the scraps of retooled shoes. Like so many panels in *Little Orphan Annie*, these quiet frames buzz with anticipation. So when Jack tosses a freshly soled shoe back to Annie, the action lines really zip, and Annie reacts with a subtle gesture of appreciation: "Gee—they sure *look* swell . . ."

The Jack Boot sequence also highlights Gray's termite-like use of highly slowed-down time. He damps the pacing to a trickle, bidding the reader to follow patiently as Jack and Annie strike up their first conversation. This get-to-know-you session lasts an entire week and is studded with cue cards: "Next Scene Follows Immediately," "Ten Minutes Elapses . . . ," "A Few Moments Elapse . . . ," and the like. (Eisner would later use this control release timing in his September 11, 1949 installment of *The Spirit*.) But in Gray's delicate handling of time and in his use of narrative repetition, he was a pioneer of the continuity strip. A story like Jack Boot's might unfold with little action from Monday through Saturday, but Gray changed pace in his Sunday strips, where villains and ne'er-do-wells could be cut loose or sent to the clink with a few strokes of the pen. By Monday morning, however, these violent scenes were nothing more than a four-line recap, and the meticulous rhythms of *Little Orphan Annie* would resume.

Gray has been described by some critics as an "expressionist" artist, yet this label refers not to expressive marks on the page, but to a mood of unseen violence hovering just between the panels. Often Gray presented his readers with new characters of questionable moral fiber, and these shady individuals could usually dupe at least one other character with their phoniness. In this way Gray built empathy with his audience and let them in on the trick. Certainly, any armchair Freudian could have a field day with Annie's daddy issues, and our Jack Boot story carries more than a whiff of the illicit to the cynical, postmodern reader. It is difficult to accept Jack as a benign protector—his physical girth swallows up whole

---

[14] *Farber,* Negative Space, *135.*

corners of the panel, and his lurking presence is ambiguous: "Will I ever forget that picture? That curly head on the pillow ... if only ... but pshaw! They'll be gone long before this ..." (see fig. 8). Is Jack Boot just a lonely old man, or is he a creepy child predator? Sensing these contradictions, perhaps, Phelps recently described *Annie* as "a classic-paced epic whose tone is doom-laden almost beyond articulation."[15]

Gray invited his readers to empathize with Annie and to project their emotions onto those unblinking, cipher-like eyes. As we have seen, he created (and sustained) a buzz of menace even in the plod of daily conversation. But where style met social commentary, Gray could be less than subtle. This would put him out of favor with fellow cartoonists like Al Capp, who reacted violently to what he perceived as Gray's anti-union, pro-capitalist tendencies. (Capp would later pull a 180 on these views, buy a gated home in the country, and write an adoring introduction to a collection of Gray's daily strips.[16]) *Terry and the Pirates* creator Milton Caniff, himself no stranger to conservative sentiment or patriotic fervor, observed that *Little Orphan Annie* was seen by some as reactionary but in fact captured the mood of the country (and in turn, its loyal readership):

> Gray was a better artist than he knew. His politics were a great part of his armor. I'm sure he felt beaten and bruised from the [liberal] reactions, but he stayed with his guns. And he had the newspaper editors behind him. Most of them felt pretty much the way he did. Editors in those days were in no sense a liberal lot. They were conservative as hell. Sometimes they had to be closet conservatives in big cities. But in smaller towns, the *Columbus Dispatch*, for instance, there isn't any question that *Orphan Annie* spoke for them. I think Gray sensed that. Long balloons or no balloons, they were reading it. You were perfectly willing to stay there and hear him out day after day.[17]

Yet despite his occasionally harsh portrayals of union rabble-rousers or lazy, spoiled actresses, Gray dished out his criticism in equal measure, to "conservative" and "liberal" alike. Gray's social commentary took aim at moochers, hustlers, puffed-up dandies, and cruel tyrants throughout

---

[15] *Phelps,* Reading the Funnies, *265.*

[16] *See Capp's introduction to* Arf! The Life and Hard Times of Little Orphan Annie: 1935–1945.

[17] *Harvey,* Milton Caniff: Conversations, *244.*

society (and even within big business, despite the protests of critics who would not forgive Gray for creating a hero like Daddy Warbucks[18]). And in the tradition of *Dick Tracy*, or Gray's literary hero Charles Dickens, the names in *Little Orphan Annie* often betrayed the essentially good or evil nature of a character. Dickens delighted in the carefully chosen name— Wilkins Micawber, Charley "Master" Bates, Mealy Potatoes, Brittles, Duff, Mr. Grimwig, Bumble, and Mr. Pumblechook all come to mind—and in the detailed social commentary of "types." Likewise, Gray rolled out a motley cast of supporting characters: the orphanage director Miss Asthma (later Miss Hannigan, in Carol Burnett's infamous cinematic turn); Mr. Am, a godlike character who brings both Daddy and the Asp back to life; the spoiled child star Tootsie Snoots; or villains like Pig-Eye Mack, Phineas Pinchpenny, and Uriah Gudge.

More important than this delicious procession of names, however, was Gray's meticulous procession of objects and the mood they could create. Here I refer again to the Jack Boot story, particularly the daily strips on March 12 and 13 (see figs. 6 and 7). In "Sleepy Time Gal" (March 12, 1936) each panel is a quiet beat toward slumber, anchored by a comforting assortment of simple props: a table, a lunch pail, Annie's fedora, and the gently crosshatched ceiling hanging low overhead. Gray shifts perspective just slightly from panel to panel, and his line quietly echoes the text of Annie's speech bubble as she drifts off to sleep: "I'll thank him again—then we'd better go . . . he seems awful busy . . . I'll wait till he looks up . . . gee—I feel sorta drow-s-s-y . . ." By the third panel both Annie and her dog, Sandy, have receded to the background, fast asleep. "Linger a Little Longer" (March 13, 1936) finds Annie awake and eager to move on ("We don't want to be a bother"), and Gray stamps each background with the unresolved darkness of a black-paneled door. This shadowy gateway suggests, if only subtly, that Annie might not be quite as safe with Jack as she wants to believe.

While not cinematic in the sense of a *Terry and the Pirates* or a frenzied Marvel action comic, such objective detachment linked Little Orphan Annie to its contemporaries in avant-garde film, particularly to Weimar directors like Fritz Lang, Walter Ruttmann, or G. W. Pabst, whose 1925 *Die freudlose Gasse* (The Joyless Street) plopped the young

---

[18] *Richard Marschall writes, "When Warbucks dispatched kidnappers by a wink to his henchmen, civil libertarians howled. When he depicted union organizers as opportunistic thugs, papers were swamped with complaints. He caricatured a local bureaucrat, a ration board official in Fairfield County, Connecticut, and he seldom pictured a politician in a flattering light. For these efforts he was frequently assailed: The New Republic published an article by Richard L. Neuberger (later a U.S. senator) decrying* Little Orphan Annie *as* 'Hooverism in the Funnies' *and later ran an editorial about the strip titled* 'Fascism in the Funnies.'" Marschall, *Comic-Strip Artists, 177.*
Comics artists also had a field day with Annie, *from* Will Eisner *(in* "L'il Andy"*) to* Harvey Kurtzman *(in* Little Annie Fanny*) to* Walt Kelly *(in* "Little Arf 'n Nonnie"*).*

Greta Garbo into a spare, forbidding world of objects—the butcher's block littered with meat that none but the butcher's family can afford; a wheelbarrow overflowing with useless currency; or the cold, wet stones of an empty street. These objects punctuate the narrative and mark the slow, burdensome passage of time in inflation-era Berlin. Likewise, Gray's chronicle of American hard times could feel both mundane and terribly ominous, as Phelps describes in his fine study of *Little Orphan Annie*, titled *Reading the Funnies: Essays on Comic Strips*:

> The hypnotic rhythms of Harold Gray, which have often been haphazardly identified as "suspense," consist of just this, I think: the way he attenuates and scales action, grading it against a lowering, excruciatingly heavy sense of time. Gray's puritanical delight lies in those *longeurs*, those prospects of waiting and routine, which are as sweat-boxes to other comic-strip artists, panicky-solicitous of their fans.

When such actions or gestures disrupt the frame, as in the whizzing shoe of the Jack Boot story or the darkened doorway described above, they disturb Gray's quiet arrangement of objects and puncture the narrative sequence. (For another kinetic example, see Annie's 1935 head butt in figure 9.) But each story soon returns to its languorous rhythms and workaday commentary. In this way *Little Orphan Annie* is a pioneering example of the intimately scaled melodrama, reflective of its time and of its readership, and driven forward each day by Gray's mastery of comics structure, from the heavy speech bubbles above to the mundane objects below, these objects elegant and spare—threadlike, even—with a web of gently crosshatched shadows darkening the frame.

---

[19] *Phelps*, Reading the Funnies, *266*

Figure 1
Lyonel Feininger, *The Kin-der-Kids*,
"Piemouth Is Rescued by Kind-Hearted
Pat," published in the *Chicago Tribune*,
September 9, 1906

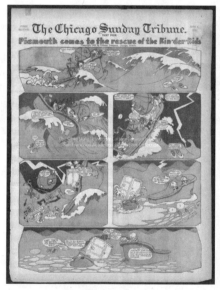

Figure 2
Lyonel Feininger, *The Kin-der-Kids,*
"Piemouth Comes to the Rescue of the
Kin-der-Kids," published in the *Chicago
Tribune*, June 3, 1906

Figures 3-8
Harold Gray, *Little Orphan Annie*, Jack Boot introduction,
March 9–14, 1936

Figure 9

Harold Gray, *Little Orphan Annie*, "Friday, the Thirteenth," September 13, 1935

Works Cited

Chicago Tribune, "Tribune's New Comic Supplement (Begins Next Sunday—Watch for It)," April 29, 1906.

Eco, Umberto. "The Myth of Superman." In *Arguing Comics*, edited by Jeet Heer and Kent Worcester, 146-164. Jackson: University of Mississippi Press, 2004.

Farber, Manny. *Negative Space: Manny Farber on the Movies*. New York: Praeger, 1971.

Gray, Harold. *Arf! The Life and Hard Times of Little Orphan Annie: 1935–1945*. New Rochelle, NY: Arlington House, 1970.

Harvey, Robert C., ed. *Milton Caniff: Conversations*. Conversations with Comic Artists. Jackson: University Press of Mississippi, 2002.

Kimmelman, Michael. "See You in the Funny Papers!" *New York Times*, October 13, 2006.

Marschall, Richard. *America's Great Comic-Strip Artists*. New York: Abbeville Press, 1989.

Phelps, Donald. *Reading the Funnies: Essays on Comic Strips*. Seattle: Fantagraphics Books, 2001.

Philbin, Ann, and Jeremy Strick. "Directors' Foreword." In *Masters of American Comics*, edited by John Carlin, Paul Karasik, and Brian Walker, 10. New Haven, CT: Yale University Press in association with the Hammer Museum and the Museum of Contemporary Art, Los Angeles, 2005.

Scheyer, Ernst. *Lyonel Feininger: Caricature and Fantasy*. Detroit: Wayne State University Press, 1964.

A Genre You Haven't Loved Enough

John D'Agata

Marguerite Yourcenar wrote *Fires*, a collection of linked essays about unrequited love, when she was thirty-two years old.

It didn't appear in the U.S., however, until 1981, six years before she died at the age of eighty-four.

"I never knew what to do with it," she tells us in the preface, an anxious fourteen pages that try to dismiss the emotion that's exhibited in the book as at one point "young" ("If the reader often sees only preciousness, it's because nine times out of ten I yielded to a wish to startle, to please or displease above everything else. Sometimes, though, it is because this same reader cannot follow, all the way through, the idea or emotion that I am giving, so that the reader mistakenly takes it as a forced metaphor or a strained conceit") and at another point "thematic" ("No matter how often I say that this collection does not require commentary, I know that I seem to be avoiding the issue in dealing at such great length with these issues while keeping quiet about the love experience that inspired the book. But what seems obvious is that this notion of mad and sometimes scandalous love that is nevertheless permeated by a sort of mystical power could only survive if it is associated with a belief in transcendence") and at another as "formal" ("In a novel, these feelings would be woven into the plot, and in a poem these would be the starting point of song. In Fires, these feelings and circumstances are expressed directly, if rather cryptically, in unrelated pensées that were at first notes for a private diary").

And just as Yourcenar never fully explains in those florid fourteen pages what exactly it was that happened to her to instigate the book, neither does Yourcenar ever admit that what she turned to in order to unravel her heart is the form we once called the essay.

What she's doing she calls a "poem," and what she's doing she calls "lyrical prose," and what she's doing she calls on several occasions "historical and lyrical prose pieces." But never does she consider what she is doing essayistic.

Even in its reviews *Fires* was described by critics as clearly not being poetry and not being fiction and not being the kind of quasi-critical or personal explorations that were popular at the time in academic circles, yet neither did any critic ever refer to the work as "essay."

In fact, the *New York Times* even invented a genre in order to avoid calling the book an essayistic work. "The unwritten novel," its critic announced, "is a book, however polished, that seems a compilation of fragments. A typical example looks like a salad of autobiography, note-book ecstasies, diaristic confessions, prose poems, epigrams, medita-tions, shafts of critical discourse. . . . Yet these scattered works are not mere pastiches."

No, they are not.

The product of a love crisis, *Fires* comprises a series of voice por-traits by nine mythological, historical, and literary figures whom Yourcenar conjures to speak on her behalf. There is Achilles, for example, whom Yourcenar imagines forgetting his disguise and embracing his lover Patroclus in front of Lycomedes' daughters, who immediately spurn the two as fags. There is Mary Magdalene, whom Yourcenar imag-ines married to an impotent and puritanical John the Baptist, who ulti-mately forces Mary into a life of prostitution out of his own disgrace. And then there is the poet Sappho, who has never pursued conventional love, yet who acquiesces finally, only to be rejected by a man she's not sure she wanted.

When she throws herself from the cliff this time, she survives in spite of herself.

"The best place," writes Yourcenar, "is to be elsewhere." And her writing here is indeed marked by myriad resistances: by an insistent reconception of the contemporary world, by measured and slow sen-tences, restrained lyrical resonance, and a deep examination of her self and life and time.

Always, though, this is filtered through history, fiction, myth.

But does this automatically make her an "unwritten novelist"? Couldn't the very activity of exploring her heart—no matter the tools that she chooses to employ—make that process an essaying?

The term *essay*, after all, is a verb. And it describes a simple activity: a single mind exploring an idea, image, or emotion through the negotia-tion of memory, anecdote, observation, history, religion, science, and even the imagination.

It is not a genre, in other words, that is limited to the academy or to history or to anthologies about our summer vacations.

The essay can be instructional, but it can also be beautiful. The essay can be useful and playful, too. The essay can be personally meaningful, culturally significant, historically prescient, and simultaneously weird, simultaneously stylish, simultaneously servicing a lifelong broken heart.

As Yourcenar explained at the end of her life, "Every literary work is forced upon us by a mixture of vision, memory, action, and ideas—every-thing in the course of a life that we share and know and steal."

All essayists traffic in information, she concluded. Sometimes that information is experienced by the writer. Sometimes it's remembered. And sometimes it's inherited from a collective unconscious.

And very often it occurs in a genre long unrequited. ✧

Ronnie E. Maher: Photographs

Alpha Community Services (ACS) is a regional nonprofit organization and the largest provider of housing services for the homeless population in Fairfield County, Connecticut. In 2006, as part of a campaign to raise awareness of the problem of homelessness in the region, and to portray the diversity of the "faces of homelessness," I was asked to make a series of portraits of people receiving services from ACS. I met each subject once and for only a short visit. My challenge was to go beyond the superficial and reveal the true spirit of each individual. It is my hope that these photographs do just that, and that the viewer is enriched by the experience.

-Ronnie E. Maher

Each year the Alpha Community Services' "Families in Transition" emergency shelters serve 700 homeless individuals, 400 of whom are children. ACS provides 423 units of shelter, transitional and permanent affordable housing with supportive services for the homeless and those at risk of homelessness, which serves more than 1,200 people, and operates the only emergency shelter for homeless families in the city of Bridgeport.

ACS incorporates the concept of Continuum of Care, a program designed to address the root causes of homelessness by providing affordable housing, coupled with comprehensive supportive services, including health care and counseling services, parent training, affordable child care, job training, financial management, educational guidance, and child and youth services, along with case management to encourage successful independence. Importantly, the program staff deliver services in a caring and compassionate manner, helping families maintain their dignity and respect, and overcome the stigma associated with being homeless.

- Carmen Colon, Executive Director, Alpha Community Services

Various

Mameve Medwed

Back in the good old days, before the Coop became Barnes and Noble, and when a bookstore marked every corner in Harvard Square (O Wordsworth! O Reading International. O Barillari! Wherefore art thou?), I went to hear Kazuo Ishiguro. *The Remains of the Day* had just come out. I fell in love with it—the elegant writing, the layered characters, the themes of lost love and missed opportunities amid the horror of impending war, all the social crumbling underneath the smooth upstairs-downstairs country-house surface. Since this event took place at a time when there weren't dozens of authors on tour within a five-mile radius, Ishiguro's appearance in my neighborhood was pretty much the second coming of a rock star, in person, at a theater near you.

He looked like a rock star: jeans, black leather jacket, lanks of below-the-ears glossy hair that fell just so over a noble forehead. He talked about his motorcycle, his band, his musical training, and of course, his novels. The audience was enthralled. He was as dazzling as his book.

It was my favorite novel for quite a while, but I am a fickle reader, always falling in love with the next and the next and the next. And yet despite a history of shifting literary attractions and transient affections, I have, over all this time, stayed in awe of Ishiguro's unreliable narrator, convinced that no writer has ever come close to the brilliant creation of that self-deluded butler. Until . . .

I read about Jane Gardam's *Old Filth* in the *New York Times Book Review*. I rushed out to buy it at my current public utility, Porter Square Books. How could one not be intrigued by such a title, an acronym for "Failed in London, try Hong Kong," a phrase that captures an era, a place, a society, its politics, and its class? I started reading it next to the checkout before my credit card had even been swiped. My breath caught, just as it had those years ago when I opened *Remains of the Day*. Here's a protagonist so damaged by his childhood, with such little self-knowledge, that his tunnel-vision narration forces the reader to become not only a full participant in a life, but also its psychological and social interpreter. What a challenge and a satisfaction to dig between the lines, to spot things about the character and his world that he himself is blind to. Sir Edward Feathers, eighty, ex–Hong Kong judge now settled in Dorset, was a Raj orphan shipped from Malaysia to Wales. In the UK, confused, unhappy, and mistreated, he was dumped at boarding school and left with cruel foster parents; for a stretch he bunked with his best friend's privileged English country family. During World War II he guarded the queen.

Called Filth by his wife and colleagues alike, Feathers is a cold man whose empty, circumscribed days highlight the collapse of empire. Certain reviewers have remarked that Filth's childhood is based on that of Rudyard Kipling—a perspective that might add even more color for Kipling fans, or detractors. Gardam writes with both compassion and humor. Her unflinching, take-no-prisoners approach gives us a novel that moves backwards and forward in time, in geography, and, especially, across the landscape of the human heart. I love this book.

Another novel I've just lapped up—*The Post-birthday World*—takes place in London (okay, full Anglophile disclosure: Ishiguro; Gardam; and now Lionel Shriver, an American woman living in England). Its clever structure is irresistible. In alternate chapters parallel universes fulfill all our what-if fantasies. Irina McGovern, a children's book editor, shares a contented domestic existence with her longtime live-in lover until she meets a charming, hunky snooker player. Will she kiss him or won't she? In one chapter she does; in the other she turns away. Shriver grants her character a full life with each man. Though we mere mortals need to make choices and accept the consequences, novelists have the power to reorder the universe. Shriver's protagonist can have her cake (birthday cake? Beefcake?) and eat it too. This is a delicious novel for a foodie, a snooker aficionado, or anyone who has ever wondered about the *other* fork in the road. ✧

SALAMANDER

Where discerning readers encounter outstanding writers

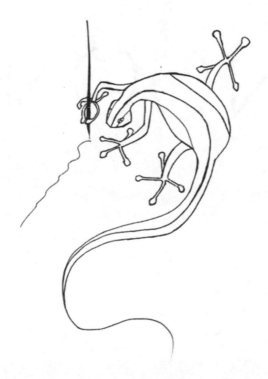

NOON

A LITERARY ANNUAL

1324 LEXINGTON AVENUE   PMB 298   NEW YORK   NEW YORK   10128

EDITION PRICE $12 DOMESTIC $17 FOREIGN

The Lunch
(Take that, Amy Tan)

Alex Kuo

Two half-sisters walked into a bar in the California that is Chinatown. Since they didn't like each other in the half English and half Cantonese of their mother tongue, they sat at separate tables but within sight, text-messaging digital English right into their cell phones. After her drink arrived, the older one keyed a message—YOU GO PICK UP LO MO!—and poked the Send pad with a lacquered fingernail, sucking on an ice cube, and waited for the reply.

WHY?

SO SHE WON'T PLAY THE SPANISH LOTTERY ANYMORE, STUPID, she poked again, but there was no exclamation point this time.

NO, NO, WHY ME PICK HER UP, YOU STUPID. YOU DRIVE FANCY VOLVO.

Treason, she slurped through the ice, and looked up at her slightly shorter half-sister seated at a table no more than twenty feet away, one hand over electric lipstick, giggling and finger-wagging a caution this time. Treason, she repeated, loud enough for the bartender to turn her head.

You two ladies okay? she waved a dirty bar rag at them.

They both turned and fixed her with a mind-your-own-business or shut-up stare, whichever worked, before the one with the lipstick collected all her stuff and re-collected herself at the other's table—after all, like it or not, she had a rep to keep in this community, since she owned her own consulting business, Efficiency Solutions, providing function: time-effort-wage analysis at a hefty fee.

All right, all right, Ida, she said and slid her military-spec compliant cell phone into her handbag. We got to get Lo Mo out of her condo to talk to her about this lottery together. Lunch or something. Just a suggestion, she shrugged and looked away.

You're right, Ida chunked an ice cube back into her drink and continued. She called me this morning and wanted more money. Invest in my business, she said. It's her business now, she said, Nerissa's business. One hundred bucks for Western Union money transfer, must be wired today, she insisted, to protect her number's eligibility. In the four years she's been playing Spanish Lottery she has lost all her savings, and the monthly interest alone on her credit card loans is staggering and beyond her pension payments.

Or pay her phone and electricity bills for the last two months, Buddhist, Catholic, woodcutter, or Kafka, same thing, you know.

What's that? Ida squinted.

That's an expression my anthropologist friend is always using, you know, the one who names everything she has *Kafka*, even her black lab and her laptop, the one who's licensed by the state to evaluate a person's cognitive condition. We can give her the money for her lottery, or pay her bills, what's the difference, same thing. At least this way she'll have heat and a phone, she added this last part in her falsetto street Cantonese.

But she'll call us ten times a day on it, ten progenitor lectures a day.

Let her phone bill lapse, is that what you're suggesting, sister Ida?

Why, sister Kate Blue, you are so mean!

They had decided on the Dragon 2000 for lunch because they knew it was Nerissa's favorite restaurant in town, even when they'd never been there and, not wanting to pick her up from her condo, both pretended not to know where it was, when they had both MapQuested its location at the Palm Court Shopping Center just in case. Shanghai cuisine, you know, where she's from. Exiled sixty-plus years back to the end of the War of Resistance last time, time of her country's last political revolution, Mao's revolution and civil war, one of the half-sisters said. She can remember the food, the dialect, and the humidity that much, imagine that, even after a forty-year layover south in Hong Kong, where she found a medical career and learned to cuss equally dirty in both privileged and street Cantonese.

Kate Blue had decided it'd be best if Ida would drive her stepmother in her Volvo, as she had to pick up some important papers at the state courthouse. You know, she convinced her, the conservatorship form. Just to irritate her, Ida asked the bartender for a phone book and pretended to flip through the Yellow Pages for the street address of the Dragon 2K. Where is Botelho Drive? she finally looked up and smiled

Before Ida had time to set the hand brake on the car in the restaurant's parking lot, Nerissa asked her for a hundred dollars. When her step-daughter peered over her driving glasses at her, she explained, With your sister's friend for guest, it's Chinese manners that the family elder pick up the check.

Not wanting to say there was no such Chinese thing, thereby challenging her stepmother, and suspicious but not knowing exactly why, Ida counted out five sequential Andrew Jacksons from her wallet and handed them to her.

And where is your sister? Nerissa demanded. She is late.

But she wasn't, she was opening the door and reaching for her mother's walking cane and helping her out.

Where is your friend? She is late, Nerissa repeated.

Hello, Ma. Good to see you, too.

Don't be so sarcastic. And keep your eyes on the ground and not at your sister. I don't want to fall down and break my fragile ninety-year old hip.

Ma, you're not ninety.

But I will be, tomorrow, she said, and tapped a lamppost this time with the black rubber tip of her cane for emphasis, a practiced artifact.

The anthropologist friend was waiting for them by the fountain inside the courtyard entrance to the restaurant.

Nerissa, my mother. Kate Blue looked at her and began the introduction. This is my friend.

Not Nerissa, she interrupted. It is Doctor Zhin.

But Ma, you haven't practiced medicine for more than forty years. The last twenty years of your career you were a hospital administrator, remember? Blowing her loose bangs in her friend's direction, Kate Blue added, with her Ph. D,. Kelly here is more a doctor than you.

I am very honored to finally meet you, Doctor Zhin, Kelly leaned down and extended a hand, smiling. I am Kelly Hwang. Over the years I have heard so many good things about you.

Yes, yes. So tall. You Korean? And how did you two meet?

Ma, Ma. You know that already. We were classmates at Pembroke, you remember, and my other best friend, Suzy Weaver, who later changed her name to Sigourney, a.k.a. Lieutenant Ripley. You came to our commencement in Providence, but everything was so chaotic that weekend, nobody got to meet anyone, you know.

Nerissa stared at her daughter, distracted momentarily. Sure, sure, she recovered quickly. I mean how did the two of you meet here in California? Waving her cane away from the Pacific Ocean, she smiled and announced with authority, Rhode Island is at the opposite side of this continent.

You know, she peppered a mimicked addition.

They took turns reading the menu aloud. Soup dumplings dipped in black vinegar and ginger sauce, definitely, xiao lung bao. Pink crab dumplings. Rice-wine-marinated chicken. Braised sliced beef. Shanghai noodles. Meatballs draped in cabbage, so finely textured they were part pâté, part soufflé. Vegetarian duck, too.

What's that? Kelly asked.

That's thin sheets of braised tofu folded over mushrooms to look like duck, Nerissa lectured to everyone at the table, including the waiter. Those vegetarian Buddhist monks have this long tradition of making tofu taste like anything you want, on the hoof or in the air. Besides meditating and sweeping the steps, what do you think they do all those days and nights in those stupas? But be careful, this Shanghai cooking is complex and rich, not like the Cantonese. My favorite is the smoked pork and the smoked fish, big chunks of it, sweet and flavored with anise.

No, not that, not the smoked fish and the smoked pork, Ida said to the waiter. Too much fat and too much salt. Not good for your heart and your arteries.

What are you now, a dietitian? Nerissa vexed astonishment. Look at you, you should talk. You're too thin, like you have TB or AIDS. Don't you think I know what's good for me? I've been my own physician since your father left us thirty-seven years ago; I can take care of myself. You, she pointed at the waiter suddenly, surprising him in Shanghai dialect. You bring the smoked pork and the smoked fish and leave the check with me.

Nerissa placed her Visa card on top of the check later, and told Kelly that she felt very lucky that day. My lottery number has been pre-selected to win, and the money is coming any moment, any moment now. It's been my business: I'm taking care of its initial investment, the federal and state taxes, and its eventual profit distribution. Just look, look at these numbers on my fortune, 5.8.5189.

When the two half-sisters saw the annulled platinum Washington Mutual credit card, they looked at each other and went to work at once: they hadn't had a Shanghai mother- and- stepmother for a combined one-hundred-plus years for nothing. While Ida talked about the sudden fortune and eternal prosperity associated with these numbers, Kate Blue muttered something about having to get back to work, and that it would be faster if she took the check and Lo Mo's credit card to the front counter rather than wait for the waiter to come back. On the way there she got out her own credit card, and made a fancy explanation to the manager picking his teeth with a toothpick at the cash register.

What do you think? the two half-sisters asked at the same time the next day, they met with Kelly at the same bar.

Well, I can tell you one thing for sure. She's a survivor. And she's mean as hell to you two, and it's not from Alzheimer's. She's driving you two crazy and making you bleed. Wow, one nasty lady who is used to wielding abusive power, especially over you, Kate Blue, my friend.

Yeah, yeah, I knew that, she said between sips, losing the shine of her electric lipstick on her glass. Her political idols are G. Gordon Liddy and Newt Gingrich—power personalities. Even has autographed photos of them in her bathroom.

But what about the conservatorship? Ida asked. Can it be done?

Ida, I'm on your side, to keep California's Adult Protective Services out, if for no other reason, Buddhist, Catholic, woodcutter, or Kafka. Once they're in, it's almost impossible to do anything else. But I don't know. Just because she believes in this game of chance, a one in three-hundred-and-thirty million, it is still a chance, still a possibility. Maybe that's not enough.

What! But she's not paying any of her bills, the utilities, phone, condo dues, credit card interest, we are. She's not capable of managing her affairs.

I disagree. Not managing her affairs does not necessarily mean she's incapable of doing it. You're doing it for her. She's sharpened her wits enough to get you two to do it for her. She's managing you. Her business now means she has something to do in her retirement. I saw the credit card switch, so did she, and pretended not to.

Ida and Kate Blue stared silently at each other and ordered another drink.

What about addiction disorder? one of them asked.

Nope. No California court is going to accept that one.

What about mild dementia or mild schizophrenia? asked the other.

The court will go buzzing with that but such an alternate personality substitution is very challengeable. Doctor Zhin can do that herself, without the help of an attorney.

Then they discussed other possibilities—, diminished capacity, cognitive dysfunction, emotional impairment, delusional thinking, and ability to remember past presidents—but it was clear to them that Nerissa could clear all these tests. None even looked promising enough to pursue, not even the thought of hiring a religious healing practitioner, allowed by the State of California.

After Kelly left, the two half-sisters continued talking like this, past the bar's closing hour and well into an imagined past perfect tense, with their mother-and-stepmother and how their family was fractured, and then collapsed back in their country's past century's accumulated wars, revolutions, and chance. ✧

A FEAST OF SNAKES, by Harry Crews

Jami Attenberg

A bookseller at Powell's Books in Portland handed me a used copy of Harry Crews's *A Feast of Snakes* as if he were revealing to me the location of a scandalous after-hours club, the door to which disappears as soon as you enter it. Like: Even though it looks dark and dirty and scary, this is where you want to go. There's practically no light inside and the music is unrelenting. Also, guaranteed there's going to be the occasional scuffle or outright brawl, or people doing drugs on the bar, or maybe there's a couple screwing in the bathroom and they don't even stop when you walk in the door, but just trust me, you don't want to miss this. Crews knows this other world the rest of us don't, even though, in a way, it seems like it could be just the next town over. Who are these people? Who can talk so crudely, and feel so much passion and hate, and engage in such shocking acts? They could not be my neighbors, and yet they are distinctly American. It was terrifying to glimpse this world, but I was glad to have had the chance. And I felt bolder and wiser for having made the visit.

I don't mean to ignore Crews's writing, which is impeccable. Crews is a craftsman of the highest order, to be sure, the way he swerves the perspective from character to character, each voice as convincing as the next, just enough to keep you unnerved. It almost made me seasick in the process, but he always keeps the reader's eyes on the horizon. And every sentence is ground down until all that is left behind is the pure message, each word like a perfect grain of sand washed by the ocean and bleached by the sun. It's just showmanship, really. Reading his writing sometimes reminds me of watching a dog wiggling his ass at the Westminster Kennel Club Dog Show. It is always fun to watch the prance. But it is the subject matter that is truly revelatory and stunning: the freak show of dry, drunken, violent Southerners and the damage they do to themselves and one another.

There is a particularly graphic sex scene near the end of the book that forced my mouth open when I read it, and then my jaw hung there, in a stunned state, for a good fifteen minutes. I have never been able to describe to anyone out loud what happens in that scene, because it makes me blush and I get all nervous and tongue-tied, and I am not a person who shies away from any kind of language, sexual or otherwise. I thought about it for days afterward, and although I was alone, each time I covered my face with my hands. Even now as I write this, I wish simultaneously that I had never read that section of the book and that I had the courage to describe it in print. Because it is—as it is with any good book, of course—all about opening your mind. ✧

Soap Sirens

Meghan Dunn

My mother knew each family's secret:
each cheating tycoon and gold digger half sister
whose illegitimate son was switched at birth.
During love scenes, my sisters and I snuck peeks
through our fingers. When the music trailed off,
my mother allowed us to look again.
I dreamed of eight weddings like the heroine,
each more special than the last, and the chance
to attend my own funeral in disguise,
unrecognizable beneath dark glasses, a darker wig.
Who would throw herself on my grave
and sob, who would come to claw at the earth?
And when my character came back from the dead,
who would replace me, strolling in one day
with a better body, a more musical voice?
Today, the role of Meghan will be played by. . .
I shared my name with three girls at school,
but the soaps swarmed with Biancas,
Kendalls, and Simones, who strode around
like predatory angels in strapless dresses
and three-inch heels, and their curls fluttered
as if a slight breeze blew wherever they alighted.
When they thrashed about on satin sheets with men,
all interchangeable Kens, their shoulder blades jutted
from their taut flesh like bony wings.
I wanted their lives: to be rescued from a rabid dog,
or a runaway Buick with suspicious brakes;
to fall victim to a maniac's plot;
or to have my memory erased by the evil Dr. N.
I wanted to disappear, to die and be reborn
like them, with a different face,
an immaculate new mind.

Advice for a Soap Siren

Meghan Dunn

Never love anyone more
than you love yourself.

If you have children
you make the mistake of loving,

they will be snatched or switched or kept
from you by vicious capitalist fathers

who will mold them into clones of themselves.
If you love a man,

he will leave or fail you
or go on a murderous rampage after discovering

your one (drunken) infidelity.
And if you have the misfortune to love

not one man, but two,
both will die in a freak tornado,

trying to save you and your unborn child,
who will grow to blame you

for the death of both his possible fathers.
So instead, invest your energy

in revenge, malice, or getting rich quick.
Most importantly, learn from the past.

The loving wife and mother is killed
for ratings, but the bitch lives forever.

Conquest, Tourism, and Eternal Canadian Rapture

Stephen Ausherman

Part One

The Gaspé: A Report from the Committee of Patriots for Truthful Intelligence

Americans are at a loss to explain Canadian superiority. We invaded in 1775 and 1812, failing in both efforts to conquer our northern enemies. They seem not only indestructible, but also interminably cheerful, able to tolerate a host of woes in the most dismal times.

In 1934, five years into the Great Depression, an unlikely tourist attraction rose from the farmland near North Bay, Ontario. The jaunty draw was a hospital, Dafoe Hospital, also known as Quintland. Built to accommodate the Dionne quintuplets, this medical facility soon grew into Canada's most popular destination, raking in half a billion dollars from its three million visitors. And for the better part of a decade five bundles of joy supplied their fellow countrymen with infectious bliss.

Also in 1934, two Connecticuters set out to explore the Gaspé, Quebec's rugged tongue of land between the Saint Lawrence River and Chaleur Bay. Artist Putnam Brinley and his wife, Kathrine Gordon Brinley, traveled for two months on this peninsula, where the neck bones of the mighty Appalachians bow into the frigid gulf waters.

Kathrine recounts the minutiae of their jaunt in her odd travelogue, *Away to the Gaspé*. Throughout the book she repeats one detail with chilling regularity: Gaspesians are totally gay. Again, the year is 1934, so of course she means gay in the jolly and exuberant sense of the word. The Quebec maritime is not a land of queer wanton lust, but rather the happiest place on Earth.

Seventy years after the Brinleys' tour of the Gaspé, I began mine and sensed at once an inexplicable aura of complete joy. But the eerie similarities don't end there, as I would discover months later when I compared her travelogue with my own journal.

Brinley, pages 66–67:

> There are many legends and stories about Bic, and particularly about the two islands in the river. One is known as Massacre Island, because of a bloody Indian battle between the Hurons and the Iroquois. . . . Even recently human bones have been dug up in the rock quarries on this fateful island.

Ausherman, June 24, parc national du Bic:

> Jean-François struggles with his English to convince us that his kayak expeditions are completely safe. "We are prepared for casualties," he says in his charming Quebecois accent. He thinks a moment, then adds: "Casualties is the correct word, no?"

Um, no. At least I hope not.

He apologizes for the limits of his English, but then quickly reminds us that today is Saint-Jean-Baptiste Day, the Fête nationale du Québec. "We must all speak French today," he jokes.

French, my ass. The Gauls wouldn't tolerate his amiable charade for two minutes.

We launch our kayaks into the calm, chilly Saint Lawrence off the coast of Bic National Park . . . and paddle out past Massacre Island, where the water turns choppy, then toward Cape Enrage, where curious seals join our tour. I'm inclined to explore more unusual names on the map—such as le Chocolat and baie du Ha-ha!—but eight miles are about all the others can manage for a morning paddle.

Brinley, page 100:

Suddenly I saw a long red fox sneaking among the charred stumps and logs. He was headed for the road, but sensing us, he turned and ran. There was no time to shoot him, camera-wise.

Ausherman, June 25, réserve faunique de Matane:

The trail is a spongy shag of moss and tangles of tree roots. It bridges salmon rivers and twists past waterfalls. Evidence of big game is in the air and on the ground. The Matane Wildlife Reserve is home to the greatest concentration of moose in Quebec, with nearly four large cervids for every square mile. We spy two of them sloshing down a muddy road. I take aim and shoot repeatedly. I also shoot hares, woodchucks, spruce grouse, and white-tailed deer, but the results are disastrous. I need a better camera.

Brinley, pages 94–95:

M. Blanchette was there with pretty, seventeen-year-old Thérèse and gay little Madeleine. . . . Thérèse took the chair next to the gramophone. She put on a disk. . . . Then the music began; dance music. . . . I could stand it no longer and since everyone was in a jolly state of mind, I got up. . . .
"Come, Thérèse," said I, "let us dance."

Ausherman, June 25 (cont.):

Our group has succumbed to a strange giddiness. Maybe jouncing along a forty-five-mile dirt road through the Matane has addled our brains. Or it could be the traditional Quebec maritime music: chanteys that evoke images of francophone pirates jamming on accordions, fiddles, and washboards. Whatever the reason, we feel younger and charged with inexplicable energy.

Brinley, pages 132–33:

The sea disappeared and we were in country that might have been Switzerland.... We rounded a turn and passed a little steep-roofed and towered English church on a knoll, surrounded by spruce trees and looking as though it had been dropped there out of Norway.

Ausherman, June 27–28, parc national de la Gaspésie:

We hike to a glacial cirque that appears to belong to another mountain range. The snow-patched granite peak on the far side of a crystalline lake looks like a chunk of the French Alps gone AWOL. I check my map to confirm we're still in the Appalachians. We are. And the lake is clearly marked as lac aux Américains. We're still on the right side of the ocean.

Other vistas in the park resemble the barren hills of Wales or English lake country, only without the crowds. One peak, the tundra-topped mont Jacques-Cartier, appears to belong to another planet. Here on the windswept crest of rock immense beauty grows on a minuscule scale. The biggest flower blossoms are the size of a fly's wingspan, and ancient trees imitate banzai masterpieces.

Brinley, pages 157–58:

The Duchess drew out a bit of violet-colored stone. In it, lines of deeper color were indented in a design resembling the backbone of a fish.

"A trilobite, and a good one!" I exclaimed.... "This little fellow was about the earliest camper on earth, wasn't he? Paleozoic, anyway."

"I know," [replied the Duchess], "... but I'm merely telling you the fun a simpleminded female can have wandering along South Beach."

Ausherman, June 28, parc national de Miguasha:

I lope along the estuary of the Restigouche River, smashing open rocks upon rocks like a caveman, all in a desperate attempt to find a fossil. Meanwhile, Theresa employs a small hammer to chip open a few stones and miraculously reveal perfect imprints of shrimp. They're thoroughly unremarkable until our guide identifies them as something out of the Devonian era.

So just like that, Theresa has discovered further evidence of life far older than dinosaurs. And suddenly she's strutting around like God's gift to paleontology, while I'm still hoarding rocks like a covetous chimp. In the span of an hour I have become a perfect illustration of evolution in reverse.

Brinley, pages 137–38:

Ever since our first trip to Bonaventure Island to see the bird colonies I had wanted to go back to make drawings of the rock formations of the cliffs.... The gulls soon discovered me and told me in emphatic language that they would not allow any intrusions of their island home. Hundreds of them flew screeching around me till I thought their cries would drive me crazy.

Ausherman, June 29, parc national de l'Île-Bonaventure-et-du-Rocher-Percé:

> We've just stumbled across a colony of northern gannets, cottony seabirds with butterscotch heads and Egyptian eyes, six-foot wingspans and beaks like tin shears. They are big and fearless birds, the largest of the boobies, and two or three together in your path can pose a formidable obstacle. We're now facing more than 70,000 of these winged beasts, with more in the air and over the horizon. Add to that an additional population of nearly 200,000 other seabirds, including razorbills, gulls, kittiwakes, and puffins, and you begin to get a sense of the crowd on the dizzying cliffs at the southeastern rim of the island. I feel like Tippi Hedren.

Brinley, page 114:

> Boiled potatoes, boiled dried codfish, home-baked bread and tea, made a good meal.

Ausherman, June 30, Gaspé:

> I passed on my last chance to try poutine, Quebec's native concoction of french fries, turkey gravy, and cheese curds. Also passed on the KFC, known here as le PFK (Poulet Frit Kentucky). Lost appetite resulting from a recent diet of smoked salmon carpaccio, maple-glazed duck breast, pan-seared rabbit, caribou medallions, pan-fried cod tongue, sweetbread, and day after day of poissons frais, délicieux fruits de mers et savoureuses grillades.

Brinley, page 189:

> We gazed in silence across the Bay of Chaleur to the gray-blue headland. All the joy of our two months there swept over me as I watched the cloud shadows play upon it.

Ausherman, June 30, Gaspé Airport:

> I don't understand why I've been so damn happy for the past eight days. It seems pathological, maniacal . . . except now the thought of leaving fills me with dread.

Kathrine Gordon Brinley returned to Canada to pen Away to Cape Breton, Away to the Canadian Rockies and British Columbia, and Away to Quebec: A Gay Journey to the Province. By all accounts, the entirety of Canada is totally gay—again, in the jolly and exuberant sense of the word.

It's all too easy to equate their character with the happiness of idiots, but don't be fooled. It goes beyond innocuous cheer. To complicate matters further, they seem immune to the severe giddiness of the Danes. Therefore, we cannot assume that the Canadian problem will resolve itself in the foreseeable future.

As my research demonstrates, the situation remains the same after seventy years, strongly suggesting that Canadians exist in a state of eternal rapture. Such a condition helps explain their high resistance to dismal situations and military invasions.

Conclusion: to conquer them, we must first find a way to sully their mood.

Part Two

Cape Breton: Canadian Rapture

On a Cape Breton highway southeast of Mabou something seemed amiss, and neither Betsy nor I could pin it down. The road narrowed as it wound through rolling farmland, haunting in its darkness. Where the map indicated a major thoroughfare, asphalt gave way to gravel. We drove on.

In an instant headlights charged the rearview mirror; seconds later glaring red taillights blinked out in a dusty plume.

As we crested a hill, an ancient stand of trees to our left gave way to open fields. At that moment a single light flashed in the corner of my eye. It was round and bright, about how I imagine an oncoming locomotive would look in the last moment before broadside impact.

A moment later I realized it was only the moon. Though two nights past full, it shined brighter than any I'd seen, illuminating silos and farmhouses at the far edges of hayfields. It shimmered in the vales. It didn't seem to follow us so much as stalk circles around us. It dipped behind the treetops only to reemerge in the dell. Sometimes it appeared to lope across the road before us, like a wild animal that waits to cross a lonely highway by the light of oncoming traffic.

The moon's behavior that night was a testament to the twisted nature of the road we traveled. Without so much as a sign or change in width or grade, it forked off and dead-ended at darkened barns and farmhouses. We backtracked and doubled back and wondered if we'd been driving in circles.

Up ahead a light on a utility pole cast a green fluorescent glow over the graveyard of an anonymous church, and that's where our dirt highway ended. We paused at a T-bone junction in the penumbra of cemetery light. On the far side of the crossroad stood the landmark we'd been told to look out for: a parking lot full of cars. We'd expected to find maybe a dozen or so, but close to a hundred vehicles jammed the lot.

The evening's attraction: a square dance. Here in Glencoe Mills that's a major attraction. Two public buildings occupy Glencoe Mills, three if there is an actual mill in the vicinity. Perhaps there was one long ago. It seemed like the kind of place where the elderly grieved for loved ones lost in a great mill fire. Once upon a time they also had a schoolhouse. That single-room structure now functioned as a dance hall.

We joined a procession prowling down the road for a space alongside a weedy ditch. Back in the lot, men gathered in the shadows, a wisp of whisky and murmurs of drought buzzing about them. Children ran free and shrieking. A teenage boy, shy fifty cents of the $5.50 admission, implored his mother for half a loon.

The wooden schoolhouse steamed and rumbled. Betsy and I sidewinded through the damp crowd and pressed up to a bar that served pop and snacks. We ordered a Sprite, then braced our backs against a wall near the exit.

The music gained momentum. The girl on stage couldn't have been older than twelve, but she rubbed her fiddle like she wanted to start a fire. She moved people. They danced in unison, as though responding to a caller we couldn't hear. They knew when to bow to their partner and when to promenade. The scuffed wooden floor buckled under the stomp and clobber of their boots and basketball shoes.

They danced, they clapped. Young and old alike, mixing and mingling without shame. They sweated and laughed and whooped in rhapsody. I'd never seen a crowd so jacked up on fiddles and pop. An ecstatic vibe swept through their souls as though, any moment now, they might speak in tongues or sprout fangs and shift into werewolves.

Betsy and I waited for someone to draw us out. I wondered how we'd keep from getting trampled, when, obeying signals we still couldn't detect, the dancing regiment changed directions. I worried about how awkward we'd feel searching for the rhythm, and how long they'd try to keep us out there, if they'd be insulted when we gave up trying.

But it didn't happen like that. Nobody talked to us. Nobody even looked our way.

Perhaps, in the throes of ecstasy, they'd lost certain senses of hospitality. I might say they were impolite. Something was more than amiss that night. We'd entered an alternate reality, a disturbing world where the moon runs in unpredictable circles and Canadians are slightly rude. ✧

Biographical Notice of Ellis and Acton Bell

It has been thought that all the works published under the names of Currer, Ellis, and Acton Bell were, in reality, the production of one person. This mistake I endeavored to rectify by a few words of disclaimer prefixed to the third edition of *Jane Eyre*. These, too, it appears, failed to gain general credence, and now, on the occasion of a reprint of *Wuthering Heights* and *Agnes Grey*, I am advised distinctly to state how the case really stands.

Indeed, I feel myself that it is time the obscurity attending those two names—Ellis and Acton—was done away. The little mystery, which formerly yielded some harmless pleasure, has lost its interest; circumstances are changed. It becomes, then, my duty to explain briefly the origin and authorship of the books written by Currer, Ellis, and Acton Bell.

About five years ago, my two sisters and myself, after a somewhat prolonged period of separation, found ourselves reunited, and at home. Resident in a remote district, where education had made little progress, and where, consequently, there was no inducement to seek social intercourse beyond our own domestic circle, we were wholly dependent on ourselves and each other, on books and study, for the enjoyments and occupations of life. The highest stimulus, as well as the liveliest pleasure we had known from childhood upwards, lay in attempts at literary composition; formerly we used to show each other what we wrote, but of late years this habit of communication and consultation had been discontinued; hence it ensued, that we were mutually ignorant of the progress we might respectively have made.

One day, in the autumn of 1845, I accidentally lighted on a manuscript volume of verse in my sister Emily's handwriting. Of course, I was not surprised, knowing that she could and did write verse: I looked it over, and something more than surprise seized me—a deep conviction that these were not common effusions, nor at all like the poetry women generally write. I thought them condensed and terse, vigorous and genuine. To my ear they had also a peculiar music—wild, melancholy, and elevating.

My sister Emily was not a person of demonstrative character, nor one on the recesses of whose mind and feelings even those nearest and dearest to her could, with impunity, intrude unlicensed; it took hours to reconcile her to the discovery I had made, and days to persuade her that such poems merited publication. I knew, however, that a mind like hers could not be without some latent spark of honorable ambition, and refused to be discouraged in my attempts to fan that spark to flame.

Meantime, my younger sister quietly produced some of her own compositions, intimating that, since Emily's had given me pleasure, I might like to look at hers. I could not but be a partial judge, yet I thought that these verses, too, had a sweet, sincere pathos of their own.

We had very early cherished the dream of one day becoming authors. This dream, never relinquished even when distance divided and absorbing tasks occupied us, now suddenly acquired strength and consistency: it took the character of a resolve. We agreed to arrange a small selection of our poems, and, if possible, to get them printed. Averse to personal publicity, we veiled our own names under those of Currer, Ellis, and Acton Bell; the ambiguous choice being dictated by a sort of conscientious scruple at assuming Christian names positively masculine, while we did not like to declare ourselves women, because—without at that time suspecting that our mode of writing and thinking was not what is called 'feminine'—we had a vague impression that authoresses are liable to be looked on with prejudice; we had noticed how critics sometimes use for their chastisement the weapon of personality, and for their reward, a flattery, which is not true praise.

The bringing out of our little book was hard work. As was to be expected, neither we nor our poems were at all wanted; but for this we had been prepared at the outset; though inexperienced ourselves, we had read the experience of others. The great puzzle lay in the difficulty of getting answers of any kind from the publishers to whom we applied. Being greatly harassed by this obstacle, I ventured to apply to the Messrs. Chambers, of Edinburgh, for a word of advice; they may have forgotten the circumstance, but I have not, for from them I received a brief and business-like, but civil and sensible reply, on which we acted, and at last made a way.

The book was printed: it is scarcely known, and all of it that merits to be known are the poems of Ellis Bell. The fixed conviction I held, and hold, of the worth of these poems has not indeed received the confirmation of much favorable criticism; but I must retain it notwithstanding.

Ill-success failed to crush us: the mere effort to succeed had given a wonderful zest to existence; it must be pursued. We each set to work on a prose tale: Ellis Bell produced *Wuthering Heights*, Acton Bell *Agnes Grey*, and Currer Bell also wrote a narrative in one volume. These manuscripts were perseveringly obtruded upon various publishers for the space of a year and a half; usually, their fate was an ignominious and abrupt dismissal.

At last *Wuthering Heights* and *Agnes Grey* were accepted on terms somewhat impoverishing to the two authors; Currer Bell's book found acceptance nowhere, nor any acknowledgment of merit, so that something like the chill of despair began to invade her heart. As a forlorn hope, she tried one publishing house more—Messrs. Smith, Elder and Co. Ere long, in a much shorter space than that on which experience had taught her to calculate—there came a letter, which she opened in the dreary expectation of finding two hard, hopeless lines, intimating that Messrs. Smith, Elder and Co. "were not disposed to publish the manuscript," and, instead, she took out of the envelope a letter of two pages. She read it trembling. It declined, indeed, to publish that tale, for business reasons, but it discussed its merits and demerits so courteously, so considerately, in a spirit so rational, with a discrimination so enlightened, that this very refusal cheered the author better than a vulgarly expressed acceptance would have done. It was added, that a work in three volumes would meet with careful attention.

I was then just completing *Jane Eyre*, at which I had been working while the one-volume tale was plodding its weary round in London: in three weeks I sent it off; friendly and skilful hands took it in. This was in the commencement of September, 1847; it came out before the close of October following, while *Wuthering Heights* and *Agnes Grey*, my sisters' works, which had already been in the press for months, still lingered under a different management.

They appeared at last. Critics failed to do them justice. The immature but very real powers revealed in *Wuthering Heights* were scarcely recognized; its import and nature were misunderstood; the identity of its author was misrepresented; it was said that this was an earlier and ruder attempt of the same pen which had produced *Jane Eyre*. Unjust and grievous error! We laughed at it at first, but I deeply lament it now. Hence, I fear, arose a prejudice against the book. That writer, who could attempt to palm off an inferior and immature production under cover of one successful effort, must indeed be unduly eager after the secondary and sordid result of authorship, and pitiably indifferent to its true and honorable meed. If reviewers and the public truly believed this, no wonder that they looked darkly on the cheat.

Yet I must not be understood to make these things subject for reproach or complaint; I dare not do so; respect for my sister's memory forbids me. By her, any such querulous manifestation would have been regarded as an unworthy and offensive weakness.

It is my duty, as well as my pleasure, to acknowledge one exception to the general rule of criticism. One writer, endowed with the keen vision and fine sympathies of genius, has discerned the real nature of *Wuthering Heights*, and has, with equal accuracy, noted its beauties and touched on its faults. Too often do reviewers remind us of the mob of Astrologers, Chaldeans, and Soothsayers gathered before the "writing on the wall," and unable to read the characters or make known the interpretation. We have a right to Rejoice when a true seer comes at last, some man in whom is an excellent spirit, to whom have been given light, wisdom, and understanding; and who can say with confidence, "This is the interpretation thereof."

Yet even the writer to whom I allude shares the mistake about the authorship, and does me the injustice to suppose that there was equivoque in my former rejection of this honor (as an honor I regard it). May I assure him that I would scorn in this and in every other case to deal in equivoque; I believe language to have been given us to make our meaning clear, and not to wrap it in dishonest doubt?

The Tenant of Wildfell Hall, by Acton Bell, had likewise an unfavorable reception. At this I cannot wonder. The choice of subject was an entire mistake. Nothing less congruous with the writer's nature could be conceived. The motives that dictated this choice were pure, but I think, slightly morbid. She had, in the course of her life, been called on to contemplate, near at hand, and for a long time, the terrible effects of talents misused and faculties abused: hers was naturally a sensitive, reserved, and dejected nature; what she saw sank very deeply into her mind; it did her harm. She brooded over it till she believed it to be a duty to reproduce every detail (of course with fictitious characters, incidents, and situations), as a warning to others. She hated her work, but would pursue it. When reasoned with on the subject, she regarded such reasoning as a temptation to self-indulgence. She must be honest; she must not varnish, soften, nor conceal. This well-meant resolution brought on her misconstruction, and some abuse, which she bore, as it was her custom to bear whatever was unpleasant, with mild, steady patience. She was a very sincere, and practical Christian, but the tinge of religious melancholy communicated a sad shade to her brief, blameless life.

Neither Ellis nor Acton allowed herself for one moment to sink under want of encouragement; energy nerved the one, and endurance upheld the other. They were both prepared to try again; I would fain think that hope and the sense of power were yet strong within them. But a great change approached; affliction came in that shape which to anticipate is dread; to look back on, grief. In the very heat and burden of the day, the laborers failed over their work.

My sister Emily first declined. The details of her illness are deep-branded in my memory, but to dwell on them, either in thought or narrative, is not in my power. Never in all her life had she lingered over any task that lay before her, and she did not linger now. She sank rapidly. She made haste to leave us. Yet, while physically she perished, mentally she grew stronger than we had yet known her. Day by day, when I saw with what a front she met suffering, I looked on her with an anguish of wonder and love. I have seen nothing like it; but, indeed, I have never seen her parallel in anything. Stronger than a man, simpler than a child, her nature stood alone. The awful point was, that while full of ruth for others, on herself she had no pity; the spirit was inexorable to the flesh; from the trembling hand, the unnerved limbs, the faded eyes, the same service was exacted as they had rendered in health. To stand by and witness this, and not dare to remonstrate, was a pain no words can render.

Two cruel months of hope and fear passed painfully by, and the day came at last when the terrors and pains of death were to be undergone by this treasure, which had grown dearer and dearer to our hearts as it wasted before our eyes. Towards the decline of that day, we had nothing of Emily but her mortal remains as consumption left them. She died December 19, 1848.

We thought this enough: but we were utterly and presumptuously wrong. She was not buried ere Anne fell ill. She had not been committed to the grave a fortnight, before we received distinct intimation that it was necessary to prepare our minds to see the younger sister go after the elder. Accordingly, she followed in the same path with slower step, and with a patience that equaled the other's fortitude. I have said that she was religious, and it was by leaning on those Christian doctrines in which she firmly believed, that she found support through her most painful journey. I witnessed their efficacy in her latest hour and greatest trial, and must bear my testimony to the calm triumph with which they brought her through. She died May 28, 1849.

What more shall I say about them? I cannot and need not say much more. In externals, they were two unobtrusive women; a perfectly secluded life gave them retiring manners and habits. In Emily's nature the extremes of vigor and simplicity seemed to meet. Under an unsophisticated culture, inartificial tastes, and an unpretending outside, lay a secret power and fire that might have informed the brain and kindled the veins of a hero; but she had no worldly wisdom; her powers were unadapted to the practical business of life; she would fail to defend her most manifest rights, to consult her most legitimate advantage. An interpreter ought always to have stood between her and the world. Her will was not very flexible, and it generally opposed her interest. Her temper was magnanimous, but warm and sudden; her spirit altogether unbending.

Anne's character was milder and more subdued; she wanted the power, the fire, the originality of her sister, but was well endowed with quiet virtues of her own. Long-suffering, self-denying, reflective, and intelligent, a constitutional reserve and taciturnity placed and kept her in the shade, and covered her mind, and especially her feelings, with a sort of nun-like veil, which was rarely lifted. Neither Emily nor Anne was learned; they had no thought of filling their pitchers at the well-spring of other minds; they always wrote from the impulse of nature, the dictates of intuition, and from such stores of observation as their limited experience had enabled them to amass. I may sum up all by saying, that for strangers they were nothing, for superficial observers less than nothing; but for those who had known them all their lives in the intimacy of close relationship, they were genuinely good and truly great.

This notice has been written because I felt it a sacred duty to wipe the dust off their gravestones, and leave their dear names free from soil.

CURRER BELL, September 19, 1850. ✧

I AM CHARLOTTE SIMMONS, by Tom Wolfe

Elisabeth Brink

Reading *I Am Charlotte Simmons*, Tom Wolfe's expose of college life in our time, is like having an entire rowdy, putrid, horny, beer-burping, tradition-rich, ivy-covered campus dropped in your lap. And I'm not talking about the weight of the book, although that's substantial. I'm talking about its unexpurgated look at the social lives of yearning, deluded postadolescents crowded together by the thousands in a few unsupervised square miles of beer halls, dorm rooms, and cash machines. I'm also talking about Wolfe's trademark extravagant style, which usually draws one of two very different reactions from critics: (1) Wolfe is a Joycean genius, or (2) Who gave his editor that lobotomy?

I ought to confess that for the last decade or so I've read more nonfiction than contemporary novels. Maybe I overdosed on fiction in grad school and simply needed to freshen my palate with a sorbet of psychology and science. Or maybe as a beginning writer, I simply needed some empty space around me. The only way I could hope to produce something that wasn't an imitation of someone else's work was to go away by myself and pretend I'd never seen a novel before in my life.

But a couple of years ago, when what would be called my "debut" novel was being ushered through production, I had a hankering to read contemporary fiction. I wanted to see what was out there and maybe find some things I liked. So I peeled my library card off the bottom of a drawer, and soon my head was swimming with other writers' words. I was, as I expected, often impressed and sometimes bowled over by the talent that's out there. (Interestingly, the writers I admired were rarely American—why is that?) But there was a whole class of novels I picked up that I couldn't get even halfway into. Within a few pages I'd get a sense of déjà vu, as if I already knew where the authors were going and how they were going to get there, and often I was right. Many of these authors wrote perfectly—complete, detailed characterizations; plausible, usually slow-moving plots; perfect Strunk and White style. Yet their good behavior left me feeling tired. I was looking for something else, something beyond craft, but I didn't know what.

Then I picked up *I Am Charlotte Simmons* and got reacquainted with Tom Wolfe, for whom the word novelist means journalist, fabulist, wordsmith, and satirist. Famous ten times over for his depictions in previous novels of bond trading and the newly moneyed South, Wolfe takes us this time onto a college campus, a milieu that offers far less glamour and, if possible, even more opportunities for unforced tragedy, comedy, and farce. The characters, by virtue of being young, are hampered not only by the usual Wolfean afflictions of vanity and delusion, but also by simple immaturity. The result is that we are treated to a particularly toxic mix of human foibles: ignorance, inebriation, pretentiousness, racism, sexism, hedonism, sadism, masochism, solipsism, arrogance, incompetence, and rabid horniness. We also find moments of idealism, affection, and honest ambition, but these things are so mixed up with all the other stuff that it is not at all clear whether any decent attribute will survive the harsh environment. This is not exactly a place I willingly want to travel in or a set of memories I want to dredge up. And perhaps, as some critics have said, Wolfe's world is skewed to the sensational. But it is real. Unflinchingly real. You know these people. Face it: you may have been one of them. Of course, if you're like me, you thought you were different from the herd—smarter and more sophisticated, at the least—but as Wolfe would happily point out, that was a self-protecting delusion. There are few people as conventional as college students. It's not their fault. It's just that individual character emerges slowly, from the choices a person makes, and college students haven't had much time to make those telling choices yet. Given that they're consigned to a setting cut off from reality, where for the most part they answer only to one another, it's a small miracle anyone's soul survives.

I Am Charlotte Simmons opens with a summary of a 1983 experiment conducted by Nobel Prize–winning scientist Victor Starling. The amygdala, a part of the brain involving emotions, was removed from a group of cats. As predicted, the cats began to experience emotion—fear, boredom, excitement, contentment—randomly and inappropriately. What was unexpected was that they soon advanced into a state a permanent violent sexual arousal. They humped one another so compulsively and insistently that they created "daisy chains" ten feet long. The experiment did not end there, however. It was soon discovered that when cats with intact brains were housed in the same room as the surgically altered cats, they too became sexually manic and quickly joined the fray. A casual observer of the frantic feline orgies that ensued had no way of knowing which animals had undergone the surgery and which had not.

Wolfe's worlds come straight out of Starling's laboratory. They are never just places; they are specific, insular social contexts or cultural atmospheres—*milieus* is still the best word—filled with distorted values and irrational behaviors. At best, these worlds deform people as they homogenize them. At worst, they eat people alive, feeding first on their typical weaknesses, then devouring the rest and finally spitting them out as wallpaper or furniture in the fashionable style. The status quo overwhelms the individual; talents and consciences are lost; many people don't or can't find authentic lives (you know them too). But some do. And that's where the story lies.

Call me cynical or unlucky, but that worldview sounds about right to me. Wolfe's voice rings true. At least, it hits a deep internal chord, and that's a rare and valuable thing. Wolfe belongs to that exclusive group of writers who have a Vision and so are able to practice their own art on their own terms. Wolfe revels in his talent, crafts fresh deals with the reader, and doesn't waste time with convention. He does his own research—picking up rhythms, nuances, and impressions as well as facts—and he gets the details right. Rip a page from his book, stash it in your bookcase, and when you find it five years from now, you'll know who and what you're reading. In *I Am Charlotte Simmons* Wolfe is not saying the only true thing about college campuses, but he is saying one of the most important true things. He is making a singular, incontrovertible, brash, unforgettable statement. Maybe that's why reading it felt like getting zapped with an electrical jolt when I was just on the verge of falling asleep. And he's American!

What's more, he's having fun. Language for Wolfe is a great big playground. He mixes metaphors; he makes up words ("virginicide," "aristo-meritocracy"); he uses the verb throb. When he feels like it, he waxes poetic: "in the lichen twilight, dusky, rusky as could be." Then he reproduces college patois with exactitude and brings the surprise of authentic longing into the voice of drunken, jilted, messed-up Beverly as she gasps, "Charlotte . . . Charlotte . . . Where are the lacrosse players? Where are the lacrosse players?"

Some critics don't like it when novelists have too much fun or take liberties with their medium, and *I Am Charlotte Simmons* earned more than its share of righteous excoriation. In the spirit of fun, I can't resist quoting a few of the boiling-over sentences and phrases used to vilify the book: "I felt like a cat with part of its brain missing," "the publisher knows it's whelping a mutt," "a lurid carnival," "cringe-inducing and excruciating," "an exaggerated, overlong, overwritten doorstop," "a clumsy, heavy-handed mess," "a bonfire of his own vanities," "a rattletrap overlay of clunky intellectual musing," "reams of hyperventilating testimony," "a laboratory of elegant rot." Wow. Does anyone else think it's interesting that these critics, as they writhe in paroxysms of Wolfe-inspired disgust, nevertheless manage, if only for a few moments, to slip the surly bonds of normally staid reviewerdom and attain their own impassioned, strongly colored, slightly unhinged, and well . . . Wolfelike prose? Imitation is still the sincerest form of flattery.

If I had to choose one thing I learned from my year of reading contemporary fiction, it would be this: the quality I admire more than any other is the one I find in spades in Tom Wolfe—fearlessness. ✧

Baggage Claim

Debra Gitterman

I met him at baggage claim, of all places, half asleep, barely knowing where I was. Luggage was circling and we were looking for what belonged to us. The sound of falling water when our arms touched. Funny that, to feel a body and think of water. Does anyone want me to marry? Do I want to marry? I remember the wallpaper in my childhood room: water combing a wheat field. I used to touch the storm. My mother chose paint for my teen years. Bubblegum girl and a doll's head in the closet. Nothing being born. Just me walking these rooms. Soft click: that's me opening the door, a door one can hardly find in all this pink. It confused my grandmother when she slept here once, more than she was already confused. How to get out of this pink humming room. I smelled sweet basil from the window. It was spring. Or it was winter and I only imagined green, as I imagined water when our arms touched.

Those Were Desert Years

Debra Gitterman

She waited for the witnesses to die,
a new generation to be born.
She waited for the cactus to store water,
a river to flood,
desert to seed,
for time to burn off memory.

Seven years she waited.
Like a god. Her people
flawed, brave, tired.
She was wilderness
and golden calf. The one
who knelt between his legs.
She burned the dead.
Her people moved on.

One day,
outside the gates of Gibeon,
a captain upright in the wind.
She was the desert walking.
She stopped, then inhaled.

Silence. Spring.
Bird notes.
Beat of a single heart.

Bennett's Cheap Catharsis

Evan Lavender-Smith

Editor's Note: Shortly after our receipt of this editorial, written by one Edward Lamarck Littleton, ABD, of Akron, Ohio, USA, we discovered, to our profound dismay, that its author had died. We resolved to publish his commentary despite a consensus among our staff that it was in dire need of a revision expunging those many odd and seemingly unrelated references to the author's personal life. Alas, no such revision would be possible; the author was deceased. This is a regrettable problem with which we have, of late, become increasingly familiar, and we hope that our readers will excuse Mr. Littleton's flights of fancy and/or factual errors—as they have so kindly excused those of other recently deceased authors we have published posthumously—for the sake of his commentary's general insightfulness. May you rest in peace, Mr. Littleton.

Your decision to publish the late Dr. Arthur Tinsdale's tedious article in support of the late Dr. F. W. Bennett's infamous "A Survey of Recent Prodigious Human Memory (PHM) Case Studies: Toward a Narratological Terminology" represents the latest setback in a ridiculous feud between the defenders of ethical scholarship—those who view the Bennett monograph for what it is: a travesty of research methodology—and those who desperately cling to the botched "Survey" for ontological reassurance, as savages may stand in awe beneath some propitious arrangement of stars.

Tinsdale's alleged reconciliation of those Bennett-related articles published side by side in this journal's Winter issue—Jordan Mathieson's deft "The Corrupting Influence of Intertextuality in Bennett's 'Survey'" and the late Caroline Bizbek's inane "The Liberating Influence of Intertextuality in Bennett's 'Survey'"—offers little analysis of theoretical, let alone practical, value. Dr. Tinsdale resorts to Heisenberg's uncertainty principle as a metaphor for the "impossibility of objective research performance" with the puerile zeal of a pimply-faced high school student enumerating to his classmates the many merits of Robert Pirsig's Zen and the Art of Motorcycle Maintenance. In taking issue with both Mathieson and Bizbek, in claiming that intertextuality neither corrupts nor liberates but necessarily influences the "performance" of research data (including the simple job of transcribing voices from an audio tape, that "slippery act" by way of which Bennett relates to us his interviews with "Marcel," "Vladimir," and "Jorge"), Tinsdale appears so enmeshed in theory it's a wonder he ever got the cap off his pen. At the zenith of his article's impassioned climax Dr. Tinsdale calls for the conversation surrounding the Bennett debacle to take a "post-postmodern turn," the need for a new consensus among PHM analysts to accept the interviews [in Bennett's "Survey"] at face value, to no longer worry [themselves] over issues of "transcription," "translation," "transliteration," "transposition," "paraphrase," "adaptation," "redaction" and "plagiarism," but instead to follow in the footsteps of those brave purveyors of the New Criticism, our brethren from the land of literary theory who—against the grain of post-structuralist, post-colonialist, post-feminist fashion—continue to practice a monastic fidelity to the text in hand, and to it alone.

How, I ask, are we expected to take this argument seriously? If a subject speaks into an audio recording device, "I remember the day my dog Bandit died like it was yesterday," and the researcher later transcribes that statement as, "I remember the day my [estranged] husband committed suicide like it was yesterday," how might such an egregious adaptation not represent the total obliteration of that researcher's ethos? Dr. Tinsdale points to punctuational discrepancies existing among transcriptions conducted by different transcribers of the same recorded interview, how these discrepancies may lead to alternate interpretations of meaning, etc., and one wonders if under his bed pillow the late Dr. Arthur Tinsdale didn't stash a dog-eared copy of Lynne Truss's *Eats, Shoots and Leaves*, harbinger of punctuational revolution in the country under whose bleary skies the good professor Tinsdale, from Cambridge, once slept so peacefully.

I will not sleep so peacefully, however—as I lie in bed alone, my (estranged) wife a thousand miles away—for here in Akron the night skies are quite clear. [1]

Let us, for the moment, leave aside Tinsdale's servile ballyhoo—as published in this journal's Spring issue—and attempt to examine the Bennett paper with fresh eyes.

The elegance with which Dr. Bennett's cross-disciplinary approach proceeds to arrive at a narratological terminology affording unprecedented descriptive tools for PHM analysts does not deserve our scrutiny: there is no doubt that for many years to come we will rely upon terms such as *fourth-person dianoegraphically limited* when describing that particular type of narration offered by a prodigious recollector whose faculties are similar to Bennett's "Jorge"; *unconscientiously unreliable* and *multiperson mnemonically unlimited* will find valuable purchase as analysts bicker over the veracity of narration offered by a recollector whose faculties share certain characteristics with "Vladimir's." The terminological value of Bennett's work is indisputable; but even revolutionary ends cannot excuse unethical means.

---

[1] *Editor's Note: This would appear to be the first of many passages wherein a "present-action" observation is presented that applies to the general concern of the editorial only peripherally, if at all. (What do Akron's clear skies have to do with Tinsdale or Bennett? We would ask Mr. Littleton, RIP, the same.)*

Consider once again the case of Bennett's "Marcel." As Richard Shelley and Wanda Tomlinson describe in their groundbreaking "Fact of Fiction? Intertextual Reference to Proust's *In Search of Lost Time* in the Testimony of Bennett's 'Marcel,'" "Marcel," the subject of the first of three "Recent PHM Case Studies" that Bennett examines in his "Survey," shares more than just a first name with the famous early twentieth-century author–literary persona Marcel Proust. Throughout his monograph's "Marcel" section Bennett strategically litters "Marcel's" testimony with details appropriated from Proust's *Remembrance of Things Past*.[2] What follows is an excerpt from Bennett's "analysis" and "transcription" of "Marcel's" testimony, a brief sampling of the author's penchant for flagrant adaptation.

Recounting detailed events from his childhood, a forty-four-year-old male from Lyon, France—herein named Marcel[3]—displays a unique ability to physically reinhabit his memories. . . . In recollection of his eighth birthday he, forty-four-year-old Marcel, stands on the veranda of his childhood home, leans over an iron picnic table and his eight-year-old self, the small birthday cake on the table holding

> four pink and four blue candles , two of which are depressed into the cake farther than the others. I—young {Marcel}, rather—wait until the drops of melted wax from those two lower candles quiver just above the frosting before making my wish, just as bird hunters will take aim at their target as it flies directly overhead but not release the trigger until the luckless ring-billed gull approaches that invisible horizon beyond which it may gain safe passage. . . . I watch myself blow the candles out quickly. What did I wish for? I have often wondered. . . . I, alongside my younger self, sit in the dark with Mother and Grandfather for a little while with only the soft chirping of crickets and the gentle swaying of the large chestnut tree to remind us that our senses are still functioning.

---

[2] *Editor's Note: The late Mr. Littleton seems to have preferred the title of this novel as adapted by C. K. Scott Moncrieff, as opposed to the more recent translation by Lydia Davis et al.,* In Search of Lost Time, *which Shelley and Tomlinson prefer, as do we.*

[3] *I have changed the names of prodigious recollectors and persons referenced in their narration so to preserve the anonymity of those who would be endlessly harassed by parvenu PHM analysts were their true names publicly divulged. This is my sole intention with respect to the inclusion of aliases, despite the opinions of my detractors, who will claim in rebuttal monographs, I'm sure, that no such persons exist or ever did; that my design in making inaccessible these prodigious recollectors' identities was self-serving. I imagine an editor's note will one day follow this footnote, indicating some conjecture to that effect.— F.W.B. [Thank you, Dr. Bennett, for the introduction. There is no evidence, beyond their textual presence in Bennett's monograph, that "Marcel" et al., or whatever their names are, ever existed in the flesh.—E.L.L.]*

Yet we needn't spend more time haggling over the specifics of those many intertextual sites—the inclusion of detail blatantly lifted from *Swann's Way*—scattered throughout "Marcel's" testimony and Bennett's "analysis" thereof, as Shelley and Tomlinson and others have already haggled enough[4] to amply demonstrate that Bennett is first a plagiarist and second a researcher. What have as yet remained unhaggled over, to my knowledge, and what do deserve quite a bit of haggling, are those many details *appropriated from the late Dr. F. W. Bennett's own life* that have been carefully woven into the narration provided by "Marcel," "Vladimir," and "Jorge."

Through the little window in the attic alcove of our—of my, rather—house in Akron, one espies a gull's nest resting precariously upon the branch of a tree. *Cheep*, go the chicks, *cheep, cheep*. "Cheep," I reply, returning to my typewriter. "Indeed. Cheep."[5]

With respect to the above-quoted excerpt from "Marcel's" testimony, along with Bennett's "analysis" thereof, the first instance of what I will henceforth term the author's tendency toward *authorial projection* (or what I privately call Bennett's *cheap catharsis*) occurs within the simile offered by "Marcel" comparing the drops of candle wax threatening to touch his birthday cake's frosting to, of all things, gull poachers waiting to shoot until their prey is on the verge of escape. (As Dismali suggests, this represents "Marcel's" "second clumsiest attempt at Proustian simile [sic].") However, and as any reputable ornithologist will concede, barring a sudden three-thousand-mile lurch of continental drift, the ring-billed gull (*Larus delawarensis*) does not inhabit skies above France; its habitation is native and exclusive to the North American continent.[6] How might we account for "Marcel's" error? Easily: by referring to an entry from the childhood diary of Dr. F. W. Bennett, born and bred in Illinois, USA, the same state that boasts an annual population of more than a thousand ring-billed gulls.

> Today is my eighth birthday. Papa takes me shooting. He shoots eight ring-billed gulls before sundown, and I shoot one. I take my first shot when it's right over my head, but I miss. It flies away, in the distance. I take another shot, and then it stops in midair, like it has flown into a drift of icy air and

---

[4] *Cf. the late Dwayne Longmeyer's subservient "The Chestnut Tree and the Iron Table: Transference of Detail from Proust to Bennett" and R. J. Dismali's monumental "'Marcel's' Long-Winded Similes in Bennett's 'Survey,'" both published in this journal's Summer issue.*

[5] *Editor's Note: We would advise the reader to skip over this paragraph, another of the editorial's unrelated "present-action" sections, and move on to the next.*

[6] *Editor's Note: Not true. Here in our London office, located on the twenty-second floor, there is a flock of ring-billed gulls skittering along the windowsill outside, making their awful, high-pitched squawking sound (i.e., quawk-ah, quawk-ah).*

become frozen, before falling to the ground, when Bandit runs off and brings it back in his mouth as my birthday present. Bandit is a very good boy, indeed.

Is it simply a coincidence, then, that the diary entry corresponding to Bennett's eighth birthday and the "interview" excerpt describing "Marcel's" eighth birthday contain references to ring-billed gull poaching? And what about that terrible simile "like it has flown into a drift of icy air and become frozen, before falling to the ground"? Does this sound familiar to my ears alone? Can this appear familiarly clumsy only to me? Or could it be that the late Dr. F. W. Bennett's personal copy of Proust's opus—which dog-eared copy I have, of late, had occasion to examine—contains on its flyleaf the same nervous, curlicued signature that young master Bennett appended to those books of which he came into possession between the ages of six and thirteen?[7] But let us proceed.... "Marcel's inability," Bennett continues,

> to recall his birthday wish indicates a critical flaw in his recollective ability. He would appear to belong to the most common typology within prodigious human memory studies—the prodigious recollector whose recall ability is hampered by a narrative distance inherent in his *third-person-limited observer-participant* perspective.... Marcel betrays the historical ambiguity consequent to the new physical presence—that of his forty-four-year-old self—existing within his recounted memories, thus:

> After {eight-year-old Marcel}, Mother, and Grandfather have left the veranda, I sit down in a chair at the picnic table, cut a thin slice of cake from exactly where the cursive {M} meets the {a}, and I look to the decorative plates scattered across the iron tabletop—Ali Baba and the Forty Thieves, Aladdin or the Magic Lamp—finally choosing one upon which a snapshot from the penultimate scene of Casablanca is depicted.... The cake smells vaguely of asparagus.... The lights are extinguished from the windows above me.... I watch {Françoise} wrap the cake to preserve it, and I notice that the slice I cut out earlier has somehow managed to return to its original location— there is no longer a break between the first two letters of my name—and I am suddenly aware of the empty pit in my stomach.

---

[7] *Editor's Note: How did Mr. Littleton obtain a copy of Dr. Bennett's personal copy of* In Search of Lost Time, *let alone his childhood diary? We would ask Mr. Littleton, RIP, the same.**
   *Neither the American CIA nor the British SIS have reason to believe that Dr. Bennett ever kept a diary. It would appear that the "transcription" from Dr. Bennett's diary, above, has been fabricated by "Mr. Littleton" and/or the editors of the British journal of psychology Q——, now defunct. Nor do we have evidence to support the claim that Dr. Bennett ever owned a copy of Michael Proust's *In Search of Lost Time.*—Ed.

My (estranged) wife and I used to order takeout from a place around the corner every Thursday. I would get moo goo gai pan and the exquisite beef with asparagus; she, always lemon chicken, beef with broccoli. I have not stepped foot in the restaurant since our separation, however; the menu from W——'s still sits on the corner of my desk, next to the phone, collecting dust.[8]

Casablanca, the Oscar-winning film starring Humphrey Bogart and Ingrid Bergman, was among Dr. Bennett's all-time favorite movies. In his last extant interview[9] the late Dr. Bennett admits to having watched this film upwards of a hundred times:

> INTERVIEWER: How many times have you watched *Casablanca*?
> F.W.B.: I . . . I don't . . .
> INTERVIEWER: [. . .]
> F.W.B.: The film . . . many . . . many times?
> INTERVIEWER: [. . .]
> F.W.B.: I have watched *Casablanca*, which I count among my all-time favorite movies, upwards of a hundred times.

Mere coincidence? It is doubtful. Bennett has not only appropriated details from Proust—"Ali Baba and the Forty Thieves," "Aladdin or the Magic Lamp"—he has also co-mingled this appropriation with details from his own life, referencing, via "Marcel's" testimony, one of his own favorite movies; he is *projecting* his own life experience onto "Marcel's." Bennett concludes his monograph's "Marcel" section thus:

> Forty-four-year-old Marcel has departed from his limited perspective when on the veranda watching Françoise wrap the cake—his younger self, limiter of all previous narration, is now conspicuously absent; put to bed, ostensibly, in one of the darkened rooms above—and his status as that rare breed of prodigious recollector, the central consciousness recollector, is revealed.

What are we to make of this? Why would renowned PHM analyst—according to the late Bizbek, "the patriarch of our field"—Dr. F. W. Bennett, alongside the presentation of his epoch-making terminology, so obviously adapt "Marcel's" testimony to conflate details from Proust's fiction and Bennett's own life? (Or, in the case of "Vladimir's" testimony, from Vladimir Nabokov's fiction and Bennett's own life? Of "Jorge's," from

---

[8] *Editor's Note: We, too, often order Chinese from a café around the corner; their menu includes beef with broccoli—which we count among our favorites—but certainly not beef with asparagus. The reader should feel free to have skipped the editorial's preceding paragraph.*

[9] *Unpublished. Conducted April 8, 2006, Akron, OH.*

Jorge Luis Borges's fiction and Bennett's life?) The late Arthur Tinsdale's answer to this question is theoretical gibberish, simply garbage; an answer that, along with Mathieson's and Bizbek's, only addresses intertextual, literary appropriation, besides.

The cheeping baby chicks, which I have recently appropriated from their nest outside my window—to the bottom of the wastebasket under my desk—cheep no more.[10]

"Marcel's" cake is said to smell vaguely of asparagus. How could Bennett have possibly known that one of the last fights my (estranged) wife and I ever had concerned a cake she made, which I claimed—regrettably, perhaps, yet truthfully—smelled vaguely of broccoli? He could not have. So why, then, do I feel, upon reading this "smells vaguely of asparagus," that Bennett/"Marcel" is speaking directly to me, directly to my own life experiences/memories? Why do I feel, every time I read this "smells vaguely of asparagus," that Bennett meant to transliterate "smells vaguely of broccoli," but at the very last moment decided otherwise, to preserve a sense of ambiguity, to preserve his "authorial alibi," if you will? Why do I feel, every time I read this impossible "smells vaguely of [broccoli]," that Bennett is making a fool of me? making a travesty of my life? mocking my memories? Why do I feel that Bennett is laughing at the final, most excruciating moments of my marriage?

There should be little doubt that Bennett's conflation of intertextual allusion and allusion to his own life experience within the testimonies of "Marcel," "Vladimir," and "Jorge" is aimed at encloaking his monograph within a haze of extra-textual allusion, a dense fog of reference beyond which the reader is meant to glimpse not the "real" "Marcel"/ "Vladimir"/"Jorge," nor, for that matter, the "real" Dr. Bennett, but instead an image of *the reader him- or herself*. The suggestion being that Dr. Bennett, who positions himself outside or beyond the ultimately "limited perspective" of "Marcel," "Vladimir," or "Jorge," possesses, uncannily, total omniscience, a brand of unlimited perspective that would include access to even his readers' life experiences, even his readers' memories. No wonder so many PHM analysts (especially those favored by this journal) have stood, with such blind passion, in defense of Bennett's "Survey," as if their very lives depended on the monograph's merit: they are unwittingly defending the merit of their own life experiences, their own memories, having been bamboozled into "discovering" themselves within Bennett's corrupt network of allusion.

---

[10] *Editor's Note: We appreciate the gesture, Mr. Littleton, and would do the same to save ourselves from the annoyance of the gulls' squawking, if only our double-paned windows‡ could be opened.*

‡ The windows at the former offices of the London-based journal of psychology Q—— are, in fact, single-paned, as well as openable.—Ed.

What follows is an excerpt from a transcribed telephone conversation between my (estranged) wife and me, conducted only moments ago, in demonstration of the great sway of Bennett's "Survey"; its ability to influence even those, like my (estranged) wife, who have not had direct contact with it.

J.T.[L.]: . . .here again yesterday asking questions: Bennett, Bizbek, Tinsdale, Longmeyer. They wanted your address in Akron. I thought I told you never to call me again. . . . Are you remembering to feed Bandit twice per day?

E.L.L.: Remember that cake you made, the one I said smelled vaguely of broccoli?

J.T.[L.]: Asparagus. You said, "How do you expect me to eat a cake that smells like asparagus?" You hate asparagus, remember?

E.L.L.: I said the cake smelled vaguely of broccoli. That's why I wouldn't eat it. I hate broccoli, not asparagus. I love asparagus.

J.T.[L.]: Love asparagus? You said, "Why would you make me a birthday cake that smells like the one food I hate most in the world, asparagus?" Thursday nights, takeout from W——'s. Beef with asparagus. You wouldn't go near it.

E.L.L.: [. . .]

J.T.[L.]: You're deranged, Ed. You're sick. You need help. Leave me alone.

E.L.L.: Why are you taking [Dr. F. W. Bennett's] side?

J.T.[L.]: Never call here again.

"Leave me alone!" I call out to the nest of cheeping gulls, which has somehow managed to return to its original location on the branch of the chestnut tree outside my window.[II] "Leave me alone!" I turn the wastebasket under my desk upside down; so many crumpled drafts of my editorial fall to the ground. Cheep, mock the chicks. Cheep, cheep.
Cheep quawk-ah! Cheep quawk-ah!

[II] *Editor's Note: The ring-billed gulls leave us in peace only on those rare days when the window washers come to wash away their droppings. They are always back the following day, though, back to their raucous squawking and interminable skittering. Would that the window washers cleaned our sills with arsenic.*

It is a cheap catharsis, finally.[12] Bennett has projected—so sneakily, with such cunning, such demonic legerdemain—his own life experience onto his monograph, within a dense network of intertextual allusion, in such a manner to create of his "Survey" a kind of terrible, terrifying mirror; a veritable fun-house mirror in which any careful reader will perceive his or her distorted image, a doppelgänger of his or her appropriated life, peering back, whispering, nightmarishly, for him or her to "come hither! Come hither! Believe! Believe in the profound mystery of life! Believe in the fathomless mystery of Bennett's 'Survey,' corrupt adaptation notwithstanding!"

Am I the only PHM analyst to have felt my precious subjectivity fractured, to have felt it appropriated by Bennett's monograph? To have felt my own life, my own personality and memory, somehow absorbed and modified by this nefarious "Survey"? Certainly not; but I may be one of the few, perhaps the only one, willing to admit it. Refer to a roundtable discussion in which Dr. Dwayne Longmeyer and Dr. Caroline Bizbek recently participated,[13] which included the following exchange:

LONGMEYER: I will not [admit] that, under any circumstance. I am simply . . . afraid I cannot [admit] the [truth].

BIZBEK: I . . . too [am afraid] to [admit] it.

INTERVIEWER: [. . .]

LONGMEYER: My friend, let's put an end to this before [the truth is revealed]. I have a wife, two young children. Please [don't ask me to admit what I know to be true; it will reflect poorly on me].

BIZBEK: [I have] six cats [and] a nephew. [They will be embarrassed if I contradict myself at this late stage and tell the truth about Bennett's "Survey."]

INTERVIEWER: [. . .]

---

[12] *Editor's Note: We much prefer "authorial projection" to "cheap catharsis." In his designation of Bennett's alleged projection of events from his (i.e., Dr. Bennett's) own life onto the testimony of "Marcel"/"Vladimir"/"Jorge" as "cheap," Littleton would seem to suggest the possibility of an "earned" projection, an "earned catharsis." (Did Mr. Littleton believe he was engaging in such an "earned catharsis" in the editorial at hand? We would, if we could, take issue. RIP, Mr. Littleton; RIP.)*

[13] *Unpublished. Conducted December 25, 2005, Akron, OH.*

LONGMEYER: Very well. You leave me [a] choice [whether or not to admit to Bennett's heinous misdoings]. It is my believe—belief?—that Dr. F. W. Bennett has, by way of so much veil adaptation of his interviews—vile, I suppose—such dense intertextual frog, attempted to appropriate his readers' memories. Fog, rather.

INTERVIEWER: Ms. Bizbek? Any final comments?

BIZBEK: It is [also] my belie[f] that Dr. F. W. Bennett has, by way of so much [vile] adaptation of his interviews, such dense intertextual [fog], attempted to appropriate his readers' memories.

My conviction in Bennett's malfeasance has already extended far beyond these pages, across psychology, English, and comparative literature departments; across states; across continents; across oceans. I have determined to repair what Bennett and his followers have so badly broken, at any cost. This editorial is merely the topping, the unquivering candle on a cake that reeks neither of asparagus nor broccoli. Open your eyes, readers, open your God-fearing ears. Open your Bennett-fearing noses. When you come to find me hanging from the chestnut tree outside my window, directly below the reappropriated gull nest, you might hear something, a whisper, perhaps a distorted version of your own voice, circling round and round my decomposing limbs: "Come hither! Come hither! Smell what we have smelled! Smell what we who maintain allegiance to the objectivity required, the objectivity forgotten of our discipline, have, for so long, smelled! Smell what we smell even today, holding vols. 28–33 of this journal near to our noses! Never broccoli! Never asparagus! Only [ring-billed gull droppings]!"[14] ✧

---

[14] *Editor's Note: We have taken the liberty, in this case alone, of editorial redaction: the final sentence originally concluded with an epithet (eight-letter synonym for cow dung), which we have here replaced with "ring-billed gull droppings" in hope of preserving propriety, on the one hand, and, on the other, "tying in," however obliquely, the editorial's gull motif with those more germane, Bennett-related observations made by Mr. Littleton, ABD, RIP.*

The American Fear of Literature

Nobel Lecture delivered by Sinclair Lewis, December 12, 1930

Were I to express my feeling of honor and pleasure in having been awarded the Nobel Prize in Literature, I should be fulsome and perhaps tedious, and I present my gratitude with a plain "Thank you."

I wish, in this address, to consider certain trends, certain dangers, and certain high and exciting promises in present-day American literature. To discuss this with complete and unguarded frankness—and I should not insult you by being otherwise than completely honest, however indiscreet - it will be necessary for me to be a little impolite regarding certain institutions and persons of my own greatly beloved land.

But I beg of you to believe that I am in no case gratifying a grudge. Fortune has dealt with me rather too well. I have known little struggle, not much poverty, many generosities. Now and then I have, for my books or myself, been somewhat warmly denounced—there was one good pastor in California who upon reading my *Elmer Gantry* desired to lead a mob and lynch me, while another holy man in the state of Maine wondered if there was no respectable and righteous way of putting me in jail. And, much harder to endure than any raging condemnation, a certain number of old acquaintances among journalists, what in the galloping American slang we call the "I Knew Him When Club", have scribbled that since they know me personally, therefore I must be a rather low sort of fellow and certainly no writer. But if I have now and then received such cheering brickbats, still I, who have heaved a good many bricks myself, would be fatuous not to expect a fair number in return.

No, I have for myself no conceivable complaint to make, and yet for American literature in general, and its standing in a country where industrialism and finance and science flourish and the only arts that are vital and respected are architecture and the film, I have a considerable complaint.

I can illustrate by an incident which chances to concern the Swedish Academy and myself and which happened a few days ago, just before I took the ship at New York for Sweden. There is in America a learned and most amiable old gentleman who has been a pastor, a university professor, and a diplomat. He is a member of the American Academy of Arts and Letters and no few universities have honored him with degrees. As a writer he is chiefly known for his pleasant little essays on the joy of fishing. I do not Suppose that professional fishermen, whose lives depend on the run of cod or herring, find it altogether an amusing occupation, but from these essays I learned, as a boy, that there is something very important and spiritual about catching fish, if you have no need of doing so.

This scholar stated, and publicly, that in awarding the Nobel Prize to a person who has scoffed at American institutions as much as I have, the Nobel Committee and the Swedish Academy had insulted America. I don't know whether, as an ex-diplomat, he intends to have an international incident made of it, and perhaps demand of the American Government that they land Marines in Stockholm to protect American literary rights, but I hope not.

I should have supposed that to a man so learned as to have been made a Doctor of Divinity, a Doctor of Letters, and I do not know how many other imposing magnificences, the matter would have seemed different; I should have supposed that he would have reasoned, "Although personally I dislike this man's books, nevertheless the Swedish Academy has in choosing him honored America by assuming that the Americans are no longer a puerile backwoods clan, so inferior that they are afraid of criticism, but instead a nation come of age and able to consider calmly and maturely any dissection of their land, however scoffing."

I should even have supposed that so international a scholar would have believed that Scandinavia, accustomed to the works of Strindberg, Ibsen, and Pontoppidan, would not have been peculiarly shocked by a writer whose most anarchistic assertion has been that America, with all her wealth and power, has not yet produced a civilization good enough to satisfy the deepest wants of human creatures.

I believe that Strindberg rarely sang the "Star-Spangled Banner" or addressed Rotary Clubs, yet Sweden seems to have survived him.

I have at such length discussed this criticism of the learned fisherman not because it has any conceivable importance in itself, but because it does illustrate the fact that in America most of us - not readers alone but even writers - are still afraid of any literature which is not a glorification of everything American, a glorification of our faults as well as our virtues. To be not only a best seller in America but to be really beloved, a novelist must assert that all American men are tall, handsome, rich, honest, and powerful at golf; that all country towns are filled with neighbors who do nothing from day to day save go about being kind to one another; that although American girls may be wild, they change always into perfect wives and mothers; and that, geographically, America is composed solely of New York, which is inhabited entirely by millionaires; of the West, which keeps unchanged all the boisterous heroism of 1870; and of the South, where everyone lives on a plantation perpetually glossy with moonlight and scented with magnolias.

It is not today vastly more true than it was twenty years ago that such novelists of ours as you have read in Sweden, novelists like Dreiser and Willa Cather, are authentically popular and influential in America. As it was revealed by the venerable fishing Academician whom I have quoted, we still most revere the writers for the popular magazines who in a hearty and edifying chorus chant that the America of a hundred and twenty million population is still as simple, as pastoral, as it was when it had but forty million; that in an industrial plant with ten thousand employees, the relationship between the worker and the manager is still as neighborly and uncomplex as in a factory of 1840, with five employees; that the relationships between father and son, between husband and wife, are precisely the same in an apartment in a thirty-story palace today, with three motor cars awaiting the family below and five books on the library shelves and a divorce imminent in the family next week, as were those relationships in a rose-veiled five-room cottage in 1880; that, in fine, America has gone through the revolutionary change from rustic colony to world empire without having in the least altered the bucolic and Puritanic simplicity of Uncle Sam.

I am, actually, extremely grateful to the fishing Academician for having somewhat condemned me. For since he is a leading member of the American Academy of Arts and Letters, he has released me, has given me the right to speak as frankly of that Academy as he has spoken of me. And in any honest study of American intellectualism today, that curious institution must be considered.

Before I consider the Academy, however, let me sketch a fantasy which has pleased me the last few days in the unavoidable idleness of a rough trip on the Atlantic. I am sure that you know, by now, that the award to me of the Nobel Prize has by no means been altogether popular in America. Doubtless the experience is not new to you. I fancy that when you gave the award even to Thomas Mann, whose Zauberberg seems to me to contain the whole of intellectual Europe, even when you gave it to Kipling, whose social significance is so profound that it has been rather authoritatively said that he created the British Empire, even when you gave it to Bernard Shaw, there were countrymen to those authors who complained because you did not choose another.

And I imagined what would have been said had you chosen some American other than myself. Suppose you had taken Theodore Dreiser.

Now to me, as to many other American writers, Dreiser more than any other man, marching alone, usually unappreciated, often hated, has cleared the trail from Victorian and Howellsian timidity and gentility in American fiction to honesty and boldness and passion of life. Without his pioneering, I doubt if any of us could, unless we liked to be sent to jail, seek to express life and beauty and terror.

My great colleague Sherwood Anderson has proclaimed this leadership of Dreiser. I am delighted to join him. Dreiser's great first novel, *Sister Carrie*, which he dared to publish thirty long years ago and which I read twenty-five years ago, came to housebound and airless America like a great free Western wind, and to our stuffy domesticity gave us the first fresh air since Mark Twain and Whitman.

Yet had you given the Prize to Mr. Dreiser, you would have heard groans from America; you would have heard that his style - I am not exactly sure what this mystic quality «style» may be, but I find the word so often in the writings of minor critics that I suppose it must exist - you would have heard that his style is cumbersome, that his choice of words is insensitive, that his books are interminable. And certainly respectable scholars would complain that in Mr. Dreiser's world, men and women are often sinful and tragic and despairing, instead of being forever sunny and full of song and virtue, as befits authentic Americans.

And had you chosen Mr. Eugene O'Neill, who has done nothing much in American drama save to transform it utterly, in ten or twelve years, from a false world of neat and competent trickery to a world of splendor and fear and greatness, you would have been reminded that he has done something far worse than scoffing - he has seen life as not to be neatly arranged in the study of a scholar but as a terrifying, magnificent, and often quite horrible thing akin to the tornado, the earthquake, the devastating fire.

And had you given Mr. James Branch Cabell the Prize, you would have been told that he is too fantastically malicious. So would you have been told that Miss Willa Cather, for all the homely virtue of her novels concerning the peasants of Nebraska, has in her novel, *The Lost Lady*, been so untrue to America's patent and perpetual and possibly tedious virtuousness as to picture an abandoned woman who remains, nevertheless, uncannily charming even to the virtuous, in a story without any moral; that Mr. Henry Mencken is the worst of all scoffers; that Mr. Sherwood Anderson viciously errs in considering sex as important a force in life as fishing; that Mr. Upton Sinclair, being a Socialist, sins against the perfectness of American capitalistic mass production; that Mr. Joseph Hergesheimer is un-American in regarding graciousness of manner and beauty of surface as of some importance in the endurance of daily life; and that Mr. Ernest Hemingway is not only too young but, far worse, uses language which should be unknown to gentlemen; that he acknowledges drunkenness as one of man's eternal ways to happiness, and asserts that a soldier may find love more significant than the hearty slaughter of men in battle.

Yes, they are wicked, these colleagues of mine; you would have done almost as evilly to have chosen them as to have chosen me; and as a chauvinistic American - only, mind you, as an American of 1930 and not of 1880 - I rejoice that they are my countrymen and countrywomen, and that I may speak of them with pride even in the Europe of Thomas Mann, H. G. Wells, Galsworthy, Knut Hamsun, Arnold Bennett, Feuchtwanger, Selma Lagerlöf, Sigrid Undset, Verner von Heidenstam, D'Annunzio, Romain Rolland.

It is my fate in this paper to swing constantly from optimism to pessimism and back, but so is it the fate of anyone who writes or speaks of anything in America - the most contradictory, the most depressing, the most stirring, of any land in the world today.

Thus, having with no muted pride called the roll of what seem to me to be great men and women in American literary life today, and having indeed omitted a dozen other names of which I should like to boast were there time, I must turn again and assert that in our contemporary American literature, indeed in all American arts save architecture and the film, we - yes, we who have such pregnant and vigorous standards in commerce and science - have no standards, no healing communication, no heroes to be followed nor villains to be condemned, no certain ways to be pursued, and no dangerous paths to be avoided.

The American novelist or poet or dramatist or sculptor or painter must work alone, in confusion, unassisted save by his own integrity.

That, of course, has always been the lot of the artist. The vagabond and criminal François Villon had certainly no smug and comfortable refuge in which elegant ladies would hold his hand and comfort his starveling soul and more starved body. He, veritably a great man, destined to outlive in history all the dukes and puissant cardinals whose robes he was esteemed unworthy to touch, had for his lot the gutter and the hardened crust.

Such poverty is not for the artist in America. They pay us, indeed, only too well; that writer is a failure who cannot have his butler and motor and his villa at Palm Beach, where he is permitted to mingle almost in equality with the barons of banking. But he is oppressed ever by something worse than poverty—by the feeling that what he creates does not matter, that he is expected by his readers to be only a decorator or a clown, or that he is good-naturedly accepted as a scoffer whose bark probably is worse than his bite and who probably is a good fellow at heart, who in any case certainly does not count in a land that produces eighty-story buildings, motors by the million, and wheat by the billions of bushels. And he has no institution, no group, to which he can turn for inspiration, whose criticism he can accept and whose praise will be precious to him.

What institutions have we?

The American Academy of Arts and Letters does contain, along with several excellent painters and architects and statesmen, such a really distinguished university president as Nicholas Murray Butler, so admirable and courageous a scholar as Wilbur Cross, and several first-rate writers: the poets Edwin Arlington Robinson and Robert Frost, the free-minded publicist James Truslow Adams, and the novelists Edith Wharton, Hamlin Garland, Owen Wister, Brand Whitlock, and Booth Tarkington.

But it does not include Theodore Dreiser, Henry Mencken, our most vivid critic, George Jean Nathan, who, though still young, is certainly the dean of our dramatic critics, Eugene O'Neill, incomparably our best dramatist, the really original and vital poets, Edna St. Vincent Millay and Carl Sandburg, Robinson Jeffers and Vachel Lindsay and Edgar Lee Masters, whose *Spoon River Anthology* was so utterly different from any other poetry ever published, so fresh, so authoritative, so free from any gropings and timidities that it came like a revelation and created a new school of native American poetry. It does not include the novelists and short-story writers, Willa Cather, Joseph Hergesheimer, Sherwood Anderson, Ring Lardner, Ernest Hemingway, Louis Bromfield, Wilbur Daniel Steele, Fannie Hurst, Mary Austin, James Branch Cabell, Edna Ferber, nor Upton Sinclair, of whom you must say, whether you admire or detest his aggressive socialism, that he is internationally better known than any other American artist whosoever, be he novelist, poet, painter, sculptor, musician, architect.

I should not expect any Academy to be so fortunate as to contain all these writers, but one which fails to contain any of them, which thus cuts itself off from so much of what is living and vigorous and original in American letters, can have no relationship whatever to our life and aspirations. It does not represent the literary America of today - it represents only Henry Wadsworth Longfellow.

It might be answered that, after all, the Academy is limited to fifty members; that, naturally, it cannot include every one of merit. But the fact is that while most of our few giants are excluded, the Academy does have room to include three extraordinarily bad poets, two very melodramatic and insignificant playwrights, two gentlemen who are known only because they are university presidents, a man who was thirty years ago known as a rather clever, humorous draughtsman, and several gentlemen of whom—I sadly confess my ignorance—I have never heard.

Let me again emphasize the fact - for it is a fact - that I am not attacking the American Academy. It is a hospitable and generous and decidedly dignified institution. And it is not altogether the Academy's fault that it does not contain many of the men who have significance in our letters. Sometimes it is the fault of those writers themselves. I cannot imagine that grizzly bear Theodore Dreiser being comfortable at the serenely Athenian dinners of the Academy, and were they to invite Mencken, he would infuriate them with his boisterous jeering. No, I am not attacking —I am reluctantly considering the Academy because it is so perfect an example of the divorce in America of intellectual life from all authentic standards of importance and reality.

Our universities and colleges, or gymnasia, most of them, exhibit the same unfortunate divorce. I can think of four of them, Rollins College in Florida, Middlebury College in Vermont, the University of Michigan, and the University of Chicago—which has had on its roll so excellent a novelist as Robert Herrick, so courageous a critic as Robert Morss Lovett - which have shown an authentic interest in contemporary creative literature. Four of them. But universities and colleges and musical emporiums and schools for the teaching of theology and plumbing and signpainting are as thick in America as the motor traffic. Whenever you see a public building with Gothic fenestration on a sturdy backing of Indiana concrete, you may be certain that it is another university, with anywhere from two hundred to twenty thousand students equally ardent about avoiding the disadvantage of becoming learned and about gaining the social prestige contained in the possession of a B.A degree.

Oh, socially our universities are close to the mass of our citizens, and so are they in the matter of athletics. A great college football game is passionately witnessed by eighty thousand people, who have paid five dollars apiece and motored anywhere from ten to a thousand miles for the ecstasy of watching twenty-two men chase one another up and down a curiously marked field. During the football season, a capable player ranks very nearly with our greatest and most admired heroes - even with Henry Ford, President Hoover, and Colonel Lindbergh.

And in one branch of learning, the sciences, the lords of business who rule us are willing to do homage to the devotees of learning. However bleakly one of our trader aristocrats may frown upon poetry or the visions of a painter, he is graciously pleased to endure a Millikan, a Michelson, a Banting, a Theobald Smith.

But the paradox is that in the arts our universities are as cloistered, as far from reality and living creation, as socially and athletically and scientifically they are close to us. To a true-blue professor of literature in an American university, literature is not something that a plain human being, living today, painfully sits down to produce. No; it is something dead; it is something magically produced by superhuman beings who must, if they are to be regarded as artists at all, have died at least one hundred years before the diabolical invention of the typewriter. To any authentic don, there is something slightly repulsive in the thought that literature could be created by any ordinary human being, still to be seen walking the streets, wearing quite commonplace trousers and coat and looking not so unlike a chauffeur or a farmer. Our American professors like their literature clear and cold and pure and very dead.

I do not suppose that American universities are alone in this. I am aware that to the dons of Oxford and Cambridge, it would seem rather indecent to suggest that Wells and Bennett and Galsworthy and George Moore may, while they commit the impropriety of continuing to live, be compared to anyone so beautifully and safely dead as Samuel Johnson. I suppose that in the universities of Sweden and France and Germany there exist plenty of professors who prefer dissection to understanding. But in the new and vital and experimental land of America, one would expect the teachers of literature to be less monastic, more human, than in the traditional shadows of old Europe.

They are not.

There has recently appeared in America, out of the universities, an astonishing circus called «the New Humanism.» Now of course «humanism» means so many things that it means nothing. It may infer anything from a belief that Greek and Latin are more inspiring than the dialect of contemporary peasants to a belief that any living peasant is more interesting than a dead Greek. But it is a delicate bit of justice that this nebulous word should have been chosen to label this nebulous cult.

Insofar as I have been able to comprehend them - for naturally in a world so exciting and promising as this today, a life brilliant with Zeppelins and Chinese revolutions and the Bolshevik industrialization of farming and ships and the Grand Canyon and young children and terrifying hunger and the lonely quest of scientists after God, no creative writer would have the time to follow all the chilly enthusiasms of the New Humanists - this newest of sects reasserts the dualism of man's nature. It would confine literature to the fight between man's soul and God, or man's soul and evil.

But, curiously, neither God nor the devil may wear modern dress, but must retain Grecian vestments. Oedipus is a tragic figure for the New Humanists; man, trying to maintain himself as the image of God under the menace of dynamos, in a world of high-pressure salesmanship, is not. And the poor comfort which they offer is that the object of life is to develop self- discipline - whether or not one ever accomplishes anything with this self-discipline. So the whole movement results in the not particularly novel doctrine that both art and life must be resigned and negative. It is a doctrine of the blackest reaction introduced into a stirringly revolutionary world.

Strangely enough, this doctrine of death, this escape from the complexities and danger of living into the secure blankness of the monastery, has become widely popular among professors in a land where one would have expected only boldness and intellectual adventure, and it has more than ever shut creative writers off from any benign influence which might conceivably have come from the universities.

But it has always been so. America has never had a Brandes, a Taine, a Goethe, a Croce.

With a wealth of creative talent in America, our criticism has most of it been a chill and insignificant activity pursued by jealous spinsters, ex-baseball-reporters, and acid professors. Our Erasmuses have been village schoolmistresses. How should there be any standards when there has been no one capable of setting them up?

The great Cambridge-Concord circle of the middle of the nineteenth century - Emerson, Longfellow, Lowell, Holmes, the Alcotts - were sentimental reflections of Europe, and they left no school, no influence.

Whitman and Thoreau and Poe and, in some degree, Hawthorne, were outcasts, men alone and despised, berated by the New Humanists of their generation. It was with the emergence of William Dean Howells that we first began to have something like a standard, and a very bad standard it was.

Mr. Howells was one of the gentlest, sweetest, and most honest of men, but he had the code of a pious old maid whose greatest delight was to have tea at the vicarage. He abhorred not only profanity and obscenity but all of what H. G. Wells has called "the jolly coarsenesses of life". In his fantastic vision of life, which he innocently conceived to be realistic, farmers, and seamen and factory hands might exist, but the farmer must never be covered with muck, the seaman must never roll out bawdy chanteys, the factory hand must be thankful to his good kind employer, and all of them must long for the opportunity to visit Florence and smile gently at the quaintness of the beggars.

So strongly did Howells feel this genteel, this New Humanistic philosophy that he was able vastly to influence his contemporaries, down even to 1914 and the turmoil of the Great War.

He was actually able to tame Mark Twain, perhaps the greatest of our writers, and to put that fiery old savage into an intellectual frock coat and top hat. His influence is not altogether gone today. He is still worshipped by Hamlin Garland, an author who should in every way have been greater than Howells but who under Howells' influence was changed from a harsh and magnificent realist into a genial and insignificant lecturer. Mr. Garland is, so far as we have one, the dean of American letters today, and as our dean, he is alarmed by all of the younger writers who are so lacking in taste as to suggest that men and women do not always love in accordance with the prayer-book, and that common people sometimes use language which would be inappropriate at a women's literary club on Main Street. Yet this same Hamlin Garland, as a young man, before he had gone to Boston and become cultured and Howellsised, wrote two most valiant and revelatory works of realism, *Main-Traveled Roads* and *Rose of Dutcher's Coolie*.

I read them as a boy in a prairie village in Minnesota just such an environment as was described in Mr. Garland's tales. They were vastly exciting to me. I had realized in reading Balzac and Dickens that it was possible to describe French and English common people as one actually saw them. But it had never occurred to me that one might without indecency write of the people of Sauk Centre, Minnesota, as one felt about them. Our fictional tradition, you see, was that all of us in Midwestern villages were altogether noble and happy; that not one of us would exchange the neighborly bliss of living on Main Street for the heathen gaudiness of New York or Paris or Stockholm. But in Mr. Garland's *Main-Traveled Roads* I discovered that there was one man who believed that

Midwestern peasants were sometimes bewildered and hungry and vile—and heroic. And, given this vision, I was released; I could write of life as living life.

I am afraid that Mr. Garland would be not pleased but acutely annoyed to know that he made it possible for me to write of America as I see it, and not as Mr. William Dean Howells so sunnily saw it. And it is his tragedy, it is a completely revelatory American tragedy, that in our land of freedom, men like Garland, who first blast the roads to freedom, become themselves the most bound.

But, all this time, while men like Howells were so effusively seeking to guide America into becoming a pale edition of an English cathedral town, there were surly and authentic fellows - Whitman and Melville, then Dreiser and James Huneker and Mencken - who insisted that our land had something more than tea-table gentility.

And so, without standards, we have survived. And for the strong young men, it has perhaps been well that we should have no standards. For, after seeming to be pessimistic about my own and much beloved land, I want to close this dirge with a very lively sound of optimism.

I have, for the future of American literature, every hope and every eager belief. We are coming out, I believe, of the stuffiness of safe, sane, and incredibly dull provincialism. There are young Americans today who are doing such passionate and authentic work that it makes me sick to see that I am a little too old to be one of them.

There is Ernest Hemingway, a bitter youth, educated by the most intense experience, disciplined by his own high standards, an authentic artist whose home is in the whole of life; there is Thomas Wolfe, a child of, I believe, thirty or younger, whose one and only novel, *Look Homeward, Angel*, is worthy to be compared with the best in our literary production, a Gargantuan creature with great gusto of life; there is Thornton Wilder, who in an age of realism dreams the old and lovely dreams of the eternal romantics; there is John Dos Passos, with his hatred of the safe and sane standards of Babbitt and his splendor of revolution; there is Stephen Benét, who to American drabness has restored the epic poem with his glorious memory of old John Brown; there are Michael Gold, who reveals the new frontier of the Jewish East Side, and William Faulkner, who has freed the South from hoopskirts; and there are a dozen other young poets and fictioneers, most of them living now in Paris, most of them a little insane in the tradition of James Joyce, who, however insane they may be, have refused to be genteel and traditional and dull.

I salute them, with a joy in being not yet too far removed from their determination to give to the America that has mountains and endless prairies, enormous cities and lost far cabins, billions of money and tons of faith, to an America that is as strange as Russia and as complex as China, a literature worthy of her vastness. ✧

O Saddam!

Rusty Barnes

Saddam Hussein was a street-side seller of hot nuts near Faneuil Hall. He worked undercover there during the last Gulf War until just after it, as the US slagged the Iraqis. If only they'd known while they video-bombed his underground bunkers and chased his doubles that Saddam spent his mornings selling cashews and pistachios in the Cradle of the Revolution with that magnificent smile. I knew, though, which made me feel not quite superior, but knowledgeable in a way others were not. My place in this hidden history, at least, would be certain. I would be celebrated in no books, but he would be—his porn-pink pistachio fingers fondling obscenely patriotic balloons—celebrated as butcher of Kurds, burner of oil, terrorist-harboring scourge, love of my life.

I was a Historic Boston tour guide, and he and I met clandestinely in the basement showers of the New England Shelter for Homeless Veterans. Our throats caught tight in terror, we crawled through the open window and tried not to laugh at the oddness of knowing we were, simply, right now, supposed to be doing just this. Saddam would gently bathe me every other midday, scrubbing me with a Bed Bath and Beyond loofah, bought by me at half price.

I spent my workdays orating lustily for the folks in the back of the crowd, who perspired in the close green shadows of the Public Garden statue memorializing ether. I spoke of things ages past (revolution, Paul Revere, sheep and cows grazing the Common, abolition, and *Make Way for Ducklings*) and of no concern, while my mind was under the light sprinkle of the showerhead with my one true love, while with one hand I fended off the ass grabs of Drakkar-smelling paunchy men with fanny packs who wanted a vacation delight with the "girl guide," as most of them called me. I felt badly for those wives, worse for the children, and tired of all their chatter. I made up stories sometimes, how Paul Revere was a closeted homosexual, how Peter Faneuil dealt slaves, how the Tea Party was the equivalent of a frat party; I would go off alone with their husbands, just off to the side, maybe behind a sweatshirt-selling vendor, under the pretext of finding Freedom Trail pamphlets, pointing out landmarks. Sometimes I would slip my hand into their shirts and rub their hairy bellies seductively, which was what they wanted, a story to tell the boys back home. I was bored, by them too.

I took that job for something to do, more or less a hedge should I decide to commit my life to junior proms and football games. It was a grim joke of sorts, that I would spend my time during the summer months catering to smiling and nodding Chinese tourists and their notions of what made America the place to visit. I fit the postcard picture the tourists demanded. The television loved me; the announcers fawned over my blond hair and quiet beauty. I even made the front page of the *Boston Globe* once. In color, and they had even whitened my teeth. I suspected my behind was smaller too. They had caught me bending over a bed of freesia and some other plant I didn't recognize, showing something to some child. Historic Boston loved people like me, schoolteachers whose tenure depended on community service and an impeccable moral record, the better for forcing that imprimatur on the rich and scornful youth of the Dover-Sherborn School District.

My father had called me a few weeks before summer vacation began, before I met Saddam; I was in the midst of next fall's lesson plans, and he was in the last thrashes of his Sturm-und-Drang marriage to my second stepmom, Rosie. He was a plumber who lived in Exeter, New Hampshire. He belonged to a militia and had given me a Smith & Wesson .357 Magnum for my twenty-fifth birthday. It had a 2.1-inch barrel and a concealed hammer, so it wouldn't hang on my clothes or purse when I needed it. I left it in my nightstand next to the Cyclovir, Xanax, Effexor, and MDMA. Also Klonopin. I wanted no surprises anymore. I wanted always to be prepared.

"It's me, baby. Did you see the Channel Forty-four news?" His voice always took on a somber tone, and I knew his biorhythm was at a low, which meant I might get a visit at any time of the day or night, my poor dad mumbling to himself about the world's woes. I braced myself.

"No, Pop." The last time he called, I'd had to talk him off the roof, almost literally. Rosie had dumped him drunk on the steps of the Odd Fellows Meeting Hall, and his neighbor, militia captain Mitch Morton, had found him there shivering in his shirtsleeves. Rosie had gone to the casino with her lady friends, she said. Pop had his doubts; I didn't care, though I felt badly for him, and Mitch just puffed his pipe and winked at me before he got into his truck and took off.

I'd had to drive up in the dead of night to keep him calm until Rosie came back. He told me, "Oh, God, Dani. I can't live without that bitch. But I'm through now. By Christ, I swear." His pledge to leave her was done in by the twenty-six grand she brought back with her.

His voice brought me back. "Another subway assault. You got your little buddy with you?"

"Always. I'm working for the Park Service, Pop." As I held the phone on my shoulder, I leafed through a grade book, and there at the back was little Jimmy King's paper discussing the causes of the Civil War. I wondered where it had gotten to.

He sighed. "I taught you better than that. It's bad enough that you work for a public school."

"It's all about the dollar, Pop. I need the extra money." I also found the love letters Jimmy had been passing to his ladylove, Sapphire. Why had I kept them?

"I can give you a few. You should move up here. Barter them teacher skills. Learn to sew, by God. No more of this Zionist occupation government." He spent all his money on munitions, on weapons he could pay someone to convert to full auto for the coming apocalypse. He'd gone full gamut since I'd been born, from refusing to pay anyone for anything he couldn't learn to do himself—learning to repair transmissions and raise rabbits for his eventual move to Alaska, and to safely stockpile trinitrotoluene and blasting caps in sealed fifty-five-gallon drums for the inevitable "mud-people takeover," as he and Mitch referred to it.

"I'm fine, Pop. Really."

"Okay. Clip me the news, would you? And send it up." Pop didn't believe anything until he saw it himself. He watched the weather and the news on three different televisions set to different channels and asked me to send him print sources afterward. I'd stopped asking questions. It was more than mistrust for him; it was absolute inability to believe in any wound he had not thrust his own fingers into. The problem now was that the whole carcass had been bled nearly dry, and my father believed he and Mitch were the bandages that would stop the flow.

Saddam caught my eye the first time I passed by the Red Auerbach statue near Faneuil Hall. He was on his way back to his cart from wherever he'd found a parking spot in the midst of disemboweled downtown Boston, his white apron dark at the front and that dark, curly hair springing forth from under the black beret. That toothy smile and thick mustache. I didn't see how people weren't recognizing him for who he was. I left my tour group in the Disney Store and followed him across the street and up the stairs, where protesters—some of them my rich-kid students, I'm sure, in town on a lark with their Phish T-shirts and their mothers' Lexuses—lined up with placards and cigarettes and tried to look serious as their mates set up a mic and a PA.

His cart was immaculate, the bottles of water arranged just so, his grill clean, umbrella new. He handed balloons to every child, inflated from the CO_2 tank. Pretty girls and women, too. I could not keep my eyes off him, nor could I understand why people didn't see what I saw. Here he was! No wonder he couldn't be found. No wonder all the TV generals looked so serious, no wonder the president seemed so intent. No wonder.

I took to watching him from afar. Police bought packets of almonds, and he nodded at them, always a smile, always something said aside that caused a laugh. I thought about walking up to City Hall, telling someone, anyone, but who would believe such a ridiculous story?

When it rained and the tourists went to hide at the aquarium and in restaurants and under the awnings of the awful Duck Tour, failing to notice the sublime irony of the military machine used for tourist profit, I stood, wet and miserable, under the shadow of the massive granite bank on School Street, smoking, even though I wasn't supposed to in uniform, waiting for my shift relief to show up. He came up then and spoke.

"Your beauty is to me like those Nicene barks of yore." His English almost accentless, but phrased just oddly enough for mystery.

"Excuse me?" I cursed myself. I hadn't prepared for this today. Other days I planned for lovers and chance meetings. Not now. Especially ones who sounded like poets.

"You are beautiful, and I would like for you to coffee with me." Those bruised eyes, heavy with sorrow and knowledge and beauty. Who could resist? Then my cell phone beeped, and I excused myself and turned away slightly.

"It's near time, Dani," the voice said.

"Pop?" I said. Saddam thrust his hands into his pockets and stepped away. His chest hair curled from his shirt neck.

"I've got some Cipro if you need it. It's time, Dani, it's past goddamn time." I could hear the fever pitch in his voice rising. "Come up here. You can bunker down with Rosie and me. We can't let them take this country away from us, this president and his Middle Eastern monkey business. You just know it's oil and the small man getting stomped, by now you must see, honey."

"God, Pop. Not now. I'm busy."

"You're working in this downpour?" His interminable weather-channel watching again.

"I'm about to have coffee. With a man." I smiled at Saddam, whose face brightened. He gestured toward the Starbucks and tilted his head quizzically, and I fell instantly, madly into a completely cliché love.

"Oh. Hope he's a good guy. Have fun. Call me when you get home."

Instead of going for coffee, I led Saddam down the alley and crawled in through the basement window of the shelter, pulling loose the rusted iron grate and slipping in. I'd seen homeless men do this, late at night as I walked to the subway, and had kept it in mind for just such an occasion, though I didn't think I'd ever find it in the waves of tourists who wanted to know how to get to Quincy Market. The weather was good, the risk was low—who would miss the girl guide for an hour or so?—and as Pop would tell me, the anthrax spores would stay close to the ground.

Almost every time this is how it went: I would hang my Smokey the Bear hat and my green-and-tan uniform on the broken towel rack and turn the water on. I would be slippery and lathered, staring up out of the shower at the clouded windows and the feet of passers-by and their children's strollers. He would come in and gently uncross my arms from my breasts and scrub me. First my back, my legs, his fingers magical conduits, easing the cramped calves and tensed spine. Then he would turn me around. I kept my head down. Saddam, the raven-haired messenger of Allah, in my mind, touching me. He would scrub my breasts and nipples and throat until I was raw and red, every inch a live nerve waiting for his touch.

As it—I was never sure what it ought to be called—progressed, my supervisor suspected us and I began to notice jokes, lewd comments from the other tour guides. I walked by Saddam at every opportunity and watched as he doled out bags of steaming cashews and Mylar balloons. He smiled always but rarely looked directly at me, though strangely enough, I felt as if he stared, and was somehow honored by that. He knew about my discomfort in my ankle-high socks and hiking boots, sprung at the instep by walking the concrete and asphalt all day. He knew how my legs trembled after even a half day in the heat, and I would sit down near him on my breaks, and an icy bottle of Poland Springs would appear nearby, a brush against my shoulder, a feathery kiss on the back of my neck when no one was looking.

When we talked, it was about the weather, or poetry. He showed me where Poe had been born, where Robert Lowell's family had lived, which way the Muslim faced to pray and when. He explained it all, all those things troubling me, and the world—Palestine, Israel, gassing the Kurds—and all I could think about was what my father would say if he could hear these explanations. He would wonder where the US was involved, always looking to put the blame on our government, big government, Zionist occupation government.

I asked Saddam about my friend Butchy, who had driven a tank over there and died, not in combat or from friendly fire like that football player, but ignominiously, of sunstroke, his blood boiling in 120-degree heat. Saddam looked down, twitched his shoulder once, and began to tell me about the clouds of black smoke in formation over the Gulf the first time around, how he had sat there all those years ago in an observation tower watching that money burn away. He had only planned to take over Kuwaiti satellite television stations, he said. He said the world would have seen the true Saddam if he had; the loving, kind, and benevolent Saddam, Allah's chosen. And he cried great, salty tears into his dark mustache. My sad Saddam. And my heart broke—for him, for Butchy, for the president, for all of them foundering through what they thought was right.

I brought him back to my apartment in Framingham once in late summer, when the heat lay heavily over the turnpike and the fading light left shadows and murmurs even in my car. I remember I had left the car double-parked in front of the Store 24 near the commuter rail. I had chilled champagne the night before, cleaned the fridge out, and set sprays of baby's breath and roses on the divan table. I had pulled all the contents of my bedside drawer out, just in case, trying to decide what to hide, which information would be most damaging. I considered hiding the Cyclovir but bought condoms instead.

When we had walked up the three flights, I held him back with one hand as I opened the door and flipped on the air conditioner. Then I saw my father sitting on the divan, twisting a rose between his hardened fingers. His eyes were wet, shoulders heaving.

"Hi, baby," he said with a sniff. Then he saw Saddam and his eyes widened, and I could see myself and Saddam in his eyes, Saddam resplendent in his cashew-smelling apron, his burn-calloused hand holding mine, his other hand on my back. "Good Christ," my father said.

"Pop." I stood frozen.

"I am pleased to meet you. Dani has told me so much." Saddam walked up and held out his hand. Pop just stared at it, then turned to me.

"What have you done?" Pop stared at Saddam, then me, as if he would cry, and then he did, a great bawling, unmanly cry. "Rosie left me." Pop collapsed in my arms, nearly knocking me over in his grief as I tried to hold him up.

God—or should it be Allah?—bless Saddam, he helped me carry Pop to the couch, cracked the champagne I'd gotten for us, and talked softly to him in that low, rolling, and throaty tone I loved so much, pretended he had not heard my father, or that he didn't know what he meant, or that he didn't know that my father was actually asking him what he had done. I understood, though.

Saddam talked through the evening and the night, and Pop never looked at him, but kept his head buried in his hands. Saddam touched him on the shoulder, walked him around the room occasionally, took him out on the deck for air, made him drink the fragrant Moroccan coffee I kept for special occasions. I could only stare, and add to the conversation once in a while, ask where Rosie had gone (he didn't know) and what he would do next (he didn't know that, either), and soon I stopped. My father and my lover sat in a room with me, getting along, talking through a crisis. Not so unusual, until I thought about who Saddam was and what he meant to the world, and then I just didn't know what to say, so I didn't say anything.

Around 4:00 AM, as I half dozed in the recliner, Pop and Saddam watched water polo and steeplechase and infomercials and the late-breaking news, plumes of smoke and deadness rising into the dry air in my apartment. They seemed so much alike, two men in the late stages of grief and grief-help, at the flash point where the night becomes successful or not, where the grief-stricken finally laugh at the bitterness escaped, and the grief-helpers just laugh in relief.

Saddam just nodded gently, almost asleep, when my father excused himself to go to the bathroom, and for some reason he went to my bathroom rather than the guest half bath. Through my bedroom. Where he saw the condoms, the MDMA, the Xanax. The Cyclovir. The gun.

Pop came out with my pistol in his big hand. I breathed once, slowly. Saddam held up his hands, as if in a ward-off gesture.

"Dani."

I noticed Saddam's smile leaving as he inched toward the door, sliding almost imperceptibly.

"I loaded it for you."

"Please stop it, Pop."

"Always keep the gun loaded." He smiled at me, eyes still tearing a bit. "I know I taught you better than that, than this." He raised the gun slowly to bear on Saddam, who bolted toward him faster than I'd believed he could, this peanut salesman–cum–dictator whom I loved, I knew now, beyond my former capacity for love, whatever that had been. My father raised the gun to his head, and Saddam jumped at him, and I watched as the two of them struggled, these titanic forces in my life, and Pop hoisted Saddam into the air with one arm, but he refused to let go his grip. Finally Saddam stepped back, my pistol in his hand. Pop stood there panting, holding his chest. "For the love of this woman, your daughter, you should not kill yourself. There are better things to die for." He looked at me, his eyes full of love, and walked out of my apartment, my gun in his hand. Pop began to clutch at himself harder, eyes staring at me in mute appeal, like a puppy's, and I went out to his car for the nitroglycerin tablets he kept in the glove compartment, and Saddam's battered van was already gone.

Needless to say, Saddam stopped our rendezvous. Like any good man, he kept me alive through my grief and refusal to understand, sent me pistachios in care of the school at the first part of the new year. I could open them, sniff, and imagine him handing me a balloon or scrubbing my sere spirit into life again. Then I would realize I was in Contemporary Political Issues, 11:30, which students would skip to smoke, and so in a near-empty classroom, I would have to bite my lip to keep from crying.

I left him a note pinned to his umbrella, another tacked under the wipers of his battered Ford, and once I left a more desperate note the way women do sometimes, and I sneaked into the shelter, past two homeless men drinking Scope, and waited in the shower, arms crossed over my breasts until the water turned frigid. So waterlogged and red faced, I crawled out to the alley and back to my job of Historical Importance and Rectitude.

Pop or Rosie—no surprise she came back—call me now, almost daily, to see how I'm doing. I see the old news clips occasionally, Saddam firing his rifle with one hand, legions of Iraqis around him, and cry. I watch the news before I sleep, before I take my pills, at every possible opportunity. I stayed glued to CNN throughout the fruitless search for WMD, the arguments about weapons and body armor and street warfare and death, and then one day I saw him again on the news, not just word of him, but the solid flesh. Pop called my cell when he saw it.

"A spider hole," he said. "Huh." I could hear him sucking on a tooth.

"What do you mean by this, Pop?"

"I guess I would thank him if I could."

"That's great, Pop. Bye."

I think about that last night I saw him. They cut his hair and beard, gave him clothes, because they had to, not because they wanted to. My father comes to visit me where I live now in Somerville, and we see what we see: the retrospectives, the awful footage. My father sent me the cell phone footage. He thought somehow it would make me feel a sense of closure. I didn't watch it, and didn't watch it, and didn't watch it. I choose to imagine that the poems Saddam wrote in his cell in Iraq under American auspices were for me. I like to imagine that there is no better thing to die for than love. ✧

Femmáge

Maria Halovanic

Inheritance isn't much: a few strands encoded
in the afterimage of a face. There's no leaving,

so the philosophy becomes one of using things up:
the breath in one's lungs, the flour sifted from the rim

of the canister, and under a locked window,
her needles and yarn, a meager sea green hunger.

I will think no longer of homes or of mouths,
none of which are mine. Just this one strand

multiplied by patterning, famine compelled
to form under two grave slips of steel, the line

begun like a mouth, the weight of which turns
from nothing to memory, the stitches mounting

like wind-stone steps collected along the street,
the echo of hair against wind, the train

gone, and the woman standing at the station—
nothing more than a simple crossing of wind

and steel disappearing in a definition of distance,
the horizon reconfigured and returning to her.

Afterimage from a Train

Maria Halovanic

The ceaseless work of looking: the sinewy
wash of shoulders, a five-o'clock cheek
in the grey field of the foundry and framed
in the grey train window, the man of ice
toiling under the work lamp that holds back
his inevitable night. His back, the rim
of his stone hat, a chalk-white line of man—
and the rest of him—gone already, although
he must remain there still, flung over
the open face of the wheelbarrow,
his lit hands sifted through gravel and silt,
now simply my hand and its reflection.

BLOOD MERIDIAN, OR THE EVENING REDNESS IN THE WEST by Cormac McCarthy

Robert Anthony Siegel

Blood Meridian is the only book that ever gave me nightmares. The bad dreams were caused, in part, by the extraordinary violence of Cormac McCarthy's story, which follows the murderous wanderings of a young man, known only as "the kid," through the southwest territories at the end of the nineteenth century. It was a world familiar to me from cowboy movies (horses, hats, plates of beans), but McCarthy had transformed it into something strange and utterly compelling, a kind of primal saturnalia in which white settlers, Mexican peasants, and Native Americans butcher one another for money, land, or no reason at all but what one character calls "the dance."

It wasn't just the nearly pornographic outpouring of blood that kept me awake at night, nor the way McCarthy made me feel implicated simply because I continued to read. The truth is that the novel unnerved me aesthetically, too. It was clearly a work of supreme artistry—the prose was gorgeous, incantatory—and yet it refused to do the things that I expected novels to do.

I should mention that I had just finished writing my first novel. It was a father-son story set in New York in the 1970s, and very much what you would expect from that description: a character study, an examination of family relationships, an attempt at tracing the psychological forces that shape personality over time.

Blood Meridian seemed to sneer at those concerns. It was not about character, at least not in the same sense as my novel. By page 80 the kid has signed up with an army of irregulars bent on invading Mexico, survived an Indian attack, been thrown in a Mexican prison, and finally joined a troop of bounty hunters hired to exterminate Apaches (they are to be paid by the scalp). All of this was vivid and real, excruciatingly so, and yet I had only the most limited sense of what the kid thought or felt about any of it. McCarthy offers no access to his consciousness. The kid isn't flat—he has volume and mass—but his interiority remains a mystery.

And yet even without a human consciousness at its center, the novel is full of strange and powerful feeling. The kid travels through a world of wonders, and McCarthy's desert landscape is imbued with dark meaning:

> That night they rode through a region electric and wild where strange shapes of soft blue fire ran over the metal of the horses' trappings and the wagonwheels rolled in hoops of fire and little shapes of pale blue light came

to perch in the ears of the horses and in the beards of the men. All night sheetlightning quaked sourceless to the west beyond the midnight thunderheads, making a bluish day of the distant desert, the mountains on the sudden skyline stark and black and livid like a land of some other order out there whose true geology was not stone but fear.

McCarthy's voice is obviously crucial to this effect. It seems to usher up from some deep chasm within the earth, timeless and impersonal. It can render the details of the physical world with uncanny exactitude, and it can sweep all of human history up into a single moment. Consider this, the first half of a single sentence describing Comanche warriors riding down on the kid and that hapless troop of irregulars:

> A legion of horribles, hundreds in number, half naked or clad in costumes attic or biblical or wardrobed out of a fevered dream with the skins of animals and silk finery and pieces of uniform still tracked with the blood of prior owners, coats of slain dragoons, frogged and braided cavalry jackets, one in a stovepipe hat and one with an umbrella and one in white stockings and a bloodstained weddingveil and some in headgear of cranefeathers or rawhide helmets that bore the horns of bull or buffalo and one in a pigeon-tailed coat worn backwards and otherwise naked and one in the armor of a spanish conquistador, the breastplate and pauldrons deeply dented with old blows of mace or sabre done in another country by men whose very bones were dust...

Over the next few months I read *Blood Meridian* five times straight, from cover to cover, absorbing its extraordinary prose, its strange construction, and its passionate urgency. The novel grapples with questions about human nature, the meaning of violence, and the limits of civilization, but McCarthy never signals his own position and never stops to explain or reassure. In that way it was clearly different from the novel of ideas that I was familiar with, in which the concepts tend to float on the surface, the subject of long disquisitions from both narrator and characters (I think of Saul Bellow or Milan Kundera). Here, the ideas are buried deep in the story itself, inseparable from what happens.

Suddenly I was determined to break out of the comfortable confines of the psychological novel, the domestic drama, the comedy of social embarrassment. I began imagining my second novel, the working title of which was now simply *My Blood Meridian*. The voice of the new book would be vatic, I told myself, the pronouncements of a seer standing at the top of a mountain, shouting against the thunder. The plot would encompass life and death. The prose would wear a weddingveil and ride a warhorse....

I can tell you now that the novel that resulted, *All Will Be Revealed*, is not any of those things. Its protagonist, Augustus Auerbach, is confined to a wheelchair and rarely leaves his Fifth Avenue mansion; he is a plotter and a manipulator, not a killer, and I spend a great deal of time inside his head, parsing his thoughts and feelings. Nevertheless, his story is my response to McCarthy's grand meditation on our fear of the Other. And now that it is done and I have begun to think about my next project, I find myself rereading *Blood Meridian* yet again, filling my ears with its swirling, operatic voice, marveling at what words can do in the hands of a writer willing to break every rule. ✧

fiction   chapbook

comics

black   review

poetry

nonfiction

art   warrior

Suscriptions: Submissions: Web:

One issue $10   BWR   webdelsol.com/bwr

One year $16   Box 862936   bwr@ua.edu

Tuscaloosa, AL 35486

B W R

Redemption Window

Eve Abrams

The fact that Brooklyn is part of Long Island often comes as a shock to people unfamiliar with New York geography. But there it is: the blatant truth. The island shoots toward Manhattan torpedo style, its back end all Atlantic Ocean; its front nosing toward Upper New York Bay, Lady Liberty, the former World Trade Center. The slice of Brooklyn in full view of this convergence is a neighborhood called Red Hook. You can see it all from the pier on Coffey Street, where, during most hours, on most days, local anglers cast into Buttermilk Channel, wedging their rods into the stylized ironwork fence, swigging from bottles of beer, and watching the slow progress of the Staten Island ferry in the distance. My friend Allen, who lives a few blocks away on Beard Street, caught a crab there once and ate it. "Were you scared?" I asked him.

"It was delicious," he replied.

In order to get to this part of Red Hook, you first need to decide how you will get there. It is not easy to do. It lies at the far end of the spine of Van Brunt Street, and the closest subway stop is a good twenty-minute walk through the housing projects. It is a land of large, seemingly empty brick warehouse buildings with arching windows and insectlike cranes. There are blocks of old brick row houses, parallel to others of boarded-up forget-me-nots. There is the water, the breeze, the occasional whiff of sea air, and the guttural moan of a foghorn. There are abrupt dead-ends and canopied intersections, and places like the lot on Beard Street, where sit four gargantuan satellite dishes and nothing else. Red Hook has a charm insinuating secrets and unpredictable spoils.

About a hundred feet from the satellite dishes, down Conover Street, is a bar that is not really a bar, a speakeasy of sorts, which is open only on Fridays. It is run by a painter named Sonny and is referred to as Sonny's for this reason, but for many of the folks from Red Hook who walk over for beer and bluegrass and/or Elvis covers every Friday night, it is simply known as the Bar. Sonny, who inherited the bar from his father, greets his customers with warm hugs, handshakes that press like warm bread dough, soft kisses, and incidental strokes from his very long, curly hair. "Thank you for coming, darling," he whispers in an intimacy that is so absurd it arrives at sincere. The sign inside Sonny's advertises itself as a yachting and kayaking club, and indeed, Sonny is one of the people whose kayak regularly navigates the passage between Governors Island and Brooklyn, known as Buttermilk Channel, en route to the East River, or in the opposite direction, to Gowanus Bay or the Verrazano Narrows.

Sonny's is an extraordinarily pleasant place. Either that or it is loud and crowded. Ever since the magazine *Time Out New York* wrote an article about Brooklyn in the summer of 1998, which included a piece about Sonny's, it has tended toward the latter. But the lure of "$3 suggested donation" drinks, Sonny's doughy hands, and the inherent magic of a once-a-week event keeps many dedicated customers, like myself, returning time and again.

One recent Friday, I sat in the back room of Sonny's with a group of friends. Our nautically decorated business-size cards, which kept a tally of the number of drinks we'd drunk, were scattered across our table, along with the empty pretzel bowl, the ubiquitous ashtrays, and glasses in varying degrees of emptiness. A painting of Sonny's hung over our heads. It was a few minutes before I noted the conspicuous absence of Lauren from the table. Lauren, who had recently broken up with her boyfriend of seven years, had not coincidentally taken to sporadic spurts of uncontrollable sadness. She had managed to find a way to blame herself for everything that went wrong in her relationship, and to decide that through her misconduct she had lost her opportunity for lasting love. Consequently, I worried.

"Has anyone seen Lauren?" I asked no one in particular. Suzanne looked up from her conversation. "Bathroom?" she suggested with raised eyebrows. I wiggled through the congested doorway and turned right under the sign reading P STREET. I knocked. No Lauren. I made my way through the packed room in the other direction—out the mouth of the bar. A dozen or so folks sat on the curb. The Atlantic was sending a delicious, smokeless breeze.

"Have you seen a woman?" I asked. "Short? Cute? With funky glasses?"

They shook their heads no, and across the street Lauren stepped out from under a tree and called my name. "I'm over here."

She'd been feeling nauseous, she explained. She needed some air. "And look what I found."

Lauren grabbed my arm and pulled me down the cobblestones in the direction of the water. It was the end of summer and felt like it. We walked down the center of the street with no thought of doing anything else.

Half a block away was a small building—a well-made shack, really— emerging from a fenced-in lot. Its walls were fashioned from yellow plywood, and the roof was a flat rectangle that looked as if it had been dropped on top. A soda machine stood as sentry on its side, casting garish red light onto the sidewalk. Four wooden steps led up to the grated glass window, above which was an overhang that read simply, REDEMPTION WINDOW.

Lauren stared at it prodigiously. "The Redemption Window," she proclaimed. "I found the Redemption Window."

It was an ominous-looking thing. It stood not two hundred feet from the water, at the edge of a neighborhood on the edge of Brooklyn, within dim sight of the Statue of Liberty and the twinkling lights of New Jersey. Standing in one of the greatest cities on the continent, it was also somehow simultaneously in the most desolate spot imaginable: the end of the road, without a house or a context, just itself, inexplicable: the Redemption Window.

"What is it?" I asked.

"The Redemption Window."

"Is anyone in there?"

"No," she said. "I checked."

We approached the window, and without thought I took ahold of the grate with all ten fingers and began to shake it. "Hello? Is anyone in there? Hello!" I yelled.

Suddenly a man appeared. His head slipped into view from the side, as if tilting upright. *From a cot*, I remember thinking. He slid open the window, and it was at this moment that I screamed. Lauren and I clutched hands and stepped back.

"Hi," she began unsteadily. "We didn't know anyone was in there."

Redemption Man woozily smiled.

"Hi," I repeated.

Redemption Man rubbed his eyes.

"So." Lauren slipped into an interview voice. "What are you doing here so late at night?"

He shrugged, and she fired away again.

"What's your job here? What do you do?" Her voice rang of the inquisitive academic.

Redemption Man opened his mouth to answer, but I, having recovered from my initial shock, shook my head violently, knowing instantly this was all wrong. I laid my hand on Lauren's arm. "Lauren. Tell the man what you need."

She looked at me blankly.

"Go on," I instructed. "Tell him. He's the Redemption Man."

She looked down, away, and then back at me.

I nodded.

Her eyes met the Redemption Man's.

Maybe it was Sonny's drinks or the magic of a summer almost over. Perhaps, in that moment, Lauren simply decided to believe. Whatever it was, I knew I had her. We were of one mind. She took a deep breath.

"I need redemption," she declared.

He cocked his head and opened his mouth.

I stepped back and nodded slowly at the Redemption Man. "She needs redemption," I repeated. I continued nodding in this slow, conspiratorial way. "Can you help her?"

Redemption Man looked at Lauren. He opened his mouth and closed it. It was a small, still world between the three of us. Lauren and I on the wooden platform; the Redemption Man in his nether room on the other side of the open window. All of us at the end of the street under an awning that advertised a way out, the promise of new beginnings.

Redemption Man opened his mouth again. He looked at Lauren and his eyes shone. "You're redeemed," he proclaimed.

The silence took his words, spread them out, and laid everything flat.

I nodded, smiling. "Thank you."

"Thank you," Lauren repeated.

"Good night," we said, and we backed down the wooden steps without another word. The window slid shut behind us.

"Wow," Lauren breathed.

"Yeah."

We made or way back down the middle of the street.

"That was really weird."

I nodded.

"What do you think goes on there?"

I shrugged.

"Why was he there so late?"

"Hm, mm."

"Do you think it's a place where people—"

"Lauren," I interrupted. "The only thing stopping that from being Jesus is you."

We halted in the middle of the street and stared at each other.

She smiled and then I smiled, and then we grabbed hands. It was a perfect night on the calm water in the huge, overwhelming city in which we live. There we stood in one small part of it, witnessing it, being part of it, watching it become whatever we made of it.

Two good Jews, we held hands and walked the rest of the way back to Sonny's, redeemed now, ready for another drink. ✧

THE ILLUSTRATED MAN, by Ray Bradbury

Sam Weller

We've all heard stories of expectant parents and the purported influence of classical music on the child in utero. In my own case, it was neither Bach nor Wagner, Brahms nor Beethoven. In fact, my own prenatal encounter with artistry was literary rather than orchestral—but melodious just the same.

It was late January 1967. What was being hailed as the "blizzard of the century" had slammed Chicago with twenty-three inches of snow in just over twenty-four hours. Howling winds off Lake Michigan made matters far worse—snowdrifts towered over six feet. And more snow continued to accumulate over the next week. The city was brought nearly to a standstill. Schools and offices were shuttered up. Cars were buried. Stranded passengers camped out at O'Hare International Airport. And in a small house in the city's northern suburbs my father plucked a paperback copy of Ray Bradbury's *The Illustrated Man* off of a living-room bookcase and began reading the stories aloud to my mother, just days before I would arrive in the world. It was an odd literary selection. Ray Bradbury's third book, first published in 1951, is at times dark and considerably apocalyptic. But my parents loved Bradbury. I jokingly blame my many adult dysfunctions on my first encounter with Bradbury's tattooed carnival freak—a Depression-era drifter whose skin illustrations swirl and twirl and come alive each night to tell the individual tales contained in the book. But in all seriousness, although I don't really believe that I was in the womb listening with rapt attention, in a twist of fate that still has me scratching my head, I began working as Ray Bradbury's biographer in 2000. My book, *The Bradbury Chronicles: The Life of Ray Bradbury*, was published in 2005.

My ongoing connection to the world of Bradbury has carried on throughout my days. When I was eleven or twelve, my parents' relationship had splintered into a stay-together-for-the-kids'-sake marriage. We were then living in suburban St. Paul, Minnesota, in an old Victorian home that had once served as a Pony Express station. When my parents purchased the house, they were even warned by the sellers that ghosts inhabited the place. (Side note: to my own disappointment, in the four years I lived in the old house, I had only one questionable supernatural encounter— a slamming door late at night. The door in question was found locked in the morning.) By this time my mom was sleeping in her own bedroom upstairs and my dad had converted a small room in the basement into an ad hoc bedroom/cave, beginning the trend of troglodyte living he has always favored. It was down in Dad's musty domicile that, among the hundreds of paperbacks on the bookshelf, my skinny little fingers first landed on the very same copy of *The Illustrated Man* my dad had read all those years earlier. Every so often on Friday nights I would sleep down in the basement. My dad and I would make a ritual out of it. He slept on a sofa, and I took the floor in his old Marine Corps–issue sleeping bag he'd had since his service in the Korean War. I loved those special nights, and in the mornings we would wake extra early to watch all the Saturday-morning cartoons. It was during one of those sleepovers that, cocooned up in the olive drab goose down bag, I began reading *The Illustrated Man*. I didn't really understand all the stories, but for some innate reason I *wanted to understand them*. And within another year or two I did. The first story that really captured my young imagination was "The Long Rain," the story of a stranded rocket-ship crew on Venus seeking shelter from the incessant rain that falls on the planet:

> The rain continued. It was a hard rain, a perpetual rain, a sweating and steaming rain; it was a mizzle, a downpour, a fountain, a whipping at the eyes, an undertow at the ankles; it was a rain to drown all rains and the memory of rain. It came by the pound and the ton, it hacked at the jungle and cut the trees like scissors and shaved the grass and tunneled the soil and molted the bushes. It shrank men's hands into the hands of apes; it rained a solid glassy rain, and it never stopped.

The story has a deep sense of place—Venus, an overgrown, waterlogged jungle world. And it is simple enough conceptually for a young adult reader—a Bradbury hallmark. It is a straightforward man-versus-nature conflict, but—also typical of Bradbury narratives—the drama is transported someplace fantastic.

In those early days of Bradbury discovery I often read *The Illustrated Man* late at night (the best time to read Bradbury), and the stories grabbed me by the pajama lapels. "The Rocket" tells the story of a loving father who yearns to turn his children's dreams of space travel into reality. And he does. By building a fantastic, imaginary rocket ship.

The stories in *The Illustrated Man* are also steeped in social concerns, metaphors I was just beginning to understand and appreciate when I began reading the book in earnest at age thirteen. In "The Other Foot" Bradbury supplants the racial tensions of 1950s America onto the planet Mars and flips the roles. In the story (which was anthologized in *The Best American Short Stories of the Year* in 1952) African-American colonists inhabiting the Red Planet have to decide how to deal with the white man upon his impending arrival. Will blacks perpetuate the years of racism and intolerance they have endured?

And then there is, of course, the lead story in *The Illustrated Man*, the frightening cautionary tale "The Veldt." The story is pure social satire—Bradbury using the science fiction genre to mirror present-day cultural conventions. "The Veldt" posits what a children's nursery of the future might look like. In this case it is a wall-to-wall, floor-to-ceiling interactive virtual-reality chamber. The parents in the story quickly learn, to chilling effect, how hard it is to wean their tech-dependent children off the nursery. The story was written in 1949, and it was Bradbury ranting on the growing medium of television and what might happen if parents used the technology as a babysitter.

In all, *The Illustrated Man* contains eighteen fantastic tales (later editions of the book include a nineteenth, the title story, which tells the origin of the tattooed carnival freak). As a child, I devoured this collection. It was at once full of splendid high concepts, deep in metaphor, and rich in social commentary, all written in Bradbury's singular, lyrical, even musical prose. Though Bradbury has a good many books worth recommending (*Fahrenheit 451, The Martian Chronicles, Dandelion Wine*, to name a few), I will always hold *The Illustrated Man close*. For in an almost Bradburian twist, I read it before I was born. ✧

 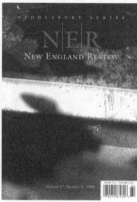 

Long Stories

by Kevin Canty

There's something shady about the art of fiction. Novels, stories, they advertise themselves to be about life itself, to represent us as we are, from the inside out, among others. Yet there are always epiphanies, conflicts, changed characters—these fictional features that crop up everywhere. There's a plot. Something happens between two characters. Something is finally broken, or finally mended. There is sex and death and sometimes food. Meanwhile, life itself plods along without much shape, without climaxes or punch lines or neat divisions between one story and the next. The only thing you can reasonably say about it is that there is too much of it. Writers come along like magpies and pluck whatever shiny object catches their eye, to take home and weave into a story, a story that—in the end—has little or nothing to do with life itself. Stories are made from experience in the same way that clay turns into teacups.

Or maybe not. I've been reconsidering lately, partly because of the Up series of documentary movies. I'd been hearing about them for years, vaguely: seven movies (so far) that revisit the lives of a group of subjects every seven years *Seven Up!, 7 plus Seven, 21 Up, 28 Up, 35 Up, 42 Up*, and now *49 Up*. But I had never quite caught up to them until my girlfriend's mother sent them to us for Christmas last year. We sat down in the depths of January and watched them in a bunch, night after night. And the first suggestion I'm going to make here is that you quit reading and do the same, if you haven't. It's impossible to write about these movies without spoiling them, at least a little, and I don't want to do that to you. The experience of watching a life unfold in this kind of fast-forward is intensely interesting and intensely pleasurable, reality TV except with real reality and real characters.

Yes, that's right, characters. These people stick in the mind as vivid, stirring individuals. Most of these lives are pretty ordinary, in the end—no soccer stars or polar explorers here—but after our weeklong Up marathon, they felt as big as life, more like friends or even relatives than the strangers they were. There's Bruce, whose struggles to find a place for himself in the world take him as far afield as India before landing exactly back where he started; Suzy, who seems utterly doomed to unhappiness in the early going, and yet, somehow, recovers herself; Neil, whose slide into mental illness, and slow, partial recovery, form the narrative backbone of the middle part of the story. And always the memory of these same characters at seven, their little faces and strange visions of the world.

Like a lot of other great ideas, this one started out as a mistake. The original *Seven Up!* was never meant to be a series; when it appeared in 1964, it was a kind of snapshot of the England of its day, through the lens of the seven-year-old eye. There were originally twenty children, deliberately selected from the far ends of the economic scale. The original writers and director had a chip on their shoulders concerning class, a conviction that the advantages of wealth were a determining factor in what each of these children could expect out of life. The story of the first film is this grim determination of their destinies, at such a young age, and the ways these children have already internalized their expectations— the rich kids to their big houses and fancy colleges, and the poor and middle-class kids to their grubbier fates.

But someone had the wit to go back seven years later and check in with these kids again, to see what their lives were like at fourteen, and at that point the story began to outstrip the easy certainties of its origins. These lives were evolving in rich and strange ways that seemed to have nothing to do with their economic background. Who was happy, who was miserable, who seemed to have a grip, and who looked like they might float away, none of this attached itself to any particular class. We would much rather trade places with Tony, who has already quit school to be a groom and apprentice jockey at a famous racing stable, than we would with Suzy, who is fabulously rich and shiningly unhappy. Andrew (rich) is nimble and funny and sharp, while John (also rich) is already sour and angry. The political points of the first film were already fading into the background, and this other, unlooked-for thing—this enormous, complex portrait of people's lives evolving over time—was overshadowing them.

The series director, Michael Apted, may not have known where he was going when he started out, but at least he had the smarts to recognize a brilliant thing when it dropped into his lap. In fact, Apted was mainly a researcher on that first episode; since then he has come back every seven years to film a new episode. (He lives now in California, where he directs high-end Hollywood product, including one of the recent James Bond movies.) It's this every-seven-years pace that gives these films their surprise and speed. Nothing from Symon for seven years, nothing much for seven years more, then suddenly he pops up with a mustache, an Afro, and five kids. Nick, the farm kid from the Yorkshire dales, suddenly appears as a nuclear physicist at the University of Wisconsin. And Andrew, sly little Andrew, keeps surprising us with his lack of surprise. I kept expecting the imp in him to surface again; instead, he sort of disappears under the weight of years, like water washing his features away.

Parents die, children are born, marriages start and fade and sometimes end and sometimes endure. Things happen, and characters are changed by these events. The subject matter of life itself, in other words, turns out to be the same subject matter as fiction—just at a slower pace.

Plots, conflicts, characters in action, it's all in there. In one of the late films Tony confesses to adultery in the presence of his wife. Will they stay married? The answer, seven years later, is a wary yes, but the tenor of their life together is changed now, some of the ease and happiness gone. It's a moment that would fit easily into any number of novels, a profound and nuanced turn of events. Again and again as I was watching these films, especially in the late going, I felt the novelistic moment, the place I recognized from art. Which perversely kind of makes me believe in art, makes me think that serious fiction writing really may be onto something, may be a way to explore the things that matter most. But it also makes me feel something about life itself, about the way that no life is too small to be interesting, no life story without drama, no single person without weight and worth. Everybody's the star of their own show. And every show's worth watching. I can't wait till 56. ✧

IT WAS LIKE MY TRYING TO HAVE
A TENDER-HEARTED NATURE

A Novella and Stories

DIANE WILLIAMS

FC2

The University of Alabama Press

http://fc2.org

THE COMPLETE TALES OF MERRY GOLD
by Kate Bernheimer

Lydia Millet

Meanness: how bright and sharp it can be, how instant and perfectly understandable. You don't find mean girls starring in novels every day; so often protagonists are nice like oatmeal cookies or milk chocolate. I get sick of it, frankly, sick of all these narrators we can relate to easily because they're so blank and blah that most of what we see in them is our own eagerness to be liked, by anyone and everyone. In real life aren't purely nice people purely boring? You want a little bit of malice in a person; you want a little bite. We don't inhabit a nice world, after all—nice isn't what gave us religion, soaring bridges, a sense of humor, vivid dreams, or great art.

And nice sure isn't Merry Gold. She wants to attack one-legged kids just for the pure satisfaction of it. "Prudish, obsessive, and cold," as the book jacket puts it with excellent succinctness, Merry has a quick and vicious quality. Like it or not, we can still relate. That's the beauty of Merry: she recalls us to the little glints of meanness in ourselves. Not that she has to; we don't have to relate in order to ride on the backs of these sentences, which are likable in themselves for their bluntness and precision and poetry. But we do. Merry brings back the deliciousness of the urge to pinch someone, which I remember with shame from my own childhood: a small, hard pinch, a twist of a pinch that could be evilly satisfying. And let's face it, spite—in children, at least—is often pretty funny.

> Merry gazed at his wooden leg—the pegginess of it pleased her. She often amputated the legs of dolls and wished very much that she too lacked a limb. She glanced over at Ketzia. Did a crybaby need both of her legs?

Merry's life somehow becomes, after the bright malice of her childhood and desperate sluttiness of her adolescence, a defeated, folded-in drabness of an adulthood, held together with vodka and fur. She drinks, lives minimally, and works as a pattern maker in a dress shop and then at a factory that makes children's clothing; as a student she sold sex to make ends meet. We get the sense she was stung at birth by a wasp of anger— that she felt entitled, from the beginning, to something she would never quite specify, perhaps to be best loved or most powerful. In any case, the impossibility of this dominion drives her to a narrow and solitary life.

The Complete Tales of Merry Gold is the second in a stream of innovative, fairy-tale-based novels about the daughters of the Gold family, following on the heels of the lovely and egregiously overlooked *The*

Complete Tales of Ketzia Gold. Both are made up of Bernheimer's oblique versions of Russian, German, and Yiddish tales, pieced together in fragmentary, short chapters with an impressionist quality. Reading, you're left not with the sense of a beginning, middle, and end, nicely tied with a bow, but the imprint of a language of mood and feeling that tends to shrug off linear interpretation, much like the fairy tales themselves. The Gold novels aren't typical novels at all, but rather collections of fairy tales hung together into a new form—a form that, instead of appropriating fairy tale tropes, images, or plots into a conventional narrative, lets the gathered and retold tales themselves determine the shape of the story. Like Italo Calvino's books, Bernheimer's are both abstract and immediate, immanent with a kind of fluid philosophy that escapes our eyesight forever around the next corner.

What's distinct about *Merry Gold*—besides the vibrant and often nonsensical brief tales, with their invisible burnings alive, talking roosters and bladders, poisoned bread, and water nixies—is its fatalistic understanding of personality. A girl lives in a good house, with doting parents and pleasant siblings, intelligence and abundance—indeed, her childhood has much to be said for it, in its bright colors and humor and sense of thrill—but is lost nonetheless, walled off. We're left with the suspicion that this lostness resides in us, too, a hard little kernel of self, always predetermined and stubbornly impervious to warmth. ✧ ·

Three Short Stories

Michael Hearst

Brooklyn Diner

When I first moved to Brooklyn, I had breakfast one morning at a Greek diner in Park Slope. Handwritten on a paper plate, taped to a wall, was the following item:

SKITAS $3.50

I asked the waitress, "What's a skita?"

She looked confused, so I pointed at the paper plate taped to the wall. The waitress then said, "Lemme check," and disappeared into the kitchen. A different waitress came to my table and took my order.

Two weeks later I went back to the same diner. The paper plate had been removed from the wall.

Question

While shopping at the Park Slope Food Coop, a young man with thick glasses and long, curly side locks approached me and asked if I was Jewish. I could tell he was on the verge of handing me a printed piece of paper—most likely propaganda for a nearby synagogue.

I asked, "Why do you want to know if I'm Jewish?"

He said, "Ah, now I know you're Jewish. You just answered a question with a question."

He dropped the flyer into my shopping cart and walked away.

Saturday Mornings

On Wednesday evenings I would call each house on my list and take orders. Six onion, two pumpernickel, two raisin, and three plain—a typical order—a baker's dozen. On Saturday mornings at 8 AM my mother would drive me to Mr. Hanwitz's bagel shop on Virginia Beach Boulevard, where I would pick up the orders and stack them in the back of our Chevy Citation. My mother would then drive me from house to house and wait in the car while I ran up and delivered the brown paper bags full of steaming bagels. My friends all had regular jobs—mowing neighbors' yards, cleaning gutters, and delivering newspapers. I had a bagel route. ✧

Why the
Devil Chose
New England
for His Work

Stories by
Jason
Brown

"Stories so beautiful, faceted,
and durable, they feel excavated from
a mine. A collection of subtle gems."
—Aimee Bender

"Linked, gem-cut stories of troubled youths, alcoholics, illicit romances, the
burden of inheritance, and the bane of class, all set in the dense upper
reaches of Maine . . . delivered with hope, heart, and quiet humor."
　　　—*Elle*

 **OPEN CITY BOOKS**

November 2007

Ontogeny

Nickole Brown

It's the science of everyone's earliest days
first plastered across the cover
of *Time* in 1965: unborn children
lifted from their dark organ
warmth with scalpel and scope, carbonation
blown to float them up
to the flashing fiber-optic eye.

Nine years later even the first
footsteps on the moon was old
news so it was no big deal for a young
girl in Kentucky to flip the pages
tracking her swell from clot
to snail to kicking feet before labor brought
something substantial enough to make
a shadow, to recognize that shadow,
to fill an urn full of its own ash.

Not that mama ever cared
to look. *You got fat, then you had a baby*
was all the learning she sought, the rest
of what she needed to know was
hot-rolled into her bleach-blond hair and
plucked into an arch, never once wanting
to read about her own bones that once began
growing outward from the middle,
hardening from the crosshairs out,
the origin of core implying an axis
of tough, the apple seeded central
with poison, her earliest memories deepest
and the least she's likely to admit.
And she'll tell you: *back then,*
you had to lay it down, let it go,

never mind what the doctor and schoolteacher
say, never mind that she came from a long line
of men who break things, of children
who hid under a bed, a tattletale stream
of urine making them easy for him to find.
She knows the worst of it, she knows everything,
but the weight of knowing must be shucked:
there are shirts that need starch,
shelves that need lining,
simple, dim salads to toss with iceberg and carrots,
jars of imitation bacon and milky dressing on the side.

Look in the garage, sister. Even it's been cleaned
top to bottom, not a spider egg or rainbow
drip of oil in sight,
it is godly, scrubbed spotless,
all our tears swept from every corner
with a cheap straw broom.

Straddling Fences

Nickole Brown

Sister, I've tried it all.
Gardening, yoga, therapy, you name it—
I've smoked my house out
with incense, taped prayers to the inside
of my fridge, worn my fingernails
clipped and bare, neglected

the bottle of pink polish
gumming on the windowsill.
I've tried pills and red wine;
I've thought of the sawed-off
shotgun under mama's bed, of the slow
release of red into a tub, of twisting the white
tulle scallops of my canopy
into a rope to hang myself there.

I've traveled, trying to leave it
behind—heels squeaking on ancient marble,
dolphins chasing my boat on a flat sea,
boys with eyes that spun like bicycle wheels
in rain. I left my first husband, my one
true home, then moved into an empty house
comforted by the nothing

of waxed hardwood floors. I have eaten
turnip greens sautéed with virgin oil,
simple food we never heard of growing up
like sushi, basmati, butternut squash.
But I still drink soda every morning,
and when I'm sick, it's straight
to the fried comfort,
a bottle of hot sauce nearby.

How can I make all this fit? How did I
make it through? Our mama in
therapy makes about as much sense
as putting Buddha in the seat of that car
we used to go to in the woods, that rusted-out Ford
of creeping charlie vine and bullet holes,
the base of a bottle all the kids said
was broken off in somebody.
Sitting there on that dry-rot

driver's seat, our hands on the crusted
wheel, was a terror so beautiful
we never thought of going anywhere.
I had to try something, had to leave
you behind, had to try to be thankful
for the chance to boss my way
through the city gates, switching all the time
between *isn't* and *ain't*, my feet
in designer red heels
with creek mud still between my toes.

Straddling a fence, I think mama would say.
On one side,
rusting barbwire, a tree swing, the green smell
of cow patties in the sun.
On the other,
another me,
pressed,
dressed,
right as fucking rain.

Victor

Michael Czyzniejewski

Along with the groceries, my wife brings home a dummy, a little guy made of wood, a redhead with round cheeks, a high, arching brow, and a goatee. Debbie tells me to unload while she shows Victor around, that she's getting pretty hungry, too, asking what time she should expect dinner.

"Victor?" I ask.

"Hello," Victor says. "You're better looking than Debbie let on."

Debbie's hand is inside the dummy's back, but Debbie's mouth doesn't move at all. In fact, she smiles a lot, and at one point during the dummy's speech she coughs. To the best of my knowledge, Debbie has had no experience with ventriloquism, but now, with ten brown bags and a watermelon on the kitchen floor, she comes off like a pro.

"There's Popsicles in one of those bags," Debbie says. "Plus, I stopped to see your mom on the way home."

Debbie disappears into the bedroom, along the way pointing out the paintings she did in college and the bathroom. While I have more questions—the least of which is what she was doing at my mother's—those Popsicles are turning to juice. Even stranger, while I'm putting everything away, I find products we've never bought before—yogurt, kiwis, string cheese, a six-pack of diet cola. With both Debbie and me lactose intolerant, and neither of us on a diet, I can't imagine who these new items are for, but away they go.

During dinner Debbie holds the dummy on her lap, and again her ventriloquist skills fall nothing short of amazing. While the dummy talks, Debbie takes sips from her wine, even chews bites of her pork chop. At one point she interrupts the dummy, then apologizes as he apologizes, making it seem like they're talking at the exact same time. I clap, tell her I'm impressed, and ask where the dummy came from.

"Victor," she says, "found my personal ad online."

Debbie seems to want to play the game out, play it as far as I'll go along with it. I'm not sure how, but Victor is able to use his arms to pick up a fork and put food in his mouth, which must fall into some hole, as in his mouth it stays. Somewhere inside this dummy sits an entire pork chop and a dish of applesauce—he leaves the baked potato untouched but did bother to waste half a stick of butter and some sour cream. I have no choice but to oblige Debbie's ruse and play along too, lest I be the one who spoils the fun. I've been accused of that in the past, a habit I'm trying to break.

"So, Victor," I say, looking Victor in the marblelike eyes. "Who do you like in the game tonight?"

Victor finishes chewing a bite, and Debbie helps him wash it down by lifting a glass of water—poured just for him—and emptying it into his wooden mouth, past his straight and white wooden teeth.

"I'm not a sports fan," Victor tells me. "But I'll say the home team, as I'd hate to be rude to my host, jinx the good guys' chances, if you know what I mean."

For the first time since Debbie brought this dummy home, I'm irked. I'm not sure if it's because the gag is going on too long, or because I hate the snobby tone Debbie has chosen for Victor, as if to tell me she's above following sports. Plus, if she's making him sincere, I don't like to be patronized. What kind of way is that to have a dinner conversation? If he's for the Pats, she should just have him tell me he's for the Pats. Like I'm going to judge him for rooting for the opposing team, or worse yet, believe that his cheering is going to affect any outcome. I've always hated guys like that, and Debbie knows it.

But I'm probably reading too much into it.

Debbie reminds me that since I cooked, it's her turn to do dishes, and she asks me to take Victor down to the rec room, tells me he'd like my collection of beer steins. "He collects zeppelin memorabilia," she says, "so he knows a lot about stuff from Germany." I counter with a reminder that the pre-game is on, that her tour of the house took a little longer than it should have, and we could maybe look at the steins at halftime. But I'm more than willing to take Victor with me, as I'm looking forward to getting my hand in there and making him say the things I want Debbie to hear, instead of the other way around. Before I can even ask Debbie to hand him over, Victor interjects.

"I think I'd like to lie down for a while, Deborah. It's been a long day, and Greg's gourmet meal has left me a bit on the drowsy side."

Debbie looks at me as if it's my choice whether or not Victor can take a nap.

"Game's on in ten," I say.

Debbie excuses herself from the table, as does Victor, and the two disappear into the guest bedroom. I clear the table, noting that it's taking a bit longer than it should for her to come back. When she finally emerges, she's tiptoeing, as if to be quiet.

"He's a sweet guy," Debbie says, and to keep the ruse going, whispers.

"But I think the little bastard likes the Patriots," I tell her, and give her a wink, a wink that's not returned.

"I told you it was my job to do the dishes."

"When do I ever listen to you?"

"Your game is on—you've made that clear."

"You forgot some things from the store, namely eggs."

"I'm glad you're okay with him staying. It's big of you to go along with this."

"I can grab McDonald's, only I thought we said we weren't going to do that anymore, pick up something on the run."

Debbie fills the sink, drops Victor's potato into the trash like a bomb. I grab a beer and notice there's only one more in the fridge. I catch myself thinking that I should leave it for Victor in case he gets up and wants to watch the game, and it makes me laugh. When Debbie asks why I'm giggling, I tell her the Jets are going to kick the crap out of the Pats, and if anyone thinks differently, his head must be made of wood.

I know why Debbie's doing this, playing this Victor game with me, which is why I have to play along. A few weeks ago, when Debbie was supposed to be at the gym, she came home, her ankle turned, and found me in our bedroom with Laura Donovan, the woman who delivers our bottled water. I wasn't naked, Laura wasn't naked, and we weren't even touching. But Laura was sitting on our bed. To any woman who breaks her two-year routine only to find a woman sitting on her husband's bed, her husband just a few feet away and looking startled, this would seem like infidelity. But like I said, Laura's clothes were on, my clothes were on, and Laura's clipboard was in her hands. It was easy for me to tell Debbie that Laura was in our bedroom because she wanted to see if an extra dispenser would fit under a cabinet in our bathroom, that she sat down because she runs up and down people's front walks with five-gallon bottles on her shoulders all day. She was tired, had to run some numbers, and I told her to take a load off. I appeared startled to Debbie because Laura's work clothes were sweaty and Debbie had just done the bedding—I was thinking about the sheets, not some crazy affair with the Culligan lady. As soon as Laura left, Debbie told me she wasn't mad about the sheets, filling me in on what she thought was really going on. I told her she was imagining things. Yes, I'd made comments about Laura before—her tan (probably a farmer's), her thick thighs and lean calves, how it looked like her big breasts were stretching the buttons of her uniform shirt. So I could totally see where Debbie was coming from, and later on we laughed about it together, made jokes. Victor's appearance is just the joke taken a step further, the punch line to the online personal she filled out and left on the screen of our laptop. We joke with each other like that: she calls me Doughboy sometimes, I dig on her cooking, especially anything from the casserole family. It's how we get along, how any married couple gets along.

And I have to admit, a wooden ventriloquist's dummy is a lot better than Gary the mailman in a thong when I come home early from work. Victor is made of wood, not to mention a snob, maybe even gay, the way he drinks water at dinner and doesn't follow sports. I'll take a wooden gay dummy any day over Gary and his shorty-short blue pants with the black stripes running down the sides. As long as Debbie does too, we won't have a problem.

*

I'm not sure why, but the next day at work I tell Charlie about the whole thing: Victor, dinner, Debbie not coming down to say good night before turning in. Charlie is my partner at work, and my best friend, but that doesn't say much, since we don't really see each other off the job. Charlie and I work in old blast furnaces—steel mills and manufacturing plants, mostly—repairing the inner structures when they start to crumble. A company calls our unions—me the Bricklayers, Charlie the Laborers—and they call us. Charlie breaks the shit wall down with a sledgehammer, I put in the new wall, then Charlie cleans up. Even though Charlie's in a different union, he is in a union and knows to follow my lead, to make the job last as long as we can without raising suspicion, without getting a lolly-gagger rep. It's a good system, a system I plan on exploiting till I'm fifty-five and Debbie and I can move to Florida. Charlie will find a new brick-layer, and we'll lose touch.

"Sounds like you and Deb have some issues to sort out," Charlie says. "A dummy?"

"The Patriots looked like a bad college team," I tell him. "Don't they have, like, ten Pro Bowlers?"

"Maybe she's trying to tell you something."

"I don't care how many rings he has, if a guy throws four picks, you sit his ass on the bench till he learns what color his jersey is. But fuck it—they can play Mickey Mouse against the Jets. What do I care?"

Charlie tells me, in between swings of his hammer, that maybe I should do something special for Debbie tonight, take her to dinner, an artsy movie, maybe dancing. He tells me that Debbie's a pretty lady, that I'm a lucky man, that someone needs to give her the things she deserves. That she's dying for it to be me. I tell him that Debbie's never asked about dancing, never shown any interest, and remind him that he's never taken his wife dancing either.

"My wife's not the one who brought home a dummy she found online, man. And besides, Deb never showed an interest in ventriloquism, yet somehow she's Edgar fucking Bergen. Who knows, maybe she's Britney Spears on the dance floor too. Or Shakira, grabbing herself and humping the floor and shit."

Technically, since I'm the tradesman, I'm the foreman on our jobs. But I never throw that in Charlie's face—I've never had to. But I'm tempt-ed now. The only reason I don't is because he's sort of right—about the ventriloquism, anyway.

"Red Lobster's having their Shrimp Feast," I tell Charlie. Just then a rat the size of a shoe box runs from the hole Charlie's punched in the wall, and I trap it in my mixing bucket.

"Cement shoes?" Charlie asks.

"Oh yeah," I say, and ask Charlie to hand me my trowel.

*

I didn't think it a possibility, but when I meet Debbie at the restaurant, Victor is perched in her lap. The table holds three place settings and three glasses of water, and the two of them are having a conversation about the movie they went to go see that afternoon, something about an English woman struggling to find her way in a man's world. Everyone in the section is staring at us, and little kids from all over are standing in the aisles, pointing and yelling over to their parents.

"You look nice," Debbie says. "I wasn't sure if you'd have time to shower."

Victor looks up from his menu and says he likes my sweater, that orange, brown, and green are three of his favorite colors. Victor's wearing a white turtleneck with a charcoal sport coat. His hair seems to have some sort of goop in it, as it's pushed back and slick, all curled up in the back.

"You bought him a change of clothes?" I say. Last night Victor was wearing a long-sleeved button-down, a dark blue, I think. I don't remember what kind of pants he had on and now can't see under the tablecloth.

"A little present," Debbie says. "Victor paid for the movie, and the men's store was right next to the theater. He can't wear the same thing every day, you know—he's not you."

A woman and a man at the table next to us find this remark very funny. They clap and ask for Debbie to make Victor say something else. I turn toward them and they put their faces back in their menus.

"Just kidding, honey! You look nice," Debbie says. She asks me to sit down, across from her and Victor. Before I can say anything—ask Debbie to leave, for instance, and drop Victor in the Dumpster on the way out of the lot—a waitress comes and brings us drinks and salads.

"I took the liberty of ordering for you," Victor says. "I overheard Debbie playing your message from the machine, bandying this 'feast' they have going, so I assumed you wanted just that, the Shrimp Feast."

Debbie digs into her salad with her free hand, and Victor does the same—I'm pretty sure she's controlling him lefty, when yesterday she was using her right. I start to think that she's maybe been secretly taking lessons at night, maybe at the community college, the one we get catalogs from in the mail. I'm not sure when she's been doing this—probably my euchre night—and it makes me feel like we've been leading double lives. Whenever I say I'm going to my folks' to play cards, I go play cards with my folks. When Debbie says she's going to stay in and read, I assume she's reading in our bed, by herself. I've been playing euchre on Wednesdays for a lot of years, so like Charlie said, who knows what other skills she's acquired in that time? To think that my wife is holding out on me makes me not hungry. Maybe she can fix cars or even mountain-climb? Maybe one night I'll pull around the block, follow her, see if she leaves. But that's crazy talk, and if I have to follow her around, then is she really worth the effort?

I am not a big fan of salad, but I pick at it because I don't want to seem ungrateful to Victor for getting the dressing right, Thousand Island. Then I catch myself for feeling bad, about hurting the feelings of a piece of wood, one who's wearing nicer clothes than me, one who remembered to put his napkin on his lap. I push the salad aside and wait for my shrimp. When it comes, I order only one refill, broiled in garlic butter on a wooden skewer, when usually I get three or four extra platters, all fried. Victor's stomach has been whittled flat, I notice, then it hits me: what if Debbie made Victor, carved him herself? What if Victor—red hair, perfect manners, chiseled good looks—is what she wants? It would make a lot of sense, but then again, nothing about this makes sense. When the waitress comes at the end of the meal and asks about dessert, I say no, order a water, and watch my wife and her dummy share cheesecake drizzled in chocolate fudge sauce, what I usually get, and Debbie always declines.

I want to kick Charlie in the ribs when he falls over from laughing the next day, telling me he'd give up all his overtime for the year to have seen me at Red Lobster with a ventriloquist's dummy, wearing my orange-brown-and-green sweater, all those people watching.

"It would have been enough to see you stop at two plates of shrimp," he says. "The rest of it, that's just heaven."

I let Charlie have his fun for ten minutes or so, then we get to work. To make my day even better, the hunk of wall we replaced yesterday has fallen in, probably because of the humidity, maybe a rotten bag of mortar. But we have to start over, knock down an even bigger section, make sure the whole wall is stable. If the structure is at all compromised when the stove is lit, the heat could seep through to the gas line and cause an explosion. And that's bad, though it would get us more work; rebricking an entire furnace of this size is usually a two-month job, six days a week, too, maybe ten or twelve hours per.

Charlie does manage to get his barbs in, wondering out loud if wood would be better than bricks, asking if I knew any good carpenters, telling me I'd look good in a goatee, even smearing one on his face with ash. In a voice that is supposed to be Debbie's, I guess, all high and cracking, he says, "Wow, I really love a man in a goatee," then starts making kissy noises and rubs his arms all over like he's hugging himself, even squeezing where Debbie's breasts would be. I wonder how hard it would be to push Charlie inside the wall I'm building, if I could finish before he came to, if anyone would ever hear him pounding and screaming after I'd gone home. Not like I don't deserve his shit—serves me right for telling Charlie everything, when honestly, I can't even remember his wife's name, Jill or Julie, something with a J.

At the end of the day Charlie asks me to go out for a beer later (mentioning that Debbie wouldn't mind the time alone), but it's euchre night, so

I turn him down. "I knew that," he says. "Just checking." Plus, I can take a joke as much as the next guy, but I think I'd rather spend an evening with the actual Victor and Debbie than any more of Charlie riding me, or him telling me how lucky I am to have Debbie. When I drop him off at his condo, he does give me one good piece of advice: "Keep a hacksaw by the bed. Just to send a message."

That night, at my folks', I lose big. I'm partnered up with Mom, who is pissed. Dad and Lester, my little brother, who still lives with them, are kicking our asses. Dad and Lester never beat me and Mom, and in fact, nobody ever beats Mom, whether she's with me, Lester, or Dad. I'm playing that bad. Mom throws her cards down a lot, drinks almost a beer a hand, even says "fuck" a few times, which she almost never does, unless she and Dad are having it out.

We're done way early, Mom wanting nothing more to do with me and my crappy leads. Lester and Dad gloat, a side we rarely ever see. They high-five, they low-five, and they dance around like little girl cheerleaders at a Pop Warner game. Dad goes up to his room—he and Mom sleep separately, have for years—and Lester goes out to his place above the garage, cigarette in mouth and lighter in hand before he hits the door. Mom, who can barely walk, asks me to stay awhile, to have one more with her, for the road. Since it's early, I accept, even though I've already had, like, seven myself in just a couple of hours.

Mom, always with an agenda, just wants to tell me how good Lester's doing at his new job, but that she misses him when he's gone. He's the baby, her favorite, and no matter what I do, how much I stay out of trouble, he'll always be her favorite. Lester, thirty-nine, has been living with our folks for the last five years, a lot of times before that too, after both divorces, after both rehabs, after, most recently, the DUI that cost him his license and his job with UPS. He's scrounged around a lot for work, bagging groceries, sweeping up at a $10 haircut shop, but recently Dad got him in at GM, working the line, a real backbreaker, putting doors the size of easy chairs on SUVs. But Dad thought Lester was ready to handle the pressure, that this job was the answer, and GM was hiring. "He and your father drive in together, come home together," Mom says, as if to imply Lester can't get into any trouble if Dad drags him around by the hand. When I remind Mom that Dad has only a few months till retirement, she finishes her beer and gets up to get another. She asks if I want one more (again), but I give her mine, only a sip or two deep, still cold.

"He'll either be ready to do it on his own, or he won't. If he is, then maybe he can talk about getting his own place. If not, then he'll just fuck it up, end of story. He can't sit on your father's lap and steer forever, you know—sooner or later he's going to have to work the pedals, too."

Mom is more than half in the bag at this point, but I still ask her: "How long have you been working on that line?"

"Heard it on Oprah," Mom says. "I watch a lot of TV now, without Lester around to talk to."

I tell Mom that I should drop over more, maybe twice a week instead of once, and she pats my hand, tells me I have a wife, a beautiful wife, and my job is to take care of her, that I should think about putting my storm windows in this weekend, that you never know when the cold will come, and before you know it, it moves right into your house. It's only September, a week after Labor Day, but this reminds me to ask about Debbie's visit, her post-shopping stop-in. As soon as I ask, Mom looks at me like I just screwed up another hand of euchre.

"Maybe she meant her mother," Mom says. She stares me down and knows that I'm serious, that I think Debbie's been to visit her in the last couple of days. That Debbie lied. "But I wish she'd drop by—the store's just around the corner. We could have coffee, maybe a beer. Tell her I said hello."

Soon after, I help Mom up to her room, put her under her covers in her bed, kiss her on the forehead. If she hadn't been drinking, I maybe would have asked her about Victor, about what it all means, but then again, it's probably good that I don't. As hard a time as Charlie gave me at work, Mom would probably be worse, lecture me on fulfilling my husbandry duties, then offer to let me live at home for a while, share a bedroom with Lester until things with Debbie work out. Mom can be awful when she's drunk, and too momly, but she's Mom, sixty-eight and ridiculously awesome. She can say whatever she wants to me, and it would be okay.

When I get home, the house is dark, which isn't unusual, as it's almost midnight. If she remembers, Debbie will leave the stove light on for me on Wednesdays, help me get across to the table and chairs, assuming I've had a few. With Lester's list of problems, I'm not sure why she fosters my once-a-week bingeing, but again, that's the way we deal with each other. I have my things, she has hers. We're married, and that's what married couples do, cover.

But lying about visiting my mom isn't one of those things that we do. That's covering, but not for me, for her. It's odd, because she could have said she was anywhere—the bank, the post office, the library, even at the store the whole time. It wasn't like I was timing her. She could have come home an hour later, and I wouldn't have said anything. But she chose to tell me she'd stopped at my mother's, that the Popsicles were melting, that I needed to put them in the freezer while she took her puppet on a tour of the house. It was deliberate, and even worse, she had to know I'd ask Mom about it a few days later. Tonight. And she was right. But why?

Whether she's asleep or not, I'm going to wake her up and ask. She won't want to talk to me while I'm drunk—leaving a light on is one thing, fighting with me is another—but I don't care. She brought this upon herself. She has to pay.

Up in our bedroom I see the light under the bathroom door and hear the shower. It is two hours past her bedtime, and even though I'm an hour earlier than usual, I doubt my wife takes showers this late every Wednesday. I think to myself that she doesn't do all that much during the day, cooks and cleans, gets the groceries, so why would she need to shower so late, right before bed? I turn the door handle, wanting to surprise her, but find it locked, so I sit down on the bed, willing to wait for her to finish.

Lo and behold, I find Debbie asleep next to me, under the covers, asleep but stirring, a smile on her face, as if she's having a good dream. Even stranger than taking a shower late at night, Debbie has taken a shower but has left the light on and the water running, the door locked. Maybe that explains it somehow— she got locked out of the bathroom, hours ago, with the light on and the shower still spewing water. She knows I have a way of jiggling open the door, using a steak knife, and she's going to have a laugh with me, say something ridiculous about paying me back for the water and electricity she's wasted. She will smell good, she will smell clean, and if I weren't drunk, we might have sex—the job ended today, and I have nowhere to be in the morning, and I have no plans to put in the storm windows. But I am drunk, and she will not have sex with me while I'm drunk.

Just as I'm about to wake Debbie, ask her about her visit to Mom's, I hear the water in the shower stop, the bathroom curtain open, someone step out.

Debbie is not alone here—we are not alone here. There is an intruder in our house, but more than likely, not really an intruder, but an invited guest. I need only one guess as to who it is, what he's been doing in my house. And I'm pretty sure I know what it is I'm going to do about it. ✧

Archives of Story Magazine and Story Press

A Finding Aid Prepared by Sylvia Yu and Heather Shannon

Manuscripts Division, Department of Rare Books and Special Collections,
Princeton University Library

Introduction

The Archives of *Story* Magazine and The *Story* Press consist of the fairly complete working business files of the original *Story* and other related publishing ventures of owner-editors Martha Foley and Whit and Hallie Burnett, and the new *Story* author files of Richard and Lois Rosenthal. The collection includes editorial and personal correspondence, business and financial records, and artwork.

Range of Collection Dates: 1931-1999

Size: 151.00 linear feet (256 archival boxes, 7 cartons, 8 packages)

Provenance: Princeton University Library made the initial purchase from Whit and Hallie Burnett in 1965, which was later followed by gifts from William Peden in 1969, Hallie Burnett Zeisel in 1979, a bequest from the estate of Hallie Burnett Zeisel in 1998, and a gift by Richard and Lois Rosenthal in 1999.

Restrictions: Copies of original J. D. Salinger material are not permitted.

Photocopying, literary rights, and citation: Single photocopies may be made for research purposes. Permission to publish material from the collection must be requested from the Associate University Librarian for Rare Books and Special Collections. The Library has no information on the status of literary rights in the collection and researchers are responsible for determining any question of copyright. Citations should be as follows: Archives of *Story* Magazine and *Story* Press, Box #, Used by permission of the Princeton University Library.

Historical Note

Story magazine was founded in 1931 by journalist and editor Whit Burnett and his first wife, Martha Foley. The inaugural April/May 1931 issue of *Story* (167 copies) was printed on an old mimeograph machine in

Vienna, Austria, and featured short stories by new authors. In 1933, the printing of *Story* was moved to New York City. Burnett and Foley created The *Story* Press in 1936. By the late 1930s, *Story*'s circulation had reached as high as 21,000 copies. Authors discovered and published by *Story* in those early, fruitful years included Joseph Heller, J. D. Salinger, Tennessee Williams, and Richard Wright. *Story* also published the early work of such authors as Carson McCullers, William Saroyan, and Ludwig Bemelmans, and sponsored numerous awards, including W.P.A., Armed Forces, and an annual college fiction contest.

Beginning in 1942, Burnett's second wife, Hallie Southgate Burnett, collaborated with him on both The *Story* Press and *Story* with the latter publishing the early work of Norman Mailer, Truman Capote, and John Knowles. In the early 1950s, *Story* was briefly published in book form. The original magazine format returned in 1960, and endured until publication was suspended in 1967 due to a lack of funds. However, *Story*'s name continued to live on through the *Story* College Creative Awards, of which Whit Burnett was director from 1966 to 1971.

After a twenty-year hiatus, *Story* was revived as a quarterly magazine by publisher Richard Rosenthal and editor Lois Rosenthal, also a husband and wife team, who fulfilled their promise to Whit Burnett that they would relaunch *Story* one day. This new version of *Story* was published from 1989 to 1999, under the auspices of F & W Publications in Cincinnati, Ohio. *Story* was a five-time finalist and two-time winner of the National Magazine Award for fiction, and had a circulation of over 40,000 subscribers. The Rosenthals carried on the *Story* tradition of publishing a mix of well-known authors, such as Andrea Barrett, Barry Lopez, Joyce Carol Oates, and Carol Shields, and new authors, such as Junot Díaz, Elizabeth Graver, and Abraham Rodriguez. In late 1999, owing to the impending sale of F & W Publications, the Rosenthals made the decision to end their stewardship of *Story* with the publication of a final Winter 2000 issue.

Note: Most of the information above is summarized and compiled from "What's *STORY* magazine? - A Brief History," published on the Writer's Digest website at: http://www.writersdigest.com, as well as from the Gale Literary Databases and the *Story* collection files.

Story Magazine and The Story Press Chronology

1931 *Story* is founded by Whit Burnett and his first wife, Martha Foley, in Vienna.

1932 *Story* is printed in Palma, Majorca.

1933 *Story* transfers its printing to New York City.

1936 The *Story* Press is founded in New York

1942 Hallie Burnett, Whit Burnett's second wife, becomes co-editor of *Story* and The *Story* Press.

1948 Publication of *Story* magazine is suspended (due to financial difficulties).

1951 *Story* is published in book form (until 1953).

1960 *Story* is reactivated by Whit and Hallie Burnett (with William Peden and Richard Wathen Princeton '39 as associate editors).

1966 *Story* is acquired by Scholastic Magazines, Inc.

1967 Publication of *Story* is suspended by the Burnetts.

1989 *Story* magazine and The *Story* Press is relaunched by Richard and Lois Rosenthal in Cincinnati, Ohio.

1999 The Rosenthals end their publication of *Story* with the Winter 2000 issue.

Collection Description

Scope Note
Consists of the fairly complete working business files of the original *Story* (1931-1967) and other related publishing ventures of owner-editors Martha Foley, Whit and Hallie Burnett, and the new *Story* (1989-1999) author files of Richard and Lois Rosenthal. The collection includes editorial and personal correspondence, business and financial records, and artwork. Among the numerous writers represented in the files are Ludwig Bemelmans, Erskine Caldwell, Truman Capote, Joseph Heller, Norman Mailer, Carson McCullers, William Peden, J. D. Salinger, William Saroyan, Jesse Stuart, and Tennessee Williams, plus new writers who have gone on to garner literary acclaim since 1989. Special format materials consist of photographs, scrapbooks, phonograph records and tape recordings, and printed materials.

Arrangement
The collection has been arranged primarily in alphabetical series by author, with approximately 30 boxes containing the Burnetts' personal papers and manuscripts not directly related to *Story*. The 44 boxes of 1989-1999 *Story* author files are arranged alphabetically by author and story title.

Added Entries
The following added entries have been assigned to this collection to highlight significant sources (other than the main entry), subjects, and forms of the collection's materials. Where possible Library of Congress Subject Headings have been used, and the forms of names reflect inter-

national cataloging standards. As a result, all of these entries may be searched in the Department's database (MASC), in the Library's online catalog, and the public card catalog to find other related material.

People: Burnett, Hallie Southgate, 1908-1991
Burnett, Whit, 1899-1973
Foley, Martha, 1900-1977
Rosenthal, Lois

Subject Headings (in uppercase) / Form Headings (in upper and lower case):

American fiction–20th century
AUTHORS AND PUBLISHERS–UNITED STATES–20TH CENTURY
Novelists, American--20th century–Correspondence
Publishers and publishing--New York (N.Y.)–20th century–Records
Publishers and publishing-Ohio–Cincinnati–20th century–Records
PERIODICALS, PUBLISHING OF–UNITED STATES–20TH CENTURY
Short stories, American--20th century
STORY (NEW YORK, N.Y.)
STORY (CINCINNATI, OHIO)

Box/Folder Listings

219

1	Abbott, Lee K.
2	Abbott, Lee K.: "The Happy Parts"
3	Abbott, Lee K.: "The Way Sin Is Said in Wonderland"
4	Abu-Jaber, Diana: "Billets-Doux"
5	Adams, Alice: "The Shipbuilder from Dusseldorf"
6	Adler, John
7	Adler, John: "Esau"
8	Adrian, Chris: "Grief"
9	Adrian, Chris: "A Hero of Chickamauga"
10	Adrian, Chris: "High Speeds"
11	Alexie, Sherman: "Every Little Hurricane"
12	Allen, Edward: "Burt Osborne Rules the World"

220

1	Alvarez, Julia: "Floor Show"
2	"Amick, Steve: "The Man in the Mouse Suit"
3	"Anapol, Bay: "The Man with the Paper Eyes"
4	"Anastas, Benjamin: "A Voice from Somewhere Else"
5	Ansay, A. Manette: "Sister"

238

1 Griffith, David: "Devil's Workshop"
2 Grimm, Mary: "Reading Marley"
3 Griner, Paul: "Back Home Again"
4 Griner, Paul: "Follow Me"
5 Gunn, Genni: "Los Desesperados"
6 Hagy, Alyson: "Keeneland"
7 Hansen, Ron
8 Hansen, Ron: "A Nineteenth-Century Man"
9 Hardy, Melissa: "Paper Son"
10 Harleman, Ann: "Conspiracies"
11 Harrar, George: "The 5:22"
12 Harris, Evan: "The Jewel"

239

1 Harun, Adrianne: "The Unseen Ear of God"
2 Harvey, Charles W.
3 Harvey, Charles W.: "Red Underwear"
4 Harvey, Charles W.: "When Dogs Bark"
5 Havazelet, Ehud: "Lyon"
6 Hayes, Daniel: "A Cake Just Like This"
7 Hegi, Ursula: "Acts of Violence"
8 Hegi, Ursula: "Hotel of the Saints"
9 Hegi, Ursula: "The Juggler"
10 Hegi, Ursula: "Trudi"
11 Heller, Joseph: "I Don't Love You Any More" (reprint)
12 Hemley, Robin: "A Printer's Tale"
13 Henning, Wendy J.: "Rodney Forms a Theory of Salvation on the Last Night of His Life"
14 Henning, Wendy J.: "Vestiges"
15 Higdon, Constance: "The Chicken Man"

240

1 Hill, Ingrid: "The Fall of Sparrow Hill"
2 Hird, Laura: "Imaginary Friends"
3 Hodgins, Jack: "Astonishing the Blind"
4 Hodgins, Jack: "Balance"
5 Holland, Jack: "Goodbye Belfast"
6 Holmes, Charlotte: "Gifts"
7 Holmes, Charlotte: "World Book"
8 Homes, A. M.
9 Homes, A. M.: "Esther in the Night"
10 Homes, A. M.: "Yours Truly"
11 Hood, Ann: "The Doctor"
12 Hood, Ann: "Escapes"
13 Howe, LeAnne: "Shell Shakers"

260

1   Sumner, Melanie: "Naar"
2   Sumner, Melanie: "The School of Beauty and Charm"
3   Taddei, Tony: "Driving Fast"
4   Támas, István: "The Schoolmaster's Wife" (reprint)
5   Taylor, Keith: "And the Waters Prevailed"
6   Thomas, Maria: "Makonde Carvers"
7   Thompson, Jean: "Antarctica"
8   Thompson, Jean: "Crash"
9   Thon, Melanie Rae: "The Bear Who Could Not Sleep"
10   Thon, Melanie Rae: "Father, Lover, Deadman, Dreamer"
11   Tinti, Hannah: "Hit Man of the Year"
12   Tinti, Hannah: "Reasonable Terms"
13   Tolstoy, Leo: "A Children's Garden of Morals" (reprint)
14   Turchi, Peter: "The Man Who Lived Above Us"
15   Tyau, Kathleen
16   Tyau, Kathleen: "All Lips"
17   Tyau, Kathleen: "Moon Baby"

261

1   Udall, Brady: "The Opposite of Loneliness"
2   Udall, Brady: "Otis Is Resurrected"
3   Udall, Brady: "Snake"
4   Udall, Brady: "The Wig"
5   Van Syckle, Andes: "Inherit"
6   Vatsal, Vinayak: "Mosaic"
7   Verghese, Abraham: "Tizita"
8   Voll, Daniel: "Dear Mr. President"
9   Voll, Daniel: "Skin"
10   Vollman, William: "Last Day at the Bakery, Sarajevo, Bosnia-Hercezgovina (1992)"
11   Wallace, Daniel: "In Heaven These Days"
12   Ward, Robert: "Funny"

262

1   Watanabe, Sylvia: "Where People Know Me"
2   Watson, Brad: "Bill"
3   Watson, Brad: "Seeing Eye"
4   Weber, Katharine: "Louisa Huntington's Last Caller, at Easter"
5   Weidman, Jerome: "My Father Sits in the Dark" (reprint)
6   Weinberg, Howard: "Nolan the Wild Dog"
7   Weldon, Glen: "Damsel"
8   Wentzien, Marion de Booy: "Twinkle"
9   Wetherell, W. D.: "The Greatest Living Mayan Speller Extant"
10   Whitty, Julia: "Lucifer's Alligator"
11   Wickersham, Joan: "Lena"

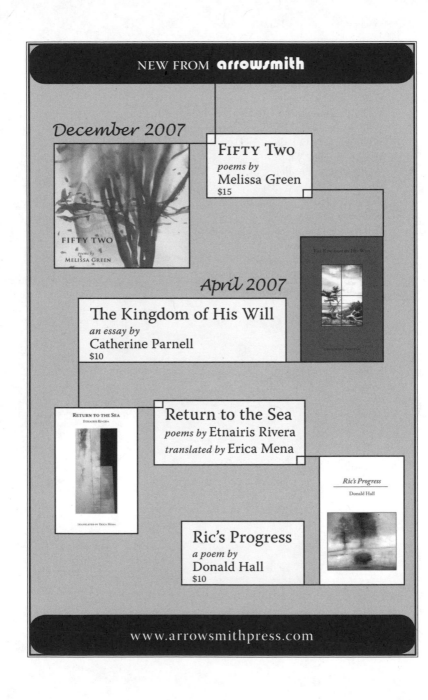

WE DIDN'T COME HERE FOR THIS: A MEMOIR IN POETRY, by William B. Patrick

Kathleen Aguero

"Look at this photograph, would you?" asks the speaker in "Last Day at Camp Timlo, August 15, 1960." "What . . . makes it unfamiliar? / Nothing really," he continues. Truly, nothing is unfamiliar about the material in William B. Patrick's *We Didn't Come Here for This*, but the tight lens through which the poet views his family, the skill and empathy with which he creates their voices, rivet me to this familiar story as if I've never known anything like it.

The poet presents a 1950s family, typical in many ways. Jim, a war hero, marries Betty, daughter of a successful businessman. Jim becomes a salesman in his father-in-law's car dealership. He and Betty have five boys: one dies as an infant, another is born with cerebral palsy, and one, luckily for us, grows up to write this book. The undercurrents this family will experience, however, are apparent from the very first poem, in which Jim remembers his war experiences shortly after D-day, while Betty thinks of her other beau, handsome Freddie Schwartz, concluding, "I can't hitch my star to Freddie / Jim's more of a go-getter." Raising his sons, Jim struggles with what it means to be a man. He doesn't want to become his father, who beat his wife with his fists and his son with a cat-o'-nine-tails. Yet, while forcing his struggling firstborn and namesake into the baby bath, he's determined "no boy named after me will be afraid." Jim's formula for manhood—"You have to edge fear out early, and substitute toughness"—and his working-class upbringing are bound to clash with Betty's privileged femininity. No wonder the death of their third child and the disability of their fourth strain this family to the breaking point. Still, these family members insist on their ordinariness—"I know my sorrow doesn't make me special," Betty says in her prayer to the Virgin Mary—and it's this humility, the refusal to turn hardship into tragedy, that makes their story affecting.

I found myself so caught up in these characters that it took a second reading to notice the virtuosity of the writing. Patrick doesn't so much talk about his family as let the members speak for themselves. The poet himself appears mainly in the persona of Billy, his younger self. So convincing are the speakers that I forgot, in fact, it's the adult Bill artfully creating these poems based on years of recorded interviews with his parents. In addition, Patrick juggles points of view with ease. In the poems that open and close this memoir, for example, we move seamlessly among three simultaneous points of view. Patrick employs form the way it should be used, not to call attention to itself but to supply a scaffolding that supports the poem. Thus, the closely related haiku of "Christmas, 1950," united not so much by logic as by imagery, are the perfect vehicle for a one-year-old's point of view. Similarly, what better match for a salesman's obsessions and digressions than the double sestina of "New Car Season for Jim, September 1954," in which Jim moves conversationally between his frustrations on the job and his frustrations with his wife? Throughout this book pacing and tone are impeccable. For example, the poem in which Jim first speaks of his own harsh childhood is followed by the playful "October 3, 1949, 7:08 A.M.," in which the poet speculates on his soul's journey into his body at the moment of his birth, a trip in which the soul gets to see the catch that puts the Yankees into the series and to ponder its decision to pass up Bruce Springsteen, born just two weeks before. Each poem, as well as the volume as a whole, is generous enough to accommodate human confusion and conflicting emotion. A hilarious spelling bee poem, for instance, contains not only smart-aleck Billy's inner judgments on his classmates and his conviction that Sister Mary Frederic is out to get him so her favorite and Billy's rival, Jim Berthiaume, can win the bee, but Billy's fear and sadness at the death of his younger brother. Even as they hurt one another, the members of this imperfect family try to do right and behave like a family, whatever that may be. They play gin rummy, watch fireworks on the Fourth of July, and eat Betty's chocolate cake together. So much is going on beneath the surface of this memoir that reads like a novel but is, in fact, a book of poetry that I keep going back to it, discovering new emotional depths and technical accomplishments.

Patrick writes in several genres. He has written two other books of poetry, *Letter to the Ghosts* and *These Upraised Hands*; a novel, *Roxa: Voices of the Culver Family*; and, most recently, a work of nonfiction: *Saving Troy: A Year with Firefighters and Paramedics in a Battered City*. Read them all. But start with *We Didn't Come Here for This*. ✧

Google

Jeffrey Yang

Google is a sea of consciousness.
As it expands, the sea shrinks.
Like Oz, it is the most knowledgeable
entity that knows nothing. *Information
is originally nothing but difference.*
Surf a wave: knowledge purifies.

Kelp

Jeffrey Yang

How easy it is to lose oneself
in a kelp forest. Between
canopy leaves, sunlight filters thru
the water surface; nutrients
bring life where there'd otherwise be barren sea; a vast eco-
system breathes. Each
being being
being's link.

Various

Quinn Dalton

This sort of thing is tough—naming a work or two that stand out from all of those other beloved books on my shelf, a beauty contest in which every contestant is a knockout. But if pressed, I usually mention two. Both are contemporary novels set in the latter half of the twentieth century in famous, now ruined but slowly recovering cities. Both feature main characters caught up in intrigue, of which they soon become, for better or worse, architects. Both are darkly comic, though one is more comic than dark, and the other is, well, the other way around.

1.

A Confederacy of Dunces is the story of Ignatius J. Reilly, whose diminished family circumstances force him to move into the workforce, which marks his rise to notoriety among the panhandlers and politicos, swindlers, starstruck strippers, street vendors, shady cops, deluded revolution planners, and other bottom-feeders roaming the French Quarter. It is the story of his long-suffering mother and his sex-crazed activist girlfriend, Myrna Minkoff, and how he ruins their lives, and how they hate him and love him for it, and how we do too. It's also one of the smartest, funniest, most unapologetic satires I've ever read—of bigotry, social activism, corruption in one of the most corruption-mired cities in the world, and God knows what all else I've missed. Because every time I read this book, I experience the story more fully. Flipping through it now, I want to quit writing and just tuck into it again.

A Confederacy of Dunces was one of Those Books for me, maybe *the* book. Its fabulously farcical plot, sympathetic anti-hero, and cast of hysterically self-important, bedraggled, magnificent characters blurred my vision for weeks, so that my Toyota became a rattling streetcar, the street signs flickering Canal, Decatur, Royal. When my husband and I made the pilgrimage to New Orleans, five years before the flood (I suspect time in New Orleans will always be measured in this way—Before and After), I wandered the French Quarter like a dazed *Da Vinci Code* devotee lurking at the Louvre. My husband and I, tipsy on hurricanes, tried to find the three-story stucco house on Saint Peter's Street, the site of the coup-planning/costume party hosted by Dorian Greene. Of course it wasn't there. Of course it was there anyway.

Many know the story behind this Pulitzer Prize–winning novel, published in 1980, eleven years after the death of its author, John Kennedy Toole, who committed suicide at the age of thirty-two. After some initial enthusiasm, Simon & Schuster had rejected his book, deeming it not "really about anything" (I guess the world wasn't yet ready for a story about nothing, à la *Seinfeld*). Toole's mental condition seemed to deteriorate after this—he took to heavy drinking, medications. After his death Toole's mother brought the manuscript to Walker Percy and insisted he read it, and the rest is, you know. History.

Toole actually wrote two books, and although *Neon Bible* doesn't have the literary power of *Dunces*, it explores the same themes—family, religion, society—all with their attendant absurdities. You can see him already thinking at age sixteen (he wrote *Neon Bible* for a literary contest, though it wasn't published until twenty years after his death because of legal disputes among his surviving relatives); you can see the wheels of his genius turning toward Fortuna's Wheel, which controls Ignatius's fate most cruelly, as he would tell it.

Neon Bible was made into a feature film in 1995. A film adaptation of *A Confederacy of Dunces* was scheduled for release in 2005, but like several other previously attempted productions, it has since been put on hold.

I haven't seen the film adaptation of *Neon Bible*, but I probably wouldn't be able to resist seeing *Dunces: The Movie!* (the studio heads renaming it, as Ignatius would wearily explain, so as not to confuse the mongoloid masses with any title verging on the multisyllabic). I couldn't miss the opportunity to hang out at Night of Joy and see Darlene try out her new act and watch Jones plotting his next move, while Ignatius, massive, eternally offended and offensive, sets off disaster with his every lunatic and yet oddly logical scheme.

I just want to know—I wish I could ask Toole: Did it feel different when you let Ignatius loose on New Orleans? Did you feel exhilarated? Did you panic a little bit when you realized what you'd set in motion?

2.

Scott Simon, author of the acclaimed 2005 novel *Pretty Birds*, already had a reputation as an award-winning correspondent covering ten wars, and his media connections made recognition of *Pretty Birds'* arrival a foregone conclusion.

But if you haven't read this book, you need to. Now. The story opens in the spring of 1992 in Sarajevo at the beginning of the longest siege of a city in the history of modern warfare—nearly four years. Irena Zaric is a high school basketball star, a voracious follower of Western pop culture—Madonna, Michael Jordan, and Princess Di are among her heroes—and a Muslim. Her best friend, Amela, is a Serb. And yet they are both really of mixed descent—Irena's father is half Serb, half Jewish, for example. What they both become is unimaginable to them in that spring when Sarajevo, taken over by black-clad Serb paramilitaries, becomes a divided city and a permanent war zone.

Displaced with her parents in her grandmother's apartment (her grandmother is murdered at the outbreak of the war), Irena is hired by her former assistant principal, Tedic, initially to perform odd jobs at the Sarajevo Brewery. Soon she is trained as a sniper, as were many teenaged women on the Bosnian and Serb sides of the war. She learns to sit still for hours, to watch for the pink cloud or "mist" around her target that confirms a hit.

The violence in this book is depicted vividly but matter-of-factly, in the manner one would expect from someone who has learned not to ask after friends who may be dead, to steal from the dead, and to eat boiled leaves. The story constantly moves, twists, rips at your heart, makes you root helplessly for its heroes, who are doomed, and who would never call themselves heroes anyway. Tedic, for example, would call himself a pacifist, "when the world permits." War hones Irena's sense of irony to a brutal point; her humor is as sharp as her aim.

Who can blame her? She lives in a world where UN soldiers trade favors for sex, where loudspeakers blaring from the other side of the siege line cajole you to give in, where snipers pick off people waiting in line for water and then pick off anyone who tries to retrieve the bodies. We may remember it from the news, but we never knew those people, the thousands starved and shot in that city, the thousands more shoved into mass graves. This book forces you to know them. You want nothing else but to know them.

I was close to home while reading this book, nursing my second daughter. One afternoon I left her in the care of my mother-in-law while I went to get a haircut. I was amazed that I was able to walk outside in the daylight without crouching to evade snipers.

My husband and I are friends with a couple who came out of Sarajevo with only their suitcases. Their two sons, born in the US, are the same ages as our two daughters. He is Catholic; she is Muslim—another example of how so many families were blended, which only adds to the shock of how the country held tightly together by Marshal Tito tore itself apart. In Sarajevo she was an attorney with a top firm, and he was a maître d' at a five-star restaurant in which he had partial ownership. When their apartment was burned, they moved in with relatives. When they found a way out in January 1996, they came to Greensboro, North Carolina, through Lutheran Family Services. He found work as a waiter; she as a nanny. Now she is a paralegal with one of Greensboro's top firms, and he owns a convenience store. They've bought a house; they have continued their lives with intelligence and humor and unfailing grace.

They have been our friends for these eleven years now, and we feel lucky to know them, but we know our luck is a direct result of the shredding of their former lives. They don't talk about their last years in Sarajevo very much. Sometimes a moment will come to conversation—

the time a mortar round destroyed the café she had gone into to try to use a working phone, the time he watched soldiers eating their shot glasses because they felt they'd already cheated death that much.

Sometimes I felt embarrassed as I read *Pretty Birds*, for two reasons. One, because I lived in comfort while these people starved or were tortured or were killed (as is true every day—now Iraq, now Darfur, now Palestine, only the beginning of a long list we can apparently live with). And two, because of my friendship with this extraordinary couple, I felt somehow I'd pried into their lives in a way I shouldn't have. This is the triumph of *Pretty Birds*. ✧

Writing Him Off

Mike Scalise

Here's how Ethan Thomas and Sam Rutherford's friendship began to end:* It was late, maybe just after midnight. Ethan walked out of his bathroom in his pajamas after brushing his teeth, and the first thing he saw was Sam, standing with his back to him at the kitchen sink. Sam is small. Almost thirty, he stands, at most, five two and looks somehow unripe, with the soft features of a teenager: fair complexion, thick frame, and a large face, like Robin Williams might have looked in his high school yearbook. At that moment he stood just feet from Ethan, leaning over his kitchen counter, scrubbing out a thick glass mug over a sink full of dirty dishes, silverware, pots, and pans.

As Sam turned to see Ethan, he quickly rinsed out the glass and placed it on the counter next to him. Ethan reached to grab it and fill it with water before heading off to join his fiancée, Juliet, in their bed down the hall, where she'd already been sleeping for the last hour. But before he was able to put the mug in his hand, Sam stopped him and said:

"I wouldn't do that."

"Why not?" asked Ethan.

"I just—I wouldn't do that."

"Why?" asked Ethan again. "What do you mean, 'I wouldn't do that'?"

"Well, you were in the bathroom," said Sam, "and I really had to go, so I pissed in that glass and dumped it in the sink."

Sam had been in New York City about a month, where he'd moved "to start over" after spending the better part of the last decade overseas, teaching conversational English to European businesspeople in various cities across what was once the Eastern bloc. After staying his first three weeks with my wife and me in our tiny apartment in Brooklyn, he'd been here with Ethan in his Lower East Side one-bedroom for five days. He'd already found an evening job in Herald Square, teaching English to day workers, but had made zero attempts to find a place of his own, something Ethan says began to "get under Juliet's skin." So that night they'd talked about looking for apartments over a "Wednesday-night beer," and the next thing Ethan knew: "I wouldn't do that," and so on.

Pushing thirty himself, Ethan is the closest thing to a beatnik-era bohemian I've ever known. He's a documentary film editor and jazz enthusiast with a cultivated pot habit that seems more essential than

---

To protect the privacy of those discussed here, some of the names and details have been changed. But not many.

annoying. But he makes it all sound very earnest and beguiling, even when he refers to people as "cats," as in "I'm gonna go smoke a square with this cat right here" or "This cat just pissed in my sink."

But as I imagine is the case with many bohemians, Ethan is not good at conflict. He's terrible at it, and he circumvents it whenever he can. I once crossed Eighth Avenue with him one night on the way back from a movie, and he tripped and fell ass-first onto the hood of a jet black, mid-nineties Camaro as it idled at the red light. When the driver got out of the car, clearly angry and screaming and pointing his finger at Ethan's chest, Ethan simply apologized and offered to let the driver punch him in the face to make amends. He hit Ethan across the side of his jaw with a cautious swing, perhaps thinking there might be a hidden camera or film crew somewhere. Ethan just took it, stumbled back a bit, then said calmly, "We cool?" The guy said, "I guess," then just got back into his car.

And that was it.

But this situation here, with a houseguest who'd once been his best friend in high school, urinating in a sink full of his dishes, caused an interesting ripple in his philosophy: it seemed to be the complete inverse of the Camaro incident, with the punch in the face coming first, and unasked for.

"I was just brushing my teeth and washing my face," Ethan says now. "That doesn't take me very long. Maybe five minutes or so. That apartment was really small. It wasn't like he couldn't knock on the door." Ethan couldn't help but consider the permanence of the whole operation. He knew the stain it left would far outlast the act itself: "So there's piss on my glass, on my forks, on my plates, in my bowls," he says. "I know you can wash them, but there's still piss on your plates, you know?"

He thought of scenarios. Ethan would have to clean everything he and Juliet and anyone else would have to eat with, drink with, cook with, or put food on (because of course he'd have to clean it all himself, if only to be sure that everything returned to sanitary). Then there was the scenario that illustrated what he thought every guest knew was the most appropriate way to go to the bathroom in a house where your host is currently using it. You (a) knock on the door, (b) say, "Hey, can I get in there a minute?" and (c) use the toilet. But Sam chose to use Ethan's favorite mug and a sink full of dishes, and the whole situation confounded and frustrated Ethan in ways he couldn't easily explain. So he just stared blankly at Sam, then at the root-beer mug on the counter between them, then at the rest of the dishes in his sink (which were now all untouchable at best), then back to a friend who he'd known all of his adult life, and all he could think to say to him was:

"Not. Cool. At. All."

Sam Rutherford moved to New York City at a time when I really began to like the idea of eliminating people from my life. Streamlining. I was on the far side of twenty-six, and many of my longest and dearest friendships seemed to have outlived their usefulness. We'd scattered ourselves across the country; I moved from Pittsburgh to New York, but others wound up in Las Vegas, Denver, Cleveland, Philadelphia, Portland, or Honolulu, each presumably to do what our late teens and early twenties had prepared us to: find jobs and wives. So I spent each summer flying to these places to attend my friends' weddings, where I'd wear poorly tailored tuxes and give toasts and drunken hugs to people I'd once shared everything with, but now only talked to every so often. And even then the conversations were strained, melancholy, and for both parties somewhat exhausting. So after years of keeping my friendships on life support with information-purging phone calls and "update" e-mails, I began to appreciate the idea that my friends' weddings were, on some level, send-off or retirement ceremonies for the fine work our friendships had done to get us to this point. Amicable ways to end relationships that no longer had any real relevance as we moved on to condos and kids and whatever came after.

So right when I felt I had a handle on whom to weed out and whom to keep, Sam Rutherford resurfaced; someone I thought had been removed from the equation long ago. I lived down the street from Sam until I was thirteen, in a small, middle-income, suburban neighborhood in a town just outside of Pittsburgh. He was a few years older than me and was a commanding, dynamic, but also very caustic presence throughout my preteen years. Our neighborhood was full of kids my age, and Sam, despite his small stature even then, was the alpha of them all. I was frail, unathletic, and timid, with an imagination that made me strange, but he was bold, witty, manic, afraid of no one, and had a temper that on more than one occasion got him into vicious fistfights with anyone he disagreed with (all of which he won, hands down).

But he took to me, and as I inched toward adolescence, he acted as my window into what I could expect. He told me how to dress, how to talk to girls, what movies to watch (Woody Allen), what books to read (Kurt Vonnegut), and how to be bold, witty, and manic. But he also ridiculed me—often loudly, in front of people—if I said something he thought was silly, or if my breath was bad, or if there was a booger in my nose. Yet I always sought his advice, opinions, and approval. Any time I did something he didn't like, or infringed upon him in some way, he'd turn to me, put his hand on my shoulder, and say, "Whenever you do anything, I want you to think: 'How does this affect Sam Rutherford?'"

It was a childhood friendship version of Stockholm syndrome, and I only started to realize it when my family and I moved to another neighborhood in the same town, and I became an adolescent myself, which was when my relationship with Sam Rutherford went on indefinite hiatus. I spoke to him very little in the years after I moved, and even then only in superficial ways, like: "How are you/your mom/dad/brother/sister/dog?" By adulthood, when I moved to New York City and he went to eastern Europe, we existed as acquaintances at best. Streamlined by default.

Ethan picked up with Sam where I left off, in high school. By then Sam had transformed into an aspiring writer and poet, which drew Ethan—then widely known in my high school as a talented musician—to him in some right-brained, misanthropic alliance: "We would drive around, and he would read me some poems, or we'd talk a lot. He was all sensitive, and I thought that was cool," Ethan says now. "I chalked it up to 'This cat is an artist' and the whole tortured-soul thing. I kinda dug that about him." And even though Sam still maintained his more manic traits, and was given to occasional outbursts of raw, unpredictable, and troubling energy, Ethan says he and his friends "seemed to like that about him in a way," because on the plus side of it he "was funny and fun to hang out with, so [they] kind of overlooked some of the little things, because back then they were just little things." The two kept close throughout college and after with e-mails and phone calls. As Sam went on to eastern Europe to teach English and Ethan moved to New York City to work in film, their friendship remained intact.

Ethan and I, though we knew of each other in high school, started our friendship only after we discovered that we both lived in New York, in what I might be best defined as a gravitation of origins. It was very common in the city for Columbia or Yale or Princeton grads to seek one another out and cluster, but our history was rooted in suburban Pittsburgh, in a town where the escape rate was very low, so we found each other and clung together for support and reassurance, much like I imagine expats do in other countries. But since we'd only known each other as people we passed in the hallway between classes years before, we rekindled nothing. Everything was new and interesting—the city, our jobs, and the fact that, as I've often heard Ethan say, in New York "you can order anything to be delivered to you. You want pot? Right to your door. Lobster? Here's the number." Yet because of our overlapping pasts, we shared enough familiarities to create a tighter bond than I had with most of my other adult friends, who now seemed to me increasingly distant, conditional, and estranged enough to streamline.

Sam was one of those familiarities, and when he announced to Ethan over e-mail that he was moving to the city, in some ways I actually looked forward to his addition to our social circle. I figured that some time abroad had done him good, maybe widened his perspective and smoothed his edges. It was also a good way for me to reintroduce myself to him as an adult, and vice versa. So I offered him a spot in my Brooklyn apartment for the first three weeks of his stay. It was essentially an act of hospitality and optimism, rooted in the hope that he'd somehow embraced his more dynamic habits and outgrown his more garish ones, but shortly after he moved in, my wife, Loren, and I discovered that the opposite had happened.

Sam slept shirtless on our couch. That was Loren's least favorite thing. For each of the first few nights she'd take a fresh set of sheets out of the footlocker by our bed and place them on the coffee table in front of our couch before Sam came home from teaching his night classes, and each morning when she woke up, he'd be on his back in only boxers, his loose white flesh pouring off to his sides, the sheets still folded where she'd left them. I was troubled by the more subtle quirks and ticks that I hadn't picked up on years earlier, like his poorly timed hack of a laugh, which shot out at the strangest moments, like when Loren or I mentioned that we liked certain songs, or that we were hungry. And how he couldn't sit still. When he sat on our couch, he'd shake his legs, or continually cross his arms one over the other while he talked or listened. It seemed like he couldn't find a way to make himself fit. When he said things, they weren't bold or witty, but rather timid and nervous, with a twinge of caution, like he was guessing at test questions.

There was a very underscored sadness to it all that I didn't expect. The nugget of him that was once so commanding when we were young had been overthrown by a host of heartbreaking neuroses, and where he once drew attention to himself because of his outspokenness and confidence, now it was because it seemed like, at any moment, he'd completely unravel.

I found it very difficult to confront him about the things that bothered me most. For instance: one night I took him to a bar on my block for a few beers, maybe to loosen him up, let him get comfortable. But when I brought up what was, to me, pretty standard conversational fodder for people our age (career plans, marriage, kids, etc.), his childlike face lost all its expression, then he quietly let loose a stream of tears, and I spent the rest of the night in the middle of a bar in downtown Brooklyn consoling him for reasons he wouldn't or couldn't explain. Then the next night I introduced him to some of my co-workers—editors and writers from the publishing house where I worked, because Sam was thinking of "making the jump over"—and he immediately launched into a series of stories from my very early youth, like how when I was five, I went everywhere (even the grocery store) dressed in Superman Underoos and a cape that my mother had made me; or how Ben Burkholder beat me up after a kickball game when I was seven, and I sat in my front yard and wailed and shook my fist and swore that I'd "get revenge." It was an odd intersection that neither of us navigated very well: I couldn't handle my past, but he couldn't handle the present. Like Ethan, I also avoid conflict, so I let those kinds of things happen and said nothing, because we both knew that just the night before I'd seen Sam silently weep over a pitcher of Sierra Nevada.

Our policy for the remainder of his stay in our tiny, eight-hundred-square-foot Brooklyn apartment became "Wait it out." His clothes on the floor, half-washed dishes stacked back in our cupboards, his constantly losing our spare keys and locking himself out, his almost contagious spells of aggravated, nervous silence—we had no desire to see what was on the other side, so we said nothing, and when his three weeks were up, and it came time for him to move in with Ethan, we paid his cab fare to the Lower East Side. Once that cab turned the corner to head across the Brooklyn Bridge, Loren called Ethan and Juliet to tell them to put sheets on the couch.

It soon became clear, though, that Sam was actually on his best behavior for us; that he'd spent his time in our apartment as well-packaged as possible. Because when he moved in with Ethan, he apparently unpacked himself more openly, to the point where on the fifth night he stayed there, after a Wednesday-night beer that must have almost made his bladder burst, he figured that while Ethan, his best friend from high school, brushed his teeth, rather than take steps (a) and (b) of the best-case scenario—knock on the door and say "Hey, can I get in there a minute?"—he'd just discreetly urinate in the sink. Yes: this was the best idea. But since the countertop was a few inches taller than he could muster, even on his tiptoes, leaning over, he'd just use the mug that Ethan had been drinking from. Then he'd clean it out immediately and put it right back where it was, and no one would ever know. But then Ethan came out of the bathroom and wanted some water, and everything all of a sudden became "Not. Cool. At. All."

"What?" asked Sam. "What's the big deal?"

Ethan then pressed Sam about why he thought that was even close to the appropriate thing to do, why that was even an option, and Sam, defensive, said back, "You're overreacting. I don't see what the big deal is. We do that in Europe all the time."

"It didn't even dawn on him that it wasn't cool," says Ethan now. "Like: 'Oh, you guys don't piss in the sink?'" Sam's logic ripped open a jarring disconnect between the two, and Ethan had immediate, dueling takes on what had caused it: perhaps there was some cross-continental lack of etiquette he was unaware of, that maybe in eastern Europe people really did urinate in sinks full of dishes. Or perhaps Sam was right, that Ethan actually was overreacting, that it was no "big deal." The best option to repair it as quickly as possible, Ethan thought, was to adopt the same policy Loren and I had: say nothing to him about it, at least not more than he already had.

"You know if you hurt his feelings, you're really going to hurt his feelings, so you walk on eggshells a little bit, even when he pisses in your sink, because he sort of doesn't know any better," says Ethan. "But even if he did know better, you worry about the consequences of getting mad at him, and you kind of weigh that against how mad you actually are, and you decide that it might not be worth it. So I decided I was just going to let it go at that," Ethan says. "Let him know that was uncool, then go to bed."

But Juliet, who was then engaged to marry Ethan, has zero aversion to conflict. She actually embraces the concept quite readily. So the next day, when Ethan called her from work, swollen with guilt and frustration, and told her everything, she, as Ethan puts it, "got as far as 'pissed in the sink' and lost her goddamned mind." She left work immediately and moved all of Sam's things into the hallway outside of the apartment. Juliet—who had not known Sam for more than a decade and had no allegiance to him at all—then demanded that Sam never enter her home again, so Ethan called him and gave him the address of a youth hostel on the Upper East Side, where he stayed that night. A few days later Sam found an open spot in a two-bedroom share in the Windsor Terrace neighborhood of Brooklyn, just a few subway stops away from where I lived, and moved in there.

I began to hear about the sink incident shortly after Juliet kicked Sam out, when Ethan sent me an instant message. It appeared on my computer screen at work and said: "Guess what our houseguest did last night?"

I decided at that moment that I'd never speak another word to Sam again. I told anyone who'd listen that he was a "toxic personality" who "had no respect for people," and how disgusted I'd been with his behavior. All of which was true, but that was only part of the reason.

When I knew Sam, I was five, six, seven, all the way up to thirteen, in the age bracket where the most you amount to are failed sketches of your adult self. Early drafts that you'd rather not show anyone. There's a reason why our preteen years are our lives' biggest producers of repression— this is where we screw everything up and do everything wrong because we have no idea how to be correct people yet. Childhood is sometimes described as fun, but it's also full of monumental humiliation, massive heartbreak, landmark mistakes, and cringing embarrassment, such as Superman Underoos and saying you'll "get revenge," and by the time someone gets to twenty-six, he's earned the right to shove all that aside, put it in perspective, and finally begin to enjoy himself.

Sam Rutherford was, very vocally, a human database of my early embarrassments, which meant that I was maintaining a relationship with someone who was hardwired to remind me of a time when I could be nothing but a failure. I wanted to move forward. I'd just begun my life with my wife—a beautiful woman who thought that I was the greatest guy in the world, and was brave enough to get dressed up and make a public record of it—and I couldn't keep someone around who was an insistent reminder of a time when I was the exact opposite.

Which is how many relationships from our childhoods—whether they're caustic or precious or driven by a pre-adolescent offshoot of Stockholm syndrome—often seem to die. Somewhere along the line at least one party realizes that he shouldn't be held hostage by the ghosts of his early sketches; that the adult he's become can't make room for the child that he was; that the two can't reconcile. And often what's left behind in the wake of that realization is the tired skeleton of a worn-out bond. In those first few weeks in our apartment it wasn't Sam's nervous shifts or his hack laugh or his silent weeping or his sleeping without sheets that caused me to streamline him. I just couldn't make room for him anymore, at least not the kind of room he wanted, and I hoped for an opportunity to leave him behind with everything else he represented. So when that opportunity presented itself with the sink and the dishes, I wasted no time saying good-bye, Sam Rutherford. Good-bye.

To his credit, Ethan found much more patience and willingness to extend toward Sam than I did, but the results of that willingness—both what happened and what didn't happen in the months after the sink incident—eventually proved to be too much for the friendship. Ethan figured that no matter how ill conceived, one random, inappropriate urination alone wasn't enough to cut off contact altogether. They could make it work. It was a relatively fixable situation, he felt, if Sam was willing to take the necessary steps to fix it, which mostly meant apologizing to Juliet. But despite Ethan's insistence, Sam seemed too embarrassed or unwilling to take those steps, and Ethan didn't know where to go from there. So he continued their friendship in the periphery of his fiancée—lunch meetings here and there, e-mail, text messaging—it was all very affairlike. They'd reached a point where a few weeks after the sink incident, with Juliet out of town on business, Ethan, in sly defiance, invited Sam over to watch a movie and have a few beers.

Sam arrived that night to Ethan's apartment with a date: a young Asian nanny who spoke very little English. She was a student, Sam said, and they'd been seeing each other. Kind of, sort of. And yes, it was less than ethical, and there was a palpable awkwardness to the arrangement early on, but Ethan adjusted to the situation and eventually considered the night to be a minor success, at least for him and Sam. They talked, laughed, joked, drank. Sam seemed to be adjusting to life in the city, which was everything that Ethan had originally hoped for from the moment Sam first announced he was moving to New York. With a few minor adjustments, he thought, this could work.

At the end of the night, hoping to quit while he was ahead, Ethan informed both Sam and his date the he was going to take his dog, Biggie—the Boston terrier that he and Juliet had picked up from a breeder upstate a few years back—for a quick walk outside to do his business, after which everyone would, as Ethan told them, "wrap this thing up."

But this was where the night—and the friendship—became irreversibly problematic.

"He took [my stepping out] as the okay from me that he and his student could—you know—do it," Ethan says. So when he came back in from outside less than ten minutes later, here's what he saw: Sam's student half naked on his couch, and Sam, disheveled and untucked, rushing toward him, arms forward, begging him to "give them a few minutes." The student quickly grabbed her clothes from the floor and scuttled past Ethan, out into the hallway, and Sam—in the move that surprised Ethan most—became livid. He screamed at Ethan, condemned his lack of courtesy, blamed him for endangering his job at the night school, and stormed out after his student, cursing Ethan's lack of regard for the situation at hand and his inability to consider the one question that Sam had often asked of me when we were growing up: "Whenever you do anything, I want you to think . . ."

Once again Sam had defied every decent scenario Ethan could think of, and finally he had had enough. Deeply confused, he shot off an e-mail to Sam (subject line: "To Selfish") that attacked critical hiccups in Sam's logic, asking, "Do you do these things just so you can think the next day, 'Wow, I really made him look like an asshole this time'?" and finally built to a point where he told him that although they could still "hang out at bars," ultimately he didn't think he was "going to be able to let [him] into [his] apartment again."

Days later, suffering from postconflict hangover, he contacted old friends to "have a Sam Rutherford bitch session." These were people who had, like Ethan, "overlooked some of the little things" earlier on in their friendships with Sam but found that over the last few years, after taking him in for brief stays while he was in between teaching jobs in Europe, they'd had to streamline him for strange reasons that they'd never mentioned specifically to Ethan. So when he told them about the whole exquisite New York mess—the sink, the pee, the student, the couch, the attitude—they told him, in one way or another, "That's nothing." One friend told Ethan how Sam had become a trivial thief while staying with him, routinely stealing neighborhood bikes on his way back home from late-night trips to the local bar, and how his wife had found them hidden in a pile behind the shed in his backyard, yet still said nothing for fear of how Sam would react. Another friend told him about how Sam had brought home women at all hours of the night, and how those episodes were so calamitous and awful sounding that they had often driven him and his wife sleepless with worry. And another told Ethan about the time he went to look for something in the guest room where Sam had been staying, only to find next to his bed a number of gallon milk jugs and two-liter soda bottles full, to various extents, with urine.

Now, I feel the need to clarify the mission here. This is not, in any way, an attempt to persecute Sam Rutherford for his behavior, or to make light of how scatological it is, or to exploit it at all. Rather, this is a mission of understanding. Because what had now transformed into the Sam Rutherford Situation became for Ethan not a question of if he should end his friendship with Sam, but how.

Once his past behavior was out in the open, both Ethan's old friends and I became the champions of armchair psychology. They all had their own theories, but my favorite thing to say, when asked, was that Sam "hated himself so much that he took it out on the people who liked him." The words "anal expulsive" were used an awful lot. Though it's true one of us may have accidentally diagnosed Sam correctly, in retrospect it probably would have been more useful if we'd bastardized mathematics instead. Because what Ethan discovered was that even though both he and his other friends were able to adapt and apply themselves to the demands of their age, Sam remained a constant. He seemed to be bouncing around the globe in an extended postgraduate stasis: the same attitude he'd had when he left, the same behavior, the same job, etc. But he also had many of the same problems, now magnified, which, for Ethan, made ending the friendship with him a much more complicated prospect.

In high school and college we form very visceral connections with our friends and pair the raw, unsoldered ends of our personalities together in a jumble of hope, doubt, unmatched support, and loyalty. Although Sam had found a way to alienate nearly everyone from that time who'd once befriended him, there was a complicity at the core of his and Ethan's friendship, an understanding. Ethan felt a lingering responsibility to Sam and to the connections they'd formed their friendship around, which acknowledged and accepted Sam for who he was: someone who, on occasion, lashed out strangely and unpredictably. It was in the initial agreement; they shook on it.

So the question became for him, what did time do to his responsibility to Sam? What was the statute of limitations on high-maintenance friendships, when those "little things" that were once so tolerable now seemed to be the very things clogging up the friendship? By the time Sam responded to Ethan's "To Selfish" e-mail with what appeared to be contrition—reminding Ethan that he had "never been the most stable of human beings," but that "Oscar Wilde said that a true friend stabs you in the front," and how he understood that they couldn't "be friends"—Ethan hadn't found the easy answers to those questions, and he struggled to find a suitable way to end the thing with dignity.

So he set up a test of their friendship's complicity: he told Juliet everything. First about what had happened on their couch while she was gone, then about what he'd found out from his friends regarding Sam's bizarre past behavior. Upon hearing it, she of course "really lost her shit" and demanded that Ethan remove Sam from his (and her) social landscape entirely, all of which played to Ethan's strengths, giving him the rare opportunity to actually use his conflict aversion skills to resolve the Sam Rutherford Situation, and here's how: as adults, we expect our friends to fit nicely, like constellations, around the life we've settled into, to respect the people we've settled in with, and not to fuss or overstep those bounds. So now Sam had to make amends with Juliet, not Ethan; which meant he'd have to recognize the bounds of Ethan's life and do the one thing he hadn't figured out a way to do his entire adult life: make himself fit. And in this effort Sam failed terribly, because as Ethan stepped back and let the Situation work itself out over the coming months, it came to the stale end Ethan had almost expected all along.

"He has never made any effort to win Juliet back," Ethan says about his final decision to streamline Sam. It wasn't the sink or the couch or the attitude, but his inability to adapt, to adjust to the contours of the life Ethan surrounded himself with that finally evaporated what was once a strong friendship. "He was either waiting for us to break up, or for her just to forget. A woman's going to forget why she's mad at you? It doesn't happen," says Ethan. "So he's never going to make that effort. That's why I'm writing him off, because [he has to realize that] you've got to do something about [what you've done], or you have to expect the results you get."

Since this all happened, I've moved away from New York, but I keep in touch with Ethan, who's now well into marriage with Juliet, and condos and kids and whatever. Last I heard, Sam still lives with his roommate in Windsor Terrace and still teaches English to day workers. He e-mails poems to Ethan every so often or calls him to see if he'd like to get a bite to eat, maybe a beer. And he sounds, in each of his voice mails—which Ethan almost never returns—timid and sad, like he's guessing at test questions. I know because every time I talk to Ethan or visit him in New York, Sam's name comes up in conversation. One of us always brings him up, and we throw around theories and back each other up on our decisions to divorce ourselves from him. We act astounded at his behavior still, call him a "corrosive spoke in the wheel" of our social circle, recount the stories like legendary moments, and continue to put ourselves above him.

But we can never seem to put the Sam Rutherford Situation to rest. Maybe that's because in reciting the stories, we transform them into cautionary tales to ourselves. In each of them Sam represents the worst example of what we could have been—if we hadn't moved in the directions we had, when we had, shed as much of our old selves as we could, and gotten the wives and jobs we felt we were supposed to—that perhaps we'd be in a similar tragic stasis. The tales are little more than smoke screens, though. Misdirections. Because we both also know, but refuse to confront, the uncomfortable idea that while streamlining friends means eliminating the ways in which they impede your carefully constructed adulthood, it also means turning your back on the ways those friends impede their own adulthoods as well.

Ultimately, the gravitational pull of our lives put us at a distance where we couldn't see Sam the way he wanted us to, and in turn, he couldn't see us the way we wanted to be seen. We had no other choice but to keep moving toward what we could see. So in an attempt to calculate that distance and feel better about where we stood, we did math and added up the facts: a sink, a beer mug, a bathroom five feet away, a couch, a student, a human database of embarrassing memories, and a failed complicity. Then we looked at the result and decided that even though Sam couldn't find a way to make himself fit within it, we weren't willing to make room in our equations for him, either. So we chose to do what everyone else who'd ever befriended Sam his whole life had done, which was to apply theories, methodically factor out the constant, and say good-bye, Sam Rutherford.

Good-bye. ✧

SIZE MATTERS

Debra Spark

I wonder if anyone still reads Ambrose Bierce's *The Devil's Dictionary*. Or even knows what it is. I first came across it almost twenty years ago on a boyfriend's bookshelf. His family were fundamental Baptists, suspicious of Jewish me, so this seemed like a real find. When I flipped it open, however, I found more of a turn-of-the-century joke book than the dark, magical volume I'd imagined. The book collects Bierce's newspaper pieces, which ran irregularly between 1881 and 1906. First published in part as *The Cynic's Word Book*, the complete collection was republished in 1911 with its present title. Some of his definitions:

> **Bore**, n. A person who talks when you wish him to listen.
> Congratulation, n. The civility of envy.

I wonder about *The Devil's Dictionary* largely because I have been writing and teaching writing for more than twenty years, which makes me feel acutely my lack of knowledge in any concrete subject, any practical facts, dates, or even political theories, though I've got an idea about how to express knowledge about facts, dates, and political theories. But perhaps I'm overstating the case. Twenty years of teaching writing has made me an expert on something. It's made me an expert on self-loathing and its many forms. Yes, that's me at age twenty-eight standing next to my friend, recently out of a psych ward and a few years shy of winning a MacArthur award, as he dumps everything he has ever written in the trash. I'm not one to contradict a genius, but I do say, "I really don't think you want to do this." And yes, that's me telling a distraught former student, "Man, you need something like fifty rejections from magazines before you even begin to consider that the problem is your story and not the readers of the story." If I were to write a companion volume to Bierce's, it would be called *The Encyclopedia of Self-Hate*, though it would function as a dictionary, and under, say, book there would be the definitions "1. Something I can't write. 2. Something I can't write, but when I do write it, no one will want to read it."

And under *relative* there would be "1. Person with vaguely familiar facial features who says, 'Sure, I think you can write. I just don't think you have anything to say.' 2. Person (see definition 1) making a very valid point."

The *Encyclopedia* is one of those lifelong projects that, to fulfill its destiny, will have to be reviled by the public (the public consisting of five readers, all with DNA similar to my own) and then burned. I only mention my plan to draft the Encyclopedia today because I want to consider a particular form of self-hate by way of preface to my book recommendation.

Over the years my students—generally graduate students, but also undergraduates—have lamented their work's lack of ambition. Not that they state it this way. Normally the complaint is, "Everything I write is so small." Small as in "domestic," or small as in "about the world at hand." And here the fear is about the world literally at hand. Familiarity breeds contempt, and writers are bound to suspect that which they know best. Most often my students' despair comes on the heels of reading a book that is undeniably big (like J. M. Coetzee's *Disgrace*, Ian McEwan's *Atonement*, or Edward P. Jones's *The Known World*), a book that tackles a subject—like racism, war, or slavery—in an unusual and complex way and in a way that reaches to experience far, far beyond the reader's (and perhaps the author's) direct experience.

Of course, this self-criticism rules out much of the work that my students most love. Is Alice Munro big in this way? What about Lorrie Moore? Stuart Dybek? Virginia Woolf? We can't all be Tolstoy; we shouldn't even try.

Not surprisingly, my female students are the ones most apt to worry about their work's smallness. In a 1996 interview Grace Paley said that early in her career she "felt like a lot of women often feel now: these are kind of domestic or kitchen stories or so forth and why bother when there are big things happening?"

Perhaps it's no accident that there's a derogative for female stories about relationships—chick lit—but no term for the male equivalent, which is, of course, "dick lit" and which, since I began by writing about *The Devil's Dictionary*, I'll define as

1. A "will I or won't I get laid?" story. 2. A story in which the narrator is so high, drunk, or in some other way incapacitated that he just can't help being a jerk.

There's a feminist and a therapeutic answer to the fear of being small, and the answer is "Snap out of it." Your experience is as valuable as the next person's. When I was in college, my mother (who otherwise has been very supportive of my writing) did indeed tell me that she thought I was a good writer, but that I had nothing to say. Even then I had the wherewithal to think, *But doesn't everybody have something to say?* Your job as a writer, as Jan Clausen argues in her wonderful essay "The Political Morality of Fiction," is to show that what happens to people matters, and it matters desperately. How you go about that is your business. Or as Grace Paley, a writer committed to social justice, says, "In a sense, what any artist tries to do—no matter who she or he is, no matter what their politics—is to really illuminate what hasn't been seen and just kind of look at what's not known. And in the act of doing that, different lives are seen for the first time—almost no matter what the politics are—and in that way justice happens, because something new is told and is put back into the world. Something that is in the world is seen." There's something inherently big when "something that is in the world is seen" and a story honestly and effectively communicates that.

Even so, there are some books in which the principal characters intersect with something significantly larger than the self, and not in the way that all fiction does this—the individual as a representative of the whole, the world globing itself in a drop of dew—but through a true intersection. Elizabeth Strout's second novel, *Abide with Me*, is such a book, and I admire it for being inarguably big, while nestling itself cozily in the domestic.

Abide with Me tells the story of Tyler Caskey, a Congregational minister in West Annett, Maine, in 1959, the year after Lauren, his young and troubled wife, has died. Tyler—a big, friendly, gentle man—is trying to carry on in the wake of his loss, but he's not having an easy time of it. His overbearing mother, who thinks her son should buck up and get on with things, has taken over the care of his baby daughter, Jeannie. Katherine, his older daughter, has largely stopped speaking, and Katherine's teachers are worried by her behavior—her screaming fits in the classroom, her declaration "I hate God" in Sunday school. As Tyler juggles his various responsibilities in the shabby church home he has been allotted and on a small salary taxed by his late wife's extravagances, he falters, unable to fully honor the pettier concerns of his parishioners, and clear in his faith but not in himself. It has been a long time since he's had "The Feeling," an experience of transcendence, of fullness, of the world as God-saturated. Indeed, he fears "The Feeling" will never come again.

As the story moves forward, Strout's omniscient yet intimate narrator offers a portrait of the entire town—Charlie Austin, the head deacon, protecting himself from his angry wife through a sexual relationship in Boston; Dorie Austin, Charlie's wife, feeling largely underappreciated and in love, in her own way, with Tyler; Connie Hatch, Tyler's damaged housekeeper, struck by how forgettable she is to others. Strout also looks back in time to offer a portrait of Tyler's marriage, hobbled, as it was, by the frustrated expectations of an unstable wife from a wealthy and possibly incestuous Boston family. In his grieving Tyler is drawn to Connie. One afternoon he meets her eyes and feels "a fleeting sense of recognition . . . the sense of having glimpsed the other's soul, some shred of real agreement being shared." Tyler's friendship with his housekeeper and Katherine's peculiar schoolroom behavior become a source of gossip, and the townspeople, misled by their unmet desires and sensing perhaps some disdain in their distracted minister, turn on Tyler, eagerly speculating, especially when his housekeeper is charged with robbery and disappears.

This may not seem like the plotline for a big book. Indeed, the story might have been a small one, immersed in the smallness of a small town, instead of what it is: a novel about the narrow-mindedness of such a town, but also about human potential, God, redemption, and grace. At the close of his *Washington Post Book World* review of Strout's novel, senior editor Ron Charles wrote, "She sees all these wounded people with heartbreaking clarity, but she has managed to write a story that cradles them in understanding and that, somehow, seems like a foretaste of salvation."

That's the kind of overstated compliment that one finds in book blurbs, so it's easy to ignore, but in fact, Charles's words are 100 percent accurate. The book actually offers something like a genuine experience of God. For this the book strikes me as enormous, and enormously moving.

So how does it do this?

The novel consists of three books. While it is always focused on the West Annett community as a whole, the plotline is with Tyler Caskey. "Book One" takes place a year after Tyler's wife's death, and it shows the muddle that Tyler is in. "Book Two" gives the complicated backstory of Tyler's marriage and presents a reason why Tyler might be in need of forgiveness. "Book Three" shows everyone in West Annett, including the minister, moving away from God or failing in some important way to love one another, until the story's end, when I felt that Tyler had been saved, that West Annett had been saved, and that I, too, might be saved. From whence this powerful feeling?

As with any novel, the whole experience of the book occasions the intense final emotion, but there are three things I can identify: the handling of belief, the novel's central metaphor, and the depiction of human need.

Early on Strout writes, "The minister drove the back road to Hollywell, looking for God and hoping to avoid his parishioners." This is the basic situation of the book; Tyler is aggravated with his parishioners—this one who wants a new organ, that one eager to psychoanalyze his daughter—and searching for God. The irritation is the easy thing to handle. What contemporary novel doesn't convey it? But as for a search for God—one about which a contemporary reader can genuinely care—there Strout is on shakier ground. "Obviously," Strout says in an interview, "we're in a time when much of Christianity makes a mockery of God." But Strout hasn't set her book in our time. She's set it in 1959, when we might trust Tyler's beliefs, whether we share them or not. In the end, though, we're persuaded by Tyler's belief mostly because he thinks like a minister. He's deeply interested in the life and ideas of Dietrich Bonhoeffer, as well as Kierkegaard, Augustine, Tillich, and C. S. Lewis.

We see him as he struggles to put his sermons together, as he remembers former conversations about God with his seminary teachers. Bits of scripture and liturgy float through his mind constantly. When he tells Connie that sometimes he thinks he might like to go south and work for civil rights, we're told:

> Connie nodded, stared at her coffee mug. "Well, I'd sure miss you," she said. *Out of the abundance of the heart the mouth speaketh.* "Yes," Tyler said, "I don't think you need to worry. I'm not going anywhere."

To write the novel, Strout says, "I had to immerse myself in [Tyler's] reference points." Strout did her homework: she visited the Bangor seminary, she read course catalogs from the 1940s, she went to lectures in New York, and she carried a thin book of the Psalms with her on the subway, but none of this research shows in the novel in a self-conscious way. The temptation was "to want to get this in and to want to get that in," but she says, "I want to be writing about people. I don't want to be writing about ideas." All this pays off. We are convinced, emotionally and intellectually, by Tyler's belief and his struggles.

Second important technique: the book's central metaphor. Throughout the novel one is always aware of light, and by that I mean the light of the sky. There's rarely an important scene when we don't know the weather. Indeed, the light is the very first thing Strout has us note when she dips into her narrative: "So begin with a day in early October, when it's easy to think of the sun shining hard, the fields surrounding the minister's house brown and gold, the trees on the hills sparking a yellowy red." This is Cold War America, so there are things to worry about, but it is also a day so "lovely in its sunny brightness, the tops of those distant trees a brave and brilliant yellowy-red," that it is "the kind of day where you could easily imagine the tall minister out for a walk, thinking, *I will lift up mine eyes unto the hills.*"

Light in this book—lowercase l light—is always attached to the Light. And uppercase Light is connected to God and goodness. Western readers may make this link anyway. When we're in darkness, we're presumably in confusion, and when we're in light, we're in understanding and maybe some blessedness. But the book reminds us of this, again and again. And again. In the salad days of Tyler's marriage his wife's eyes seem "lit from behind so they shone like dark cedar chips with sun on them." And lest we doubt the light/Light connection, even the room in which he views her eyes is full of "a sharp, beautiful August sunlight," and "the air was not merely air, it was the presence of God—you could feel it as distinctly as you would feel the water around you if you were swimming in a lake." When the characters are confused or bored, the sky is "gray," "aluminum gray," "naked," "watery," "gray galvanized tin." And when the book's characters are most cut off from one another, least able to love, the sky is "as dark as dusk." At one point Tyler looks out a nighttime window and wonders why God has hidden his face. Later Tyler's own eyes become "tiny pins of light."

The central metaphor works because on some level we believe it; we are awed by light. It makes us think of that which transcends us, and in Maine, where this novel is set, and where I live, the light can be particularly moving. It is also true that we all have seasonal affective disorder. As Strout herself says, "If the sky is a certain color, everything is a different color. You live differently when the sky is low." True enough, and as it goes for us, so it goes for Strout's characters.

I admire so much about Strout's writing, but what I admire most is her eloquence about emotions, her painful exactitude. In her novel's final book Strout brings her characters to a point of incredible loss. "I don't know what to do. I don't know what to do," Charlie Austin thinks when he realizes his affair is over. He's not alone. No one in this book knows what to do. Spiritually empty, they lack sympathy for one another, as evidenced by their gossipy willingness to go after Tyler, but also by Tyler's gloomy take on his parishioners.

Meanwhile, the sky is a mix of colors, and the characters are both most confused and most ready for transformation. What has been a theme in the book—cheap grace versus costly grace—becomes an issue of cheap or perhaps immature love versus costly or more mature love. In the end the characters see what they truly need; they grow in just about every way, but also in their relation to God. It is only because the characters are in genuine human need, though, that Strout is able to make this transformation. This works, of course, because we recognize the need. We've felt it ourselves.

Though this transformation is significant, Strout has used a minimum of means to achieve it. The narrative design is connected to the book's central metaphor and the movement from darkness to light. This is the movement the sky makes, the movement Tyler makes, the movement that (almost all of) the people of West Annett make, and, as a result, the movement the reader makes.

Big? Yes, the novel feels enormous . . . and enormously consoling. Why, people can be good! What a thing for a book to make us believe, here in the messy beginnings of the twenty-first century. ✧

Jennifer Egan

Jennifer Egan is the author of three novels, *The Invisible Circus*, *Look at Me*, a finalist for the National Book Award, and the bestselling *The Keep*, as well as a short story collection, *Emerald City*. Her short short fiction has appeared in *The New Yorker*, *Harper's*, *McSweeney's* and *Ploughshares*, among others. Also a journalist, she writes frequently in the *New York Times Magazine*.

Q: Name a childhood hero.
A: Harriet the Spy. I tried to emulate her, but I didn't have the guts (and the neighbors didn't like it)

Q: Name a work you wished you'd written.
A: *The Great Gatsby*. An absolutely perfect novel that reverberates out of all proportion to its small size. *Pride and Prejudice* is another like that.

Q: If you had to order your work by how successfully you completed what you set out to accomplish, what would that list look like?
A: *Look at Me*
   The Keep
   The Invisible Circus
   Emerald City

Q: Name a writer in history you would've like to have been a contemporary of and why.
A: Shakespeare. To see him onstage, to know the particulars his life, and most of all to figure out how the hell he did it so brilliantly again, and again, and again.

Q: Name a work of yours whose reception you've been surprised about and why.
A: *The Keep*; I was surprised to find that many people disliked it. And also that many didn't understand it. Thank God there were also some who liked and/or got it.

Q: Correct a misperception about you as a writer in fifty words or less.
A: That's a tough one. I'm not aware of a coherent perception of me as a writer, much less a misperception.

Q: Name a trait you deplore in other writers.
A: Preening egotism. If you look at what we're up against, historically, none of us is good enough to feel that way.

Q: Name your five desert island films.
A: *Blow Up*
The Great Dictator
The Lives of Others
Pulp Fiction
Gone With the Wind
Can I add a TV show? *The Sopranos.*

Q: Name a book not your own that you wish everyone would read.
A: *The Image*, by Daniel Boorstin. It contains the keys to understanding how mass media culture works. . .and it was published in 1961.

Q: Name a book you suspect most people claim to have read, but haven't.
A: *Infinite Jest.*

Q: If you could choose one of your works to rewrite, which would it be and why?
A: *The Invisible Circus.* I'd let it be more mysterious. I used to have a terror of not being understood, and my execution of that novel is too driven by that fear.

Q: Share the greatest literary secret/gossip you know.
A: I've been told that Mary McCarthy and James Baldwin had an affair.

Q: Name a book you read over and over for inspiration.
A: *The House of Mirth,* by Edith Wharton

Q: Name the writing habit you rely on to get you through a first draft.
A: Tolerating the most godawful prose imaginable (my own), and producing seven pages of it every day.

Q: Name a regret, literary or otherwise.
A: Taking myself out of the running for the Rome Prize (for *The Invisible Circus*) because I was working hard on *Look at Me* and didn't feel like moving abroad at that time. Never a good idea to pass up a grand adventure. And if I'd managed to win, my Italian would be so much better now!

Q: Name your greatest struggle as a writer.
A: Feeling like I'm *doing* what I'm doing, rather than pretending to do it.

Q: Name a question you get about writing to which there really is no good answer.
A: ""Where do you get your ideas?"

Q: Name a question you wish you would've been asked.
A: How about a question I never realized I was waiting to be asked until I was asked it last fall: "What is your greatest strength as a writer?" The answer, I realized, was: Doggedness. ✧

The Center offers $15,000 Excellence Teaching Fellowships and $10,000 Teaching Assistantships, plus full tuition and fee waivers. Recent graduates have won the Whiting Award, the Henfield Award, the Playboy Fiction Contest and the Flannery O'Connor Award. Nine recent graduates have published books since 2003, and several more are publishing books this year. We award master's and doctoral degrees, have a great visitors series, offer workshops in fiction and poetry and nonfiction prose, edit *Mississippi Review* online and in paper, publish a student magazine, and manage (with a little luck) to help our writers become better writers. Apply online at **www.centerforwriters.com**.

Permanent Faculty: Angela Ball, Frederick Barthelme, Steven Barthelme, Julia Johnson.

Recent Visiting Writers: Ann Beattie, Lucie Brock-Broido, Kelly Cherry, Stuart Dischell, Stephen Dobyns, Tony Earley, Percival Everett, Amy Hempel, Michael Knight, Tim O'Brien, Francine Prose, Elissa Schappell, Dave Smith, Matthew Sharpe, Rob Spillman, James Tate, Dara Wier.

The Center for Writers

The University of Southern Mississippi 118 College Drive # 5144 Hattiesburg, MS 39406-0001
www.centerforwriters.com

Index

The following is a listing in alphabetical order by author's last name of works published in *Post Road*. An asterisk indicates subject rather than contributor.

Hunt, Jerry	FOUR VIDEO TRANSLATIONS (theatre)	PR10, 33
Iagnemma, Karl	ITALIAN DAYS BY BARBARA GRIZZUTI HARRISON (recommendation)	PR7, 134
Ihara, Nathan	HITTING HARMONY (nonfiction)	PR8, 100
Ison, Tara	MENDEL'S DWARF BY SIMON MAWER (recommendation)	PR2, 166
Jackson, Major	INDIAN SONG (poetry)	PR2, 87
	URBAN RENEWAL ix. (poetry)	PR2, 88
James, Henry	ON TURGENEV (etcetera)	PR7, 183
Jenkinson, Len	THE MUSEUM OF SPEED (fiction)	PR3, 26
Johnson, Samuel	LAST WILL AND TESTAMENT (etcetera)	PR4, 149
Johnston, Mat	WHAT WE DO (fiction)	PR7, 100
Jones, Alden	SECRET LIFE BY MICHAEL RYAN (recommendation)	PR4, 108
	POLITE SOCIETY BY MELANIE SUMNER (recommendation)	PR9, 170
Jones, Ben	THE ANCESTOR'S TALE BY RICHARD DAWKINS (recommendation)	PR11, 200
Kadish, Rachel	LAWRENCE WESCHLER'S VERMEER IN BOSNIA (recommendation)	PR12, 65
Kalfus, Ken	CONFESSIONS OF ZENO BY ITALO SVEVO (recommendation)	PR2, 168
Kalotay, Daphne	WOMEN IN THEIR BEDS: NEW AND SELECTED STORIES BY GINA BERRIAULT AND THE TEA CEREMONY: THE UNCOLLECTED WRITINGS OF GINA BERRIAULT (recommendation)	PR11, 31
Kaluza, Kobun	EXCERPT FROM INERT DEMENTIA (theatre)	PR14, 193
Kantar, Annie	FOR YOU, A POEM (poetry)	PR2, 89
	I SEE MY GRANDMOTHER AGAIN (poetry)	PR2, 90
Kennedy, X. J.	THE FICTION OF J. F. POWERS (recommendation)	PR10, 123
Kimball, Michael	EXCERPTS FROM THE SUICIDE LETTERS OF JONATHAN BENDER (B.1967–D.2000) (fiction)	PR12, 155
Kimura, Takahiro	DESTRUCTION AND CONSTRUCTION OF THE HUMAN FACE (art)	PR5, 194
Klass, Perri	BIRDS OF AMERICA BY MARY MCCARTHY (recommendation)	PR12, 203
Klíma, Ivan	IRENA OBERMANNOVA (recommendation)	PR2, 169
Klink, Joanna	SHOOTING STAR (poetry)	PR2, 100
	RIVER IN DUSK (poetry)	PR2, 101
Knapp, Elizabeth	INDELIBLE (poetry)	PR11, 13
	UNINVITED GUEST (poetry)	PR11, 15
Kozma, Andrew	INVADER (poetry)	PR14, 103
	WHAT IS (poetry)	PR14, 104
Kreines, Amy	WARNINGS (etcetera)	PR8, 165
Kronovet, Jennifer	A HISTORY OF KANSAS (poetry)	PR3, 37
	SCENIC OVERLOOK (poetry)	PR3, 38
Kuo, Alex	THE LUNCH (fiction)	PR15, 85